Webster's Secretary's Handbook with Spelling and Word Division Guide

By Beryl Frank

Published by
CASTLE BOOKS
Distributed by
BOOK SALES, INC.
110 Enterprise Avenue
Secaucus, New Jersey 07094

Credit: C. & P. Telephone Company, Baltimore, Md.

Thanks to all the secretaries everywhere who aided and assisted in the preparation of this book, as well as to their executives. Also, thanks to my personal executive for his assistance and encouragement.

ISBN: 0-89009-3644
Library of Congress Catalog Card Number: 80-67952

Table of Contents

Introduction

This book does not assume that today all secretaries are female or that all executives are male. Many modern offices have competent male secretaries as well as top-notch female executives. However, there is a need here to use singular pronouns for both positions. For purposes of clarity the secretary will be referred to in the female gender and the executive in the male gender.

Mechanization, electronic processes, and automation all have contributed to changes in office routine and procedure. Despite these time-savers of the late twentieth century, the position of the secretary is, if anything, more important than ever before. The scope of her work may have changed; for instance, she no longer has to lick postage stamps if there is an automatic stamp machine in the office. However, the secretary is still very much responsible for the contents of the letter her executive signs. A large telephone switchboard may eliminate the need for contact with the general public, but she will still be the girl Friday who greets people who want to contact her executive.

The secretary must be expert at time-management, a cordial and unhurried hostess to those waiting for an appointment, part-time bookkeeper, accountant, and purchasing agent. In short, a good secretary has at her fingertips the answers to a thousand questions — and, if she does not, she knows where to find them. Finding those answers is what this book is all about.

What Is a Secretary?

A matter of semantics often confuses a secretary with a stenographer. A stenographer, according to the dictionary, is a person who takes dictation, usually in shorthand, and transcribes that dictation in typewriting.

A secretary, also according to the dictionary, is a person employed to keep records and take care of correspondence and other writing tasks for an organization or an individual. There is quite a difference between a stenographer and a secretary.

Frequently, a secretary functions as an executive assistant who relieves the executive of many routine and specialized details of the office. She is a link between the maker of decisions—the executive—and the person or persons who implement those decisions. Her work demands initiative, as she may be called on regularly to make decisions herself. These may be as simple as deciding whether to page her executive if he is out of his office or to take a message from the caller. They may be complex decisions that will actually affect the carrying out of business for the firm.

Today's secretary is a highly specialized and well-trained member of the office team. She has been referred to as an "executive-extender."

The National Secretaries Association (International) is an organization directed toward raising secretarial standards through continuing education. It is through them that the Certified Professional Secretary Examination is given—a test that requires high standards of expertise for those secretaries who are certified.

The philosophy of the National Secretaries Association (International) is carried out by many colleges and universities throughout the country. These offer courses in all phases of business to prepare the secretary better with knowledge of the workings of the economic world in which she will be functioning.

In short, today's secretary can and should be a highly trained person whose advancement depends on her own ability.

How to Improve as a Secretary

Whether you are an executive secretary or a very small cog in a large wheel, you should be up-to-date on secretarial skills. The more you know, the more competent you can be. Check your skills and general education. If English grammar is your weakness, take a course in the subject. If you are involved with accounting or bookkeeping for your executive, check with an accountant to clear up any bugs in the system you are now using. Ask the bank for current information on checking accounts. Seek to improve your efficiency in your job by learning all you can about every phase of that job. You will be improving yourself with this knowledge and will become a more efficient member of your office team. You, the secretary, are important. Evaluating yourself in relation to your job will enhance your worth.

You will regularly be called on to set up work priorities — deciding what should be done when. An important letter takes precedence over a routine report. Both must be completed on time. Interruptions from the telephone must be figured into each day's work schedule. Each day is different from every other, and each day calls forth decisions, both large and small, that affect you and your executive.

Change a preposition and increase your stature as a secretary. Work "with" your executive rather than "for" him. This kind of positive thinking will increase your value.

This book will not give you all the answers. Hopefully, however, it will answer some of your questions as well as make suggestions as to where to find more detailed information.

Basic Secretarial Skills

Basic secretarial skills may vary from one office to another, but there are general requirements that apply to most places of business, whether large corporations or small one-man shops. Most of these basic skills are taught in a good secretarial school, and most stenographers have this knowledge, too. If it has been years since you took your secretarial training, you can improve yourself by brushing up on one or all the skills mentioned. To improve in your job, all basic skills need to be updated from time to time.

Dictation

With the increased use of machines for dictation, a secretary may not need the shorthand learned in school. However, some executives still prefer the one-to-one relationship of seated secretary with her spiral-bound notebook in hand. If your dictation is given in this way, you will be required to take down accurately the correspondence or report being dictated. This calls for intense concentration on your part. This is no time for wandering thoughts. The dictator may pause to assemble thoughts, but, once he is ready, the secretary must be ready as well.

Since secretaries are not machines, even the best may miss an occasional word or thought. When this happens, do not interrupt the dictator. When he is finished, go back over your notes before you leave, and clarify whatever is necessary.

Transcribing your notes accurately is equally as important as taking them. You must be able to understand your own shorthand to do a superior job of transcription.

Typing

It may seem elementary, but accurate typing is a basic secretarial skill. If you cannot transcribe neatly and with adequate speed, you are not competent in your basic skills. No matter how advanced your position may be as an executive secretary, you may still have occasion to type or transcribe confidential matters. Your typing skills need to be fast and accurate.

General Vocabulary

A good general vocabulary is an essential part of a secretary's tools. You must be familiar with the English language in its correct form to be of help to your executive. He may depend on you to correct grammatical errors he makes. You cannot do this if you do not have a good command of the language.

Many of the letters you send out will represent your firm and your executive. It is important to both that these letters do not go out with grammatical errors. Good use of basic English and grammar is essential to a competent secretary.

Business Forms and Punctuation

Your office will probably have a standard form to use for letters. There are several different letter formats used in business today. These are discussed in detail in a later chapter. It is up to you to know which form your company prefers and to set up your letters in that way.

Punctuation can be a real problem for a secretary if she does not know the accepted forms used in modern business. A refresher look at the proper way to use punctuation can help you solve any problems, ranging from ellipses to periods.

Office Machines

The knowledge of how to operate and care for basic business machines is essential to a career secretary. You may not be required to type on a portable, as you will probably have an electric machine. However, you should know how to handle such things as changing typewriter ribbons and cleaning the machine.

You may or may not have to be in contact with a mimeograph operation or a duplicating machine, but you should have enough familiarity with them that you can quickly learn the quirks of your own office machines. If there is a machine in the office, you probably will at some time be required to operate it or direct someone else in its operation. Learn all you can to improve your basic skills in this area.

Telephone Manner

You have probably been answering a telephone since you were able to talk, but a specific telephone manner is required in an office. Answering telephone calls and taking messages, both discussed in depth in a later chapter, reflect on you and your executive. A pleasant telephone manner is a basic secretarial skill.

Basic Filing System

Filing systems range from small 3 by 5 card files to complete file rooms with separate filing clerks in big corporations. You may even have to set up your own filing system for your executive's correspondence. Understanding how a filing system works will help you in either event. Since you will be putting into the filing system as well as locating material from it, be sure you learn how a filing system operates, particularly that in your own office.

Additional Office Requirements

These may or may not be considered as basic skills, but you may have to perform some of them. The previously listed skills will prepare you to deal with the following possibilities.

You may have to make rough drafts of executive correspondence. You may also be required to read, sign, and send out some correspondence. The basic skills already mentioned will help prepare you to do these jobs efficiently.

Writing speeches, memoranda, and reports may be part of your work. You may have to edit copy that was prepared and typed by someone else.

Another phase of your work may be research for facts that your executive needs. This will require your knowledge of where to go and how to look for research material.

There may be times when you are considered the purchasing agent for office equipment and supplies. You must make the decision as to when to order supplies or what machine will best fit in with your office needs.

All the previously mentioned basic skills will prepare you to deal adequately with these additional office requirements. Each office requires its own specifics as to what its secretary should be able to do. The best rule is to remember that the more you know, the more efficient you will be.

The Specialized Secretary

All secretaries share a need for the basic secretarial skills already mentioned here. However, there are employment opportunities that require additional and specialized skills. These are in the fields of law, medicine, and such technical firms as engineering, where technical reports and correspondence are required.

The Legal Secretary

A legal secretary must have a knowledge of law procedure and terminology to perform her job efficiently. She will need to know how to use a standard law dictionary as well as how to type formal legal documents such as briefs, proxies, and wills. She may even be required to be a notary, so that she can officially notarize legal papers. Further specialized training may be a requirement of her position. She may work in a small law office or be employed in the law department of a large corporation. Her position is important both to her employer and to the clients he serves.

The Medical Secretary

Specialized training, sometimes on-the-job, is also required for a medical secretary. She must be prepared with medical terminology and medical shorthand, as well as the office procedures of her doctor employer. Job opportunities range from offices of doctors or dentists to hospitals, clinics, and health departments. Corporate medical departments, as well as pharmaceutical houses, also offer opportunities. The duties of a medical secretary can range from a knowledge of accounting to securing medical data from patients and even to minor medical duties, such as preparing a patient for examination. A knowledge of basic sciences is a good background for the medical secretary.

The Technical Secretary

A technical secretary may be required to type chemical formulas, mathematical formulas, or highly technical reports such as those used in the field of engineering. She will need to learn the particulars of the firm for which she works. If she works with classified information, she may require government clearance. She will have a broader knowledge of her particular field, which will enable her to function more efficiently in her work.

For All Secretaries

One last thought for *all* secretaries. No matter what your employer's business is, you can be a specialized secretary. Improving your knowledge of the business requirements of your firm will improve your ability to deal with whatever may arise. Think of yourself as special—a special person with special talents who can and does do a special job.

General Office Information

Any capable newspaperman includes the what and where of the story on which he is working. The previous chapter of this book dealt with the "what" of the secretary. What she is and what her work includes were discussed there.

This chapter is the important "where" of the secretary's job. The where is your work space in the office—your office home, if you prefer—and this work space, properly arranged, will contribute to the efficiency of your work.

Take a long, critical look at your work station. It may be a private office of your own outside of your executive's office. Perhaps you share a room with several other employees or even have a section of your executive's office. Whichever is your situation, certain office rules should apply. Your work station is where you spend the major portion of most working days. Think about it both from the standpoint of doing your work as well as the reflection of you it presents.

Your Chair

You may not be allowed to select your own chair. Most offices have furniture that outlasts its employees. However, if you should select office furniture, choose carefully. Make your selections for maximum efficiency as well as attractiveness. A plush velvet-cushioned chair may be ideal for the waiting room where visitors read magazines while waiting for their appointments. It will not suit you for ten minutes if you are transcribing important dictation. The desk chair you use should be at a height that allows you to sit erect but comfortably. It may be a swivel chair so that you can turn from your typewriter to the work area. To function best, you should feel that your desk chair is in adjunct to your own body. Your feet should touch the floor, and you should be able to work in a relaxed but alert position.

Your Desk

Whether you have inherited your desk from someone else or have chosen your own, the way you arrange it is strictly up to you. Your desk will undoubtedly have a place for a typewriter, a telephone, and several storage drawers. It may have a large or a limited work surface.

Your desk may be a simple typing desk with an elevator mechanism that raises and lowers the typewriter stand, or it may be a complex work center. Whatever style desk you have, the key to efficiency is how well you utilize it.

Those things you use most often should be no farther away than one arm's length. If you have to stretch to reach for the telephone, you will waste time and physical energy every time the phone rings or you make an outgoing call. Have it within arm's reach—on the right if you are left-handed and on the left if you are right-handed. Having the telephone on the correct side frees your writing hand to take accurate messages. Correct placement of the telephone is so important that it is worthwhile to have it moved if that is necessary.

Your telephone-address book, desk calendar, and memo book all should have a place on your desk. These are items in daily use and need to be easily accessible. If you keep a copy of your executive's appointment book, this too needs its place in the sun. Easy accessibility of these items is a must; exactly where you position them on the desk depends on each individual.

Of course, it is necessary to have papers, folders, and supplies on the desk surface during working hours. But do not leave a lot of loose papers scattered around to be blown away. Make good use of some kind of work organizer, such as an expanding portfolio. Look to your office supply catalog for ideas along this line. There are many organizers from which to choose—from simple desk trays to elaborate space-makers. The old adage "a place for everything and everything in its place" applies to the desk surface.

As for the desk drawers, organize them as carefully as the top. It may sound simple, but keep paper clips, rubber bands, and the like in their own place, and know where these things are. Do not reach for a clip and come up empty. Keep desk supplies orderly and at hand. The same applies to your paper and stationery supplies that go in the large storage drawers.

Allow enough space in the back of one storage drawer for your personal needs, such as your pocketbook. Since you will not be using this too often during the day, it should be relegated to a spot in the back, out of your way.

So far, your desk organization has given you a workable surface, storage space—and sterility. If you want to have a flowering begonia to add a light touch, place it in a spot where it will not be in the way of your work. Make sure that the plant is not so large that it will interfere with your work space—and enjoy it. It is a known fact that it rests the eyes to look at green leaves.

Lighting and Noise

Correct lighting and a generally quiet office both contribute to better working conditions. Most office planners take both factors into their original planning. You may not be able to control the noise, but you can be sure you have proper, adequate lighting for your work.

If the overhead lights do not zero in on your desk, ask for a desk light. There are many different styles available, and the financial investment is minimal.

The Typewriter

The typewriter is certainly one of the most important tools of a secretary's trade. This, like the chair and desk, become very personally yours. If an inanimate object can be said to have rapport with a human, that object is your typewriter. Treat it kindly.

Dust and erasure crumbs are the demons of all typewriters. Cover your machine at night to prevent dust accumulation. Move the carriage to either side when using an eraser. This will help to keep dirt out of the machine.

Clean your typewriter regularly with a soft brush. Your typewriter repairman may have other suggestions for cleaning your particular machine. Listen to his advice and follow it.

Have your typewriter checked and cleaned at regular intervals. Once a year is the minimum. A hard-working typewriter may require professional maintenance more often.

Supplies

You may or may not be responsible for a supply cabinet. If you are, be sure that this is as organized as your desk. Try putting any liquid supplies—glue and ink, for instance—on a low shelf; paper goods should be easy to reach, and like paper should be stacked together. Do not mix letterheads with second sheets. Keep small things in their own boxes. Pens, pencils, and paper clips can go high in the cabinet. Label the shelves, and also keep labels on boxes.

When refilling the supply cabinet, put the new supplies to the back so that the older supplies will be used first. This system of rotation keeps you aware of what you have on hand and what you may need to reorder.

If your job includes reordering supplies, keep an eagle eye on that supply cabinet. Do not get down to your last pack of carbon paper and run the risk of running out. Checking supplies at regular intervals will enable you to order before you run out.

Housekeeping

Even if your office has a custodial service, you, as a secretary, still have some housekeeping duties to perform. Naturally, you will want to keep your own work station clean and dust-free. This does not mean scrubbing the floors, but it does include regular dusting of your own desk. You may also prefer to give your executive's desk the once-over to be sure it is clean, clear, and ready for a day's work. Empty and wash dirty ashtrays, and remove and clean used coffee cups. If you are in charge of the coffee machine, you must also be responsible for keeping it clean. Another house-keeping duty may be the plants in the office. Water them as needed, and keep them looking good. An expert secretary will cheerfully tackle these small but important details. They are the little things that pace the way to office comfort for all concerned.

You and Public Relations

There are as many different phases of you, the secretary, as there are secretaries. The range stretches from the top-brass executive secretary in a multimillion-dollar corporation to the one-man office secretary. There is one thing all secretaries, regardless of their individualized and specialized duties, have in common—public relations. The secretary is a link between the executive and the outside world.

Every time you answer the telephone, greet a visitor for your executive, or send out correspondence, you are dealing with the public. How you meet this public reflects on your executive as well as on you.

Personal Appearance

The day you went for your initial job interview you probably took careful stock of what you wore. It was important to you that you looked as efficient and as capable as you knew you were. You hoped that your costume and grooming reflected as much about you as did the job resumé you carried with you. You certainly scrapped the idea of wearing faded blue jeans or too-short shorts to meet your prospective employer. The care you took about your grooming for that interview must certainly extend to what you wear and how you look every single day on the job.

There is a wide range of acceptable dress in the modern office of the 1970s. The classic business suit of a jacket and skirt has not changed, although pants may complete the suit in place of the skirt. Indeed, some versatile designers have created matching slacks. In this regard what you choose to wear will depend on individual office custom.

One thing applies to any office costume—it should be clean, neat, and fashionable, but not necessarily high style. Save the extreme for after-hours. Those spike-heeled glass slippers may be fine for a cocktail party, but be a bit more conservative, with a simple pair of comfortable, plain pumps, for the workday. You will actually be more comfortable, as well as more businesslike.

Both makeup and hairstyle should be suitable for the working day—not what you wear out for a big night on the town. Simplicity in your over-all appearance will create a business atmosphere around you. From 9 to 5, you are an important part of the office team. Your basic wardrobe, well chosen, will create this impression.

One last word about personal appearance: You may not always know ahead of time when you must accompany your executive to an out-of-office meeting or a business lunch. Unexpected things do arise. Dress each day with as much care as you took for that very first job interview.

Know Your Executive

It may not be spelled out in your job requirements, but knowing your executive is of utmost importance to both of you. Your decisions as to when to approach him with a problem or an interruption should be made on the basis of what you know about him. The executive who begins his office day with a cup of coffee will not want to make important decisions until after that. When he is preparing himself and his thoughts for an important appointment or business conference, he is not ready to discuss vacation schedules or a day off for you.

A good working relationship between executive and secretary is one of mutual respect and understanding. Because you, the secretary, work closely with the executive, you are in a good position to be aware of the tensions of his work. You may also be aware of his pressures from outside sources, such as illness at home. When you understand his problems, you are better able to assist him in the heavy responsibilities he must carry.

Loyalty to your executive is part of your job. You are part of his team. He may express opinions and ideas to you that he assumes are confidential. Be sure you respect such confidences and keep them to yourself. The trustworthy secretary is not part of any office grapevine.

When you understand the responsibilities and goals of your executive, you will be best able to serve his needs. When his work goes smoothly, the chances are that yours will also go smoothly.

Telephone Personality

Every time you use the telephone, either for incoming or outgoing calls, you are representing your company. Correct use of the telephone is important not only to your personal success but to that of your executive and company as well.

Many offices have their own requirements as to how to answer the telephone. An accepted form for answering your executive's phone is: "Mr. Smith's office, Mrs. Kelly." This is a concise way of telling the caller he has made connection with the correct office, as well as the name of the person to whom he is speaking. However, there is one important thing to remember. The person calling cannot see you. His first impression is the voice he hears—that voice is your telephone personality.

When you talk on the telephone, you are actually meeting people without the benefit of any visual aids. They cannot see your neat appearance or your poise and charm. They only hear the mental picture that your voice projects. Your telephone personality comes across in your warm, friendly manner, your courtesy, and your tact.

Be alert and pleasant when you answer the telephone. Do not let the late television show you watched last night or the disagreement you had with a friend come through the wires. Put a smile on your face so that a smile is also in your voice. Sounding pleasant when you pick up the receiver can help solve many problems.

Speak distinctly. Demosthenes may have been able to talk with a mouthful of pebbles in ancient Greece, but you will have trouble if you are talking through a mouthful of candy.

Be natural. Simple, straightforward language is the best. Talk at a moderate, easy to understand rate. Let your natural intonations come through to vary the tone of your voice and to add emphasis to what you say.

Your telephone personality tells a great deal about you. Your courtesy begins from the minute you answer—on the first ring of the phone, if possible—until you thank the person for calling at the close of the conversation. You may talk to a great many more people by telephone than you actually meet in any one business day. In this case your telephone manner becomes another important aspect of you and public relations.

Listening as Well as Hearing

Effective listening is not the same thing as hearing. You hear a clock strike when you are aware of the noise. You listen to that clock strike when you concentrate on the number of chimes.

In an office it is not enough simply to hear. A large part of a secretary's skill is in listening. In this case a synonym for listening might be concentrating totally. Examples of listening in a given business day show the amount of concentration that is taken for granted and which the secretary must do.

Examples of Listening

1. Accept daily oral instruction from the executive.
2. Take accurate and precise dictation.
3. Answer incoming telephone calls.
4. Locate needed, specialized information from other members of the office force.
5. Contact and carry through messages to and from people outside the office.

A competent secretary learns her listening skills well. When you are that secretary, you concentrate fully on what you are hearing. In this way you are better able to cope with the daily problems that may arise in your office, from those of the lowliest stock boy to those of the president.

Everything and everybody in your office becomes part of you and public relations, from your nicely groomed appearance to your interaction with people both within and outside the office. A good secretary is far more than a good typist. Pride in yourself and in your job make you pay careful attention to all phases of that job, and good public relations may be the steps leading up the ladder of success.

Office Forms, Manners, and Conventions

You—A Member of the Office Team

Working in an office, regardless of the size of that office, makes you a part of the office team. Your ability to get along with people enhances the efficiency of your job and promotes cooperation all along the line. A good working relationship with all personnel may seem obvious, but it is important.

Courtesy in an office is far more than just "Please" or "Thank you." It should be extended to include pleasant greetings to co-workers and office visitors, although this is no time for long personal conversations. Normal friendliness and some awareness for the feelings of others will dictate when you should use extra understanding for a co-worker. Your own instincts are your best guide.

As a member of the office team, you have certain tools and supplies that you use regularly—so do your fellow workers. If you find that you have run out of a needed supply and must borrow, be sure to return the borrowed item promptly. Replace what you are missing from the supply cabinet as soon as possible to avoid borrowing again. It is never a good idea to borrow personal things, such as money, from a fellow worker.

Cheerful cooperation in the office is a must. The proverbial helping hand has saved many a secretary from work overloads. Reciprocation of help given aids the entire office to get the work out on time.

Personal complaints are best kept to a minimum. If a legitimate complaint that affects the work of the office must be lodged, be sure to lodge it with the person best able to resolve the trouble. Do not discuss the matter generally. Treat the complaint confidentially, so as not to embarrass a fellow employee.

Confidential business matters must be kept strictly confidential. You must be trustworthy about information you are told. Do not be part of the office grapevine. A good secretary may hear many things but says nothing.

Punctuality

A dependable secretary is a punctual person. Be ready to begin work when the workday starts. This means be seated at your desk comfortably and relaxed at the appointed time—not hanging up your coat five or ten minutes after the telephone has started ringing. Your executive depends on you to be ready for work at a given time. This is also true of your lunch hour. The extra cup of coffee that makes you late getting back to the office can be the catalyst that upsets the afternoon work routine for everyone.

Dictation

Many executives prefer a routine time of day to give dictation. Since much of your time as a secretary will be spent taking and transcribing this dictation, it is essential that you be prepared for it. You will need a spiral-bound notebook, a pen and/or several well-sharpened pencils, a file folder for papers and reference material, paper clips to mark items for special attention, and a colored pencil for insertions in the dictated copy.

Before further discussing the taking of dictation, a word should be said about machine dictation. In heavily automated offices a dictating machine may take the place of the secretary's spiral notebook. These machines range from a complex, centralized dictation system to a portable dictation unit that can fit into a pocket or handbag.

A secretary who transcribes from a dictating machine will work essentially at her own desk with little or no contact with the person dictating other than placing the finished transcribed work on his desk. However, it is important that the secretary fully understands the operation of the dictating machine to enable her to transcribe the given dictation as quickly and accurately as possible.

Even though most of your dictation may be from a machine, there are still times when your executive will dictate to you in person. These are the times you must be ready on a moment's notice to take anything from a short telegram to a long emergency report that must go out immediately.

Your spiral-bound notebook should be at hand, with a rubber band around the portion of pages already used. Date each page at the bottom. This enables you to locate old dictation quickly and easily. Some secretaries keep two notebooks ready—one for letters and reports and the other for those unexpected important things that require special and prompt attention.

Be attentive and concentrate while taking dictation. Whether your executive gives you the average 70 or rapid-fire 120 or more words a minute, it is important that you do not miss a word. Do not allow yourself any wool-gathering while taking dictation. Concentrate fully on what is being said.

If you do not understand something in the dictation, wait until the end of the letter, then clarify whatever is necessary. Never interrupt your executive in the middle of his thoughts. Ask afterwards about any points in question, then mark your shorthand accordingly. If your executive is interrupted by the telephone or a personal caller, wait quietly until he is finished, or, on his signal, go back to your own desk until he is ready to resume dictating.

Transcription

As there was a routine for dictation, there hopefully is a routine for transcribing notes. This should be when interruptions are at a minimum. Make up your own system, tailored to your needs, for transcribing. Clear your desk of other things, and concentrate on the work at hand.

Allow time at the end of the workday to check over your dictated material for anything that must be handled on that day. This material should have been specially noted in your shorthand book as different from routine work, and should be easily located.

Reordering Supplies

Most offices have their own system for ordering and reordering supplies. This system may range from special-purchase requisitions, to a supply department, to you, the secretary, actually purchasing everything from typewriter ribbons to carbon paper direct from the stationer. Whatever system applies in your office, you will probably have some responsibility as a purchasing agent for supplies.

Know your supplier. This representative will be able to tell you what is new in the line he sells. He can tell you the difference between a carbon set and carbon sheets. He can tell you the erasing qualities of letterhead paper and second sheets. In short, the supplier can offer suggestions as to what you need based on the performance of what you have previously used. If you want to make a change, you will be fully informed and able to present your new ideas to your executive.

Keep a record of the supplies you use, quantities usually purchased, supplier's name and address, and the minimum quantity to be kept in stock. This is a stock-control system that should prevent you from running short of important supplies and yet not overload the stock kept on hand. Some supplies, such as ink and typewriter ribbons, can deteriorate with age. Your supply records, accurately kept, can prevent this from happening.

The Filing System

The office you work in probably had a filing system before you were hired. However, it is essential for you, as a secretary, to understand basic filing systems. With this understanding you may be able to make suggestions that will improve the already-existing system.

Alphabetical Filing

This is by far the most usual type of filing and is particularly useful for you if you want to set up a personal telephone file, for example. Whether on 3 by 5 cards or in folders, the material to be filed is listed in 26 categories—A to Z. Your system can be kept in a file cabinet in your office or on a box on your desk. Either way you will file alphabetically according to client or firm name.

Filing by subjects or geographical areas is set up in much the same way. This may call for more organization on your part and depends on the type of business in which you are involved. A mail-order house might prefer geographical filing. Subject filing usually requires an alphabetical card index that lists headings, divisions, and subdivisions of the file. This card index makes it much easier to find needed information and can save hours of time that you might spend in searching.

Nonalphabetical Filing

This type of filing system is frequently used by professional businesses, such as a law office or an engineering firm, or by a scientist. The files are set up by number, with subdivisions under them. The division might be 000. The subdivision might be 010; if further subdivisions are needed, they can be listed 010.1.

There is no attempt here to teach you how to set up a filing system of the more-complicated type. Rather, this is a bird's-eye view of what you will find in many offices. Large businesses have completely separate files that are maintained by specialized filing clerks. It is to your advantage as a good secretary to understand how the particular system in your office works. Your understanding will help you to locate filed material that your executive may need in the shortest possible time.

Basic Do's and Don't's of Filing

Keep up-to-date with needed filing supplies. It has already been said that you should keep a running record of the supplies you need in the office. The guides and folders used in filing are no good to you if they are at the stationer's. Order more before the supply on hand is depleted.

Do not place more than 50 papers in a folder. Fifty is a nice round number and is about as crowded as most folders can be without expanding the folder so that the tab is buried. Overcrowding can cause filing errors and lost time hunting for misplaced papers. When a particular file is full, subdivide it into categories of additional folders.

Perhaps the most important "don't" about filing is—don't change a system you do not understand. Familiarize yourself with the already-established files in your office. Find out the reasons things are filed the way "they always have been." After you know all the ins and outs of what is already in use, you are ready to make suggestions for change. Make haste slowly, however. Work your new ideas in after you are sure they will work well for all concerned personnel.

The Secretary's Workbook

Take stock of your own efficiency by making up a workbook that could be used by a substitute secretary in the event of your unexpected absence. This might give you a clearer perspective of your own job and offer new insight as to ways of improving weaknesses in your operation. You may have all the answers in your head, but put them down on paper anyway.

Things a Substitute Needs to Know

1. The full name and title of your executive is the first thing a substitute must know. Who is able to make important (and unimportant) decisions if he is out of the office for any reason?

2. What is the procedure for handling mail in your office? When is outgoing mail picked up? At what time is daily incoming mail delivered? How does your executive prefer that his mail be handled; i.e., do you open it and process it before the executive sees it? Do you answer routine letters for him?

3. What procedure do you use for handling incoming telephone calls? Do you screen all calls before the executive is called to the phone? Does he prefer to answer calls himself? Do you have a special place for key telephone numbers?

4. What kind of filing system is used in your office? How is general material handled? Where is the filing system located? What particular guides are needed for the files in your own office?

5. What are your executive's rules for dictation and typing? What stationery is used? How many carbons are usually needed? What letter form does your executive prefer? Include a sample. If the executive prefers a particular time of day for dictation, make a note of this also.

6. List all directories and manuals used in the routine performance of your job. Do you keep the latest copies available? Also list those pieces of office equipment you need to know how to operate. A list of the proper people to contact for repair service on that equipment should be included.

7. How and when do you order supplies? Be sure to list any special items that you use in your routine work.

8. How is the executive's calendar handled? Do you make appointments for him? Do you check his schedule with him every day? Are you responsible for the details concerning meetings, such as room reservations, note pads, and pencils for the people attending the meeting? Do you take the minutes of those meetings?

9. Does your job include making travel arrangements for your executive? Have you listed his preferences for airlines, hotels, and car rental, for example?

10. Personal data about your own job, such as coffee breaks, lunchtime, and even smoking at your desk, should be included. In addition write down your executive's personal preference about little things such as coffee, cigars, or his lunchtime preference. You might also list any routine things you handle for him, such as Christmas gifts, reminders of special occasions (both personal and business), or even reminders of when his regular organizational meetings take place.

From time to time in the performance of your job, look back over this workbook and update it if necessary. Thinking of your job through the eyes of a possible substitute may point out weaknesses that bother you, and you may then find ways to correct them.

Communications—Lifeline of the Office

Communication, the giving and receiving of information, is truly the lifeline of the office. Every phase of your office day includes communication of one sort or another, from your first pleasant "good morning" to the last cheerful "good night."

You, the secretary, communicate in many different ways. Your pleasant, attentive manner in greeting visitors is direct personal communication. Conversations with your executive and other personnel in the office are also communication. The letters and reports you type, the directions you give, the business conferences you arrange—these are all forms of communication. Many are face-to-face communication. The people with whom you communicate have a visual aid—you and your appearance (or the appearance of the letter or report at hand) to help make communicating easier.

The Telephone

One form of communication not mentioned above is that mechanical wonder known as the telephone. The voice a caller hears when you answer your telephone is frequently the only introduction that caller has to you. Your voice communicates a mental picture of you to the caller. The caller cannot see your nice hairdo, your smart fashions, or your poise. The image created depends entirely on your voice—and your good telephone manners. Your voice is your means of communication. Your voice is you!

How to Answer the Telephone

Answer the telephone promptly. Quick service reflects on your efficiency as well as on the company's. Try to answer on the first ring if possible. Remember, the waiting time seems longer to the person calling you.

If you must leave the line, explain why and excuse yourself. When you return to the line, be sure the person knows you are back before you resume the conversation.

Identify yourself. Do not frustrate a busy caller with a plain "hello." This is not businesslike and wastes time as well. Tell the caller whom he has reached.

"Mrs. Smith's office, Mrs. Kelly" is an accepted form for answering an executive's telephone. This immediately tells the caller he has the correct office and the person to whom he is speaking.

The tone of your voice says a lot about you. When you talk on the phone, the person on the other end of the line can tell whether you are happy or dejected, excited or bored, or in a good or bad mood. If you allow emotions such as frustration or anger to creep into your voice, its tone changes and so does the picture you are projecting.

By controlling your feelings, you send across the wires as pleasing a picture of your personality as you want the person on the other end to receive. Try sending a smile across the telephone line!

The picture your voice projects is important, whether you use the phone to place an urgent business call or just for a social visit. (Be sure to limit those social calls from the office. Save them for after working hours.)

A pleasing telephone voice can do everything for you, from assuring you prompt and courteous service to selling a raffle ticket for your executive.

Any number of factors can alter your telephone voice. Emotion is a major influence, but many other things contribute, too. The speed and volume with which you speak, the clarity of your voice, and the inflections you use all combine to help form your telephone image. Make sure you are not one of the ladies mentioned below.

Miss Dreary—Is your voice so flat and expressionless that people think you look like a dreary? Remember to send a smile along the line.

Miss Bewildered—Do not know for sure what you are calling about? Before you call, be prepared!

Mrs. Bossman—A loud, rude voice never sends a pleasing picture across the wires. There is a fine and important line between sounding businesslike and sounding rude.

Mrs. Whirlwind—Do you ever send this image? Talking to someone who is trying to do ten things at the same time can be really frustrating.

Mrs. Breathless—Slow down! Talking at breakneck speed will take twice as long—because you will have to repeat everything.

Mrs. Mouthful—Are you a Mrs. Mouthful? With a pencil, a cigarette, or a piece of candy in your mouth, your voice will not come through clearly over the phone.

Miss Affected—Insincerity shows up clearly over the phone. If you are just a little bit too grateful, you may come across as being affected.

Let your telephone voice speak well for you. Show that you are alert and ready to help the person on the line. Put a smile in your voice as well as on your face. Be natural. Now is not the time to impress a caller with your large vocabulary. Use simple, straightforward language, and speak distinctly and directly into the telephone transmitter. Talk at a moderate rate and volume, but vary the tone of your voice. This will add emphasis and vitality to what you say.

Each office has its own particular form for answering the telephone. You, as a good secretary, will find out how your telephone should be answered. There are certain rules that are generally acceptable.

How to Take Messages

Be prepared! A basic rule for Boy Scouts is also good for taking telephone messages. This means keeping a pad of paper and a sharpened pencil or a pen beside the telephone at all times. You cannot record the time of your executive's business appointment if you do not have pencil and paper handy.

Be sure to include the date and the time the telephone call came, as well as the caller's name. No matter how efficient you are, do not trust important messages to your memory. Remember, you are not the judge of what is important. Be sure all messages are passed on to the intended recipient, whether or not they seem to make sense to you. In this case you must be the competent recorder who delivers the message as promptly as possible.

Telephone Message Forms

The kind of telephone message forms you should use depends on the type of messages you are called on to take in a given week. A small office with a local business will not need the elaborate setup for taking messages that a large company with constant long-distance phoning will require.

It is up to the secretary, if she is to decide on the kind of message form used, to familiarize herself with the many that are available. Again, look to your local stationery supplier for the forms that best fit your business needs.

The simplest type of message form, other than a blank piece of paper, is the message pad. These convenient pads have "WHILE YOU WERE OUT" printed on them. They have a specified place for the date, time, name of the person to be contacted, who called or came to the office, and other assorted blanks to be filled in. Naturally, they also allow blank space for your remarks as well as a place for you, the person taking the message, to sign your name. In this way, the person receiving the message has all the needed facts at his command.

There are also "LONG-DISTANCE CALL" forms which offer essentially the same blank places to be filled in. These call attention to the fact that the call was from out-of-town and therefore must be handled as quickly as possible.

For an office that receives numerous long-distance calls, there are record books set up that keep full note of all details of incoming as well as outgoing long-distance calls. These provide a very convenient method for checking telephone calls against monthly statements and are usually double-paged, leaving room for all necessary information, such as name of caller, caller's firm, party called, time, costs, and notes.

There are permanent-bound record books that provide a record of every call the office receives. Some of these have automatic duplicate sets that remain in the bound book; the original goes to the person who received the call.

One of the most convenient records of phone calls is the spiral-bound variety that also has a duplicate for a permanent record. This type takes up less space on the desk because it can be opened to the waiting blank and still offers a duplicate record that the secretary can use for referral at a later time. The original, of course, goes to the person who was called.

It is up to the competent secretary to find the best method for taking phone messages for her particular office. Even a long-established secretary should take a look at her methods from time to time and see whether the manner in which she is recording telephone messages is the most efficient way for her particular office. Check into the new things that are constantly being offered by the stationer to find out if there is a new form that might make this very important aspect of the job more efficient.

Telephone messages are very important; a well-recorded message can make the difference between a satisfied customer and the loss of business for the firm.

Your Personal Directory

Many people find it most convenient to keep a book of frequently called numbers next to the telephone. This is an ideal place for emergency numbers as well as those numbers regularly called by you or your executive.

Cross-list your telephone-number file so that you can obtain numbers for your executive as quickly as possible. You will have a listing for Harrison Tool Company under H, but, if Mr. Birmingham is the man you need to contact, list him under B also.

Another good suggestion is to list the name of Mr. Birmingham's secretary on both cards. This may seem like a duplication of listings, as the information will appear on both file cards, but a cross-file of this nature will definitely help to increase your efficiency, and you may hear your executive brag—"My secretary can find anything I need."

Before You Call

Before you place a call, do you think of what you are going to say? And in what order? Make notes so that you remember to cover every point in a logical sequence. Be sure you make sense.

Have details in front of you, such as names, addresses, and dates. If you are calling in reference to a letter or bill, have it in front of you for reference.

Outgoing Calls

When you need to make an outgoing call, be sure of the number. Before dialing, check the telephone directory of your personal call list. This will help avoid wrong numbers and save time as well.

Be sure to let the telephone ring. While most business calls are made to other businesses, allow enough time for an answer. Ten rings of the telephone equal one minute of your time. Allow this much to make your connection.

As you identified yourself for incoming calls, be sure to do the same when you are placing a call. Others may not recognize you by your voice, so begin the conversation with a good start by giving your name right away.

You may reach a switchboard operator. Be prepared to tell your story in a sentence or two, so that the operator can connect you with the proper person. If you are calling long distance, be sure to tell the operator the place from which you are calling. This extra information may get you the person you want just a little bit faster.

Giving Information

If you must leave the line to obtain information for a caller, it is courteous to say, "Will you wait? Or shall I call you back?" If the person chooses to stay on the line, use the "hold" button (if your telephone has one) or lay the receiver down gently. If it should take you longer than you expected to gather material, return to the line every 30 seconds or so to assure the caller you are working on the request. When you have the information, thank the caller for waiting.

At the close of the conversation, thank the person for calling and do your best to end the conversation in a way that will leave the caller feeling satisfied. After you say goodbye, let the caller hang up first. Then replace your receiver carefully.

Long-Distance Calls

Although much of your telephone work may be done with local calls, occasions do arise when you must make a long-distance call. The etiquette listed above applies to long-distance phoning as well as to local calls.

Remember the time differences when placing long-distance calls. It may be early on a working morning in New York, but it is before business hours in Los Angeles. This can be the difference between getting your answer or not and applies to all long-distance calls placed in the course of any office day.

There are several ways to place long-distance calls. The cost depends on the type of call placed, the day of the week, and the time of day at the location from which you are calling. The expense of the telephone call you are placing might be described as the following equation:

Time of day when call is placed plus rate mileage equals cost of the call.

Day rates apply Monday through Friday from 8:00 A.M. to 5:00 P.M.

Evening rates apply Sunday through Friday from 5:00 P.M. to 11:00 P.M.

Night and weekend rates apply from 11:00 P.M to 8:00 A.M. every night plus all day Saturday and Sunday until 5:00 P.M.

Station-to-Station Calls

When you are reasonably sure the person you want to talk with will be there, or when you will talk with anyone who answers, dial direct. It is possible to dial direct to almost any state in the United States today.

With this type of call the charge is made automatically to the phone you are calling from as soon as the distant call is answered. Rates for direct-dialed calls are lower than operator-handled calls, especially at night and on weekends. There is no longer a three-minute minimum charge for direct-dialed calls. If you talk for a minute or less, you will be billed for only a minute.

To dial direct station-to-station, you will need the telephone number of the person being called. This includes the area code as well as the local number. A numerical list of area codes, prepared by most local telephone companies, is of help when placing long-distance calls. Include such a book or booklet with your reference material.

Operator Assistance

Because it costs more to handle them, calls requiring operator assistance are charged at a higher rate than those completed without the help of an operator. Operator-assisted calls are calls such as collect, credit card, calls billed to a third number or special-billing number, calls made from coin telephones, and person-to-person calls.

Person-to-Person—Since station-to-station rates are always cheaper, it is best to use person-to-person only when it is essential to talk to a particular person or if you know there is likely to be a delay in reaching the person, such as a paging situation.

Appointment Calls

Appointment calls involve a telephone operator who is asked to put through a person-to-person call at a specified hour. The operator makes contact with the person to be called at the specified time and then notifies the caller. This service is no more expensive than a person-to-person call but does save time for the caller.

Sequence Calls

When a number of calls are to be made to out-of-town points, the secretary can supply the telephone-company operator with a list of those calls, including the names of the persons to be called, the city and state, and the correct telephone number if known, as well as the time the executive wishes to complete each call. The operator will then place the calls as arranged.

Time Difference

In the continental United States, there are four different time zones—Eastern, Central, Mountain, and Pacific. Each zone is separated by a one-hour time differential.

Eastern time .... Noon
Central time............... 11:00 A.M.
Mountain time............ 10:00 A.M.
Pacific time .... 9:00 A.M.

The earliest a business office in New York can call a business office in California is at 12:00 noon. Conversely, California knows that at 9:00 A.M., the start of their work day, it is lunchtime in New York.

Special Equipment

A competent secretary will familiarize herself with what is available from the telephone company serving her office. Phone-company personnel are only too glad to discuss the most efficient means of implementing specific business needs. The special equipment listed here does not include such specifics as telephone aids for impaired vision or loss of hearing. Such things are available, and, if you or your executive has a problem, contact your local representative about such aids.

The Call Director

This push-button telephone can handle up to 29 lines and allows one person to see the status of all lines at all times. This has taken the place of many different and separate telephones on the desk. It is a compact unit that also offers optional features such as hold calls, speakerphone, and intercom conferences.

Speakerphone

Just push one button, then dial without lifting the handset. Speak, and your voice is picked up by a microphone sensitive enough to "hear" voices clearly anywhere in the office. Listen over a loudspeaker with volume adjustable to your preference.

Using speakerphones at multiple locations permits electronic conferences that can save substantially on time and travel expenses. This is a means of getting more done faster, with hands-free telephoning.

WATS—Wide Area Telecommunications Service

If your business interests are geographically dispersed, you need all the help you can obtain to keep in touch with prospects, customers, suppliers, and diverse sources of information.

One answer is WATS—a special telephone service that lets you expand your communications ability while keeping a lid on your telephone budget. This is a special service for wide-area telephoning and allows you to make out-of-state calls within a given geographical location. Area One is composed of those states nearest your own location. WATS gives you virtually unrestricted telephoning to your chosen areas. This is a package plan that can be arranged with the local telephone company to meet your unique operational requirements.

Telegrams, Cables, and Radio Messages

When your executive tells you to wire certain information to a customer or supplier, you will need to know the basic facts about telegrams, cables, and radio messages. If speed is of prime importance, you must know the fastest and most economical way of transmitting that information. Western Union provides modern telegraph service and is an important part of this nation's business life.

You may not need to know that a Desk-Fax is a facsimile machine that sends your message in exact picture form unless you have such a machine available in your office. However, it is wise to learn about the different types of written communication that can be sent and how this is done.

The telegram, nightletter, and the mailgram can all be dictated to Western Union over the telephone. However, if you are a frequent user of any of these methods of communication, you will want to obtain blanks from Western Union or the post office direct. These not only give you the form preferred for sending your message but also enable you to keep copies for your files.

The Telegram

The full-rate telegram is basically a 15-word message that can usually be delivered in 3 to 5 hours. Additional words on a telegram are charged for at a low extra-word rate. There is no charge for the address and signature in a full-rate telegram.

Preparing a Telegram

To facilitate the preparation of a telegram message, use telegraph blanks provided by Western Union. These blanks provide places to check the type of service to be used—either full-rate telegram or nightletter. In addition, they provide full address space, ample lineage for the message, as well as the sender's name, address, and telephone number.

It is wise to make at least three copies of a telegram—one to be sent, one to be retained in the company file, and one as a record of the telegrams sent to facilitate checking the billing at the end of the given time period.

If you, the secretary, are responsible for actually wording the telegram, you will learn many shortcuts and word economies. Any word found in the dictionary counts as one word. Abbreviations are written with no spacing, such as "COD" for cash on delivery. Geographical names are written according to the number of words; i.e., Los Angeles is two words while LA is one word. If frequent writing of telegrams is part of your job, you will want to contact your local Western Union office for more specifics along these lines.

The Nightletter

The minimum charge for a nightletter is for 100 words. The nightletter may be sent at any time up until 2:00 A.M. and will be delivered from 7:00 A.M. until 2:00 P.M. of the following business day. As with the full-rate telegram, there is no charge for the address and signature in a nightletter.

The Mailgram

The mailgram is a message based on a minimum charge for 100 words and is transmitted over Western Union facilities to the nearest post office in the city of destination. The mailgram then proceeds through regular postal facilities for delivery the day following the post office's receipt of same. The cut-off time to effect delivery for the following regular mail delivery is 7:00 P.M.

The rules for a telegram apply as well to the mailgram. Forms are also available from Western Union and should be typed at least in triplicate as for a telegram.

International Messages

Few parts of the world cannot be reached by international messages. Such messages are either cabled or sent by radio in the case of shore-to-ship communication. There is a charge for every word, including the name and address. Punctuation is charged for as well. If your office is in the habit of sending many international messages, it would be wise to call Western Union to get full particulars as to international regulations.

Other Telegraphic Services

There is so much happening constantly in data-automated systems that it is impossible to go into all here. There are systems from Western Union called Telex and TWX. Other data systems come from all major data services. Companies such as Texas Instruments, General Electric, and the like will be happy to provide you with needed material on what their companies offer.

This chapter was called "Communications—Lifeline of the Office." It is important for you, the secretary, to know what is available along these lines and the best way for you to use them in your daily work. All forms of communication—from a local telephone call to an international message—will go across your desk. You, the informed secretary, are ready for them.

The Business Letter

The handling of mail and the writing of business letters were briefly mentioned in the chapter on communications. Any graduate of a secretarial school will have been taught most of the elements of a good business letter. However, questions do arise—and, if you have some, the following are general rules for writing business letters.

When to Write a Letter

When your executive dictates a letter or a memo, you have no problem as to what to do. But there may be times when you have to make a decision yourself as to whether to write or whether to use the telephone. Naturally, the telephone is the fastest means of direct communication, but there are times when the letter is a must.

When information requires confirmation, the written form is the best. This will give you a permanent record of that message for your files and will eliminate misunderstandings in the future.

If you are trying to gather information, such as credit ratings, which may be embarrassing for the other party, a written memo or letter is preferred. Likewise, if there is difficulty in contacting a specific person for information, such as a man who travels frequently, a letter or memo will reach him when he returns to his desk.

A letter will take more time than the telephone to obtain the needed answers or material, but, since it is a written form, with copies maintained in your own files, it can be considered more accurate for normal business needs.

The Format

The business organization for which you work will probably have an established format for correspondence. Before you type your first letter, look at copies of previous letters to note the form used by your company. There are four basic forms.

The Full Block

In the full-block letter all lines begin at the left margin. The advantage of this style is its simplicity, and it is one of the most popular of business-letter forms. A minor variation of the block form is to indent the date and the complimentary close to give a more balanced appearance to the letter.

The Semiblock

In the semiblock letter paragraphs are indented as well as the date and the complimentary close. Five spaces are usually allowed for the indentation, although as many as ten spaces are considered acceptable.

Indented Style

All principal lines of the indented-style letter are indented. The lines of the inside address and the closing section of the letter are all indented five spaces from the line above. Each paragraph of the letter begins with a five-space indentation. This style is seldom used in the United States, although it does still appear in foreign correspondence.

Hanging Indented

The hanging-indented letter style is frequently used as an advertising gimmick to attract the reader's attention. Both the date and complimentary close are indented. However, the paragraphs begin at the margin. Succeeding lines are then indented five spaces. This style gives an unusual but eye-catching appearance to the letter.

Full-block style

Semiblock style

Indented style

Hanging indented style

Punctuation Patterns

Punctuation patterns vary as do the letter-format styles. Again, refer to earlier correspondence in your office to see which punctuation pattern is used.

Open

As the name implies, the ends of the lines in an open-punctuation letter are left open, without punctuation. The date, address, salutation, complimentary close, and signature—none requires a punctuation mark. While the end of the dateline is unpunctuated, the comma between day and year is still used. If an abbreviation, such as Co., is used, a period is used for that abbreviation. Any punctuation marks in the lines themselves are retained. Naturally, the body of the letter will still use punctuation to end sentences.

Mixed

With mixed punctuation a colon is used following the salutation, and a comma is used after the complimentary close. This is perhaps the most commonly used style of punctuation with any of the letter formats.

Closed

The closed-punctuation pattern is rarely used in the United States but is quite common with European businesses. A period follows the dateline. Commas are placed at the end of every line of the address except the last, which is ended with a period. A colon follows the salutation. A comma is used with the complimentary close as well as after each line of the signature block except the last, which ends with a period. After the initial and/or enclosure marks, no punctuation is used.

Individual Parts of a Business Letter

The Letterhead

The letterhead can be defined as the printed heading on the business paper or as the paper itself. Here, letterhead refers to the printed heading that includes the name, address, and telephone number of the business. In some cases this also includes officers of the company. The letterhead is usually one and one-half to two inches in depth.

Dateline

The form in which the date is typed is fairly standard today. January 15, 1979 is the usual form. Note that the month is spelled out, not abbreviated, and that a comma follows the day. Since every business communication should be dated, this is most important. The date used by the secretary is usually the date on which the letter was dictated.

The dateline should be typed two to six lines below the last line of the letterhead. Placement on the page depends on which style of letter format your company uses.

Inside Address

The inside address includes the addressee, the street address, the city and state, and the zip code. Addresses should occupy at least three lines. If no street address is available, it is acceptable to type the city on one line and the state following. Avoid more than four typed lines for the address.

The inside address begins four to eight lines below the dateline. In the event of a very short letter on a large piece of paper, drop the inside address down several more spaces to improve the appearance of the letter. No line in the address should extend beyond the middle of the page. Two examples of correct inside address form follow:

Mr. Jonathan Wynne
Baltimore Sunpapers
2 North Calvert St.
Baltimore, Maryland 21202

Mr. Gary Hansell
Sun Life Insurance Company
New York, New York 10036

If the addressee holds several offices in the company, use the same title used on the signature line of his letter, as this is probably the one he prefers.

Salutation

The salutation is always typed underneath the inside address, with a blank line preceding and following it. It always begins at the left-hand margin. The first letter of the first word of the salutation is capitalized. Accepted forms of address for specific titles are listed elsewhere in this book.

The degree of formality used in the salutation depends on how well the writer knows the person to whom the letter is addressed. Examples of correct salutations are:

Dear Sam
My dear Senator Jones
Dear Mrs. Lewis
Dear Dr. Rogers
Gentlemen
Ladies
Mesdames

Body of the Letter

Most business letters are single-spaced. An exception can be made with a very short communication, which should be double-spaced to fill out more of the page. Double-space between paragraphs. If there is an insert in the body of the letter, such as an address or quoted material, indent ten spaces from both the left and right margins to make the insert stand out. Double-space before and after the insert.

Complimentary Close

The complimentary close, the end of the business letter, concludes the written conversation of the letter. Its placement depends on the format for the letter. The tone of it depends on the formality of the letter.

Formal closings   Respectfully
                           Very respectfully yours
Less formal   Very truly yours
                           Yours truly
Personal closings Sincerely
                           Cordially
                           With all good wishes

Signature Line

The signature line is normally typed four spaces below the complimentary close. The signature should be typed as the writer normally signs his name, including any degrees or titles by which he wishes to be addressed in reply. A short title may be typed directly after the signature. A longer title should be placed on the line below the signature, in line with

No courtesy title is used by a man before his name, either in his written signature or on the signature line. However, a woman customarily indicates her status by using Miss or Mrs. before her typed signature. This is often done by including the status in parentheses before the name; i.e., (Miss) Lorraine Jackson.

If you are signing your executive's name to his letter, simply write his name in the space left for the signature and place your initials beside it.

The identification initials are generally typed on the left-hand side of the page, two spaces below the last line in the signature block. The dictator's initials are typed first in caps followed by a colon. This is followed by two initials of the transcriber, usually in lower case. Again, company preference as to the style to use must be considered.

Typing Numbers

Numbers one through ten are usually spelled out. Numbers 11 and above should be typed as figures:

Please send me six copies of your magazine.
Please send me 15 copies of your magazine.

For amounts of money, use figures. Percentages are usually written, as 15 percent. Dimensions and measurements are written in figures, as 20 feet or size 4. Time is written with figures with A.M. or P.M. following, as 4 P.M.—or as four o'clock.

Where you use a series of numbers including some above and below ten, use one style to express those numbers.

My order is for three pens, five pencils, and twelve erasers.
I require 30 dresses, 15 suits, and 4 slacks.

Money in large round amounts may be written in two ways: $12 million or 12 million dollars. This only applies to whole numbers. Complicated numbers should be written entirely as figures, as $12,456,192.

Addressing Envelopes

Placement of the address on an envelope should be in the center of the envelope, or a little to the left of the horizontal center to allow for long lines. If the address is short, double-space the lines. However, if there are four or more address lines, single-space them. Customarily, block form is used on an envelope. The last line of the envelope address should include the zip-code number. Complete zip-code information can be obtained from your nearest post office.

Punctuation

Correct punctuation can be the difference between sending out the first letter typed or having to retype it. A good secretary will check on questionable punctuation before turning in an incorrect letter to the executive. Knowing when to use a comma or a semicolon can make a big difference.

Apostrophe

An apostrophe indicates possession, contraction, or plurality of different words.

Possession	John's letter
	a day's work
Contraction	it's in place of it is
	I'll in place of I will
	you're in place of you are
Plurality	p's and q's
	1's and 7's
	However: 1970s

Colon

The colon separates parts of a sentence that are almost complete and independent by themselves. The colon may also be used to introduce an extended quotation and is used after a formal salutation in a letter.

The contract said:
Mr. Jones' speech involved three principles:
Dear Sir:

Comma

A comma separates two independent clauses in a compound sentence; sets off a modifying phrase; separates words or phrases in a series of three or more.

He wrote yesterday, but you have not received the
  letter.
My secretary, Mrs. Black, wrote you.
We require paper, pencils, and pens. (In this example,
  the comma before the word "and" may be omitted.)

Dash

The dash shows a break in thought, sets off a parenthetical phrase, or serves to summarize what has already
been said.

I must say--before giving you details--
The anniversary sale--which was most successful--
Toys, puzzles, and books--all were needed.

Ellipsis

An ellipsis shows the omission of quoted material or
words needed to complete a sentence.

Friends, Romans . . . lend me your ears.
Friends, Romans, and countrymen . . . . (When an ellipsis is used at the end of a sentence, a period is
  added.)

Exclamation Point

An exclamation point indicates strong feeling or an em-
phatic saying.

Don't delay!
Call at once!

Hyphen

A hyphen is used primarily to show word division at the
end of a line. It also separates the parts of compound words.
It is used between two or more words that serve as a single
adjective preceding a noun.

resi-dent (The letters dent will appear on the following
  line.)
ninety-nine
mother-in-law
one-man office
well-to-do person

Parentheses

Parentheses are used to set off explanatory or supple-
mentary material not essential to the meaning of the sentence or to include numeric amounts in some legal documents. If they are a part of the parenthetical clause or
phrase, periods, commas, and other punctuation marks belong within the parentheses. If they belong to the words outside the parentheses, other punctuation also belongs outside them.

Included is One Dollar ($1.00) for you.

Period

A period indicates the completion of a sentence. It is also used for abbreviations.

The sentence is over.
Mrs. Jones and Mr. Smith went together.

Question Mark

A question mark is used at the end of a direct question.

Are you ready to go?

When used in conjunction with other punctuation, such as quotations, the question mark appears like this:

"Are you ready to go?" he asked.

Quotation Marks

Quotation marks are used to enclose a direct quotation, for some titles, and for unusual words that are not to be taken at face value.

"Are you ready to go?" he asked.
The third chapter of *Treasure Island* is titled "The Black Spot."
That was some "free" service!

Semicolon

A semicolon separates two clauses not joined by a conjunction and is used before connecting adverbs. It also separates items in a series when one or more of the items contains commas.

The agent lists the policy fee; he collects when there is a loss.
The trip went all over the world; however, he stopped in Tahiti.

In conclusion, this is by no means a complete course in the correct use of punctuation. There are other books on your reference shelf that will go into more detail when you require that for special questions. Such things as capitalization, underlining, and word division can all be learned from sources of grammar such as the dictionary or English grammar you have nearby. If this is your weakness, by all means take time to brush up on your basics.

Office Mail

Incoming Office Mail

Handling the daily mail efficiently is one of the duties usually assigned to a secretary and is certainly one assigned to an executive secretary. Part of the service to your executive is to open and prepare his mail in the fastest possible way, allowing him to attend to it with the greatest amount of ease. It is your job to see that he has the necessary records from the files that pertain to the request in the mail, securely attached to that letter. In this way the executive can make his decision more quickly as to what action should be taken.

Although different businesses process their mail in different ways, the rules set forth here apply to most offices, large or small, and permit a fairly routine procedure to expedite this important facet of the business day.

Sorting the Mail

In most offices mail is delivered at about the same time every day. Therefore, an efficient secretary knows when she will receive mail and plans her day to include immediate handling of it.

Whether the mail comes in by the bag-load or in a reasonably small pile, the first step in handling daily mail is to sort it. The order of importance may be this:

Telegrams, first class, second class, third class, and parcel post or fourth class.

If international mail is a regular part of your incoming mail, you may want to insert this before the second-class mail. Memos may or may not deserve an early place in your sorting. The way you sort depends on the particulars of your own office.

The reason for careful sorting of the mail is to ensure that the most important matters are laid out for the executive first. It stands to reason he will want to answer an important letter before he looks over circulars, booklets, or catalogs.

Letters marked personal or confidential should be separated from the rest of the mail and given, unopened, to the executive. If they are opened by mistake, this should be noted on the envelope. In the event that the executive is away from the office for an extended time, he will give instructions as to the handling of personal and confidential mail.

Opening the Mail

Use a letter-opener carefully, so as not to tear the contents of the envelope. A light tap of the letter on the desk before opening it will ensure that the contents move down in the envelope and prevent tearing of any part of the contents.

Be sure everything is removed from the envelope. Checks and important enclosures have been lost through carelessness. When you are certain that nothing remains in the envelope, check the letter to see if it contains a return address. If this is not on the letter but is on the envelope, attach the envelope to the letter with a paper clip. Some offices prefer that this is done with all the mail. Others allow the secretary to destroy envelopes unless they are needed for return addresses.

In attaching enclosures and envelopes to the mail, use paper clips or file folders rather than staples. Staples should not be used on the punched cards that are so frequent in this data-automated age.

Dating the Mail

Many offices use a rubber stamp with the date to be sure that incoming mail is dated on the day it is received. Whether or not you have a rubber stamp, it is wise to date the mail on the day it is received. This simplifies explanations as to why a deadline was not met or why a request was not filled sooner. The date of the letter's receipt may be supplemented with the time of receipt if there is more than one regular mail delivery to the office.

Preparing the Mail

In offices where mail preparation includes the secretary's reading of the mail, the next step may be a secondary sorting. The order of importance for letters received may need to be adjusted.

An efficient secretary, when reading the mail, will underline important points for the executive's attention. It may be necessary to make notes in the margin as to action required or other points that the executive needs to know.

While reading the letters, the secretary should note any material needed from the files, such as previous correspondence. This material can be assembled either before presenting the morning mail to the executive or while he is reading the mail. Either way, it will be available to him when he needs it.

When the mail has been opened, sorted, dated, and properly prepared, it is ready to be given to the executive for his perusal. The efficiency of the secretary will make her executive's work faster and easier to complete.

If the Executive Is Away

There are times when the boss is away from the office for hours or days at a time. When these occasions occur, the executive will usually have left instructions as to the handling of his mail. The initial procedure of the secretary will be the same. When decisions are to be made as to the disposition of the mail, she will make them. This may mean taking specific problems to the next in command in the office, or it may mean drafting a letter to the writer explaining the executive's absence from the office. Either way, careful records will be kept of any action taken and will be presented to the executive on his return.

Outgoing Office Mail

The actual letter has been discussed earlier in this chapter. However, mailing of typed letters includes a knowledge of postal rates and available fast-delivery services, as well as certain checkpoints to be made on each letter sent out.

The address on the inside of the letter should agree with that typed on the envelope. This reduces the chance of error and delay caused by an incorrect address.

If the letter is personal or confidential, this should be noted on the envelope, as well as the type of mail delivery being used. Such things as special delivery must be noted on the mailing envelope.

Before the letter is inserted, it must be checked as to signature and enclosures. Naturally, the correct postage and correct zip code must be on the envelope.

Postal Rates and Classes

Many classes of mail are available to businesses, and, as an efficient secretary, it is your business to know what they are. The place to start is the nearest post office. There are up-to-date pamphlets available free as to postal regulations and current rates. This type of material should be part of your reference shelf in the office and you should have some knowledge of it yourself. The following is a brief summary of postal classes of mail.

First-Class Mail

First-class mail is used for handwritten and typed messages, postal cards, and the transmission of checks and money orders. First-class letter mail may not be opened for postal inspection and is determined by weight (no more than 13 ounces) without regard to distance. All first-class mail is given the fastest transportation service available.

Priority Mail

Priority mail is for fast transportation and expeditious handling of mailable matter weighing more than 13 ounces on which priority-mail rates have been paid.

Second-Class Mail

Second-class mail is generally used by newspaper and other periodical publishers who must meet certain postal-service requirements. It may also be used for mailing individual copies of magazines and newspapers.

Third-Class Mail

Third-class mail is used primarily for large mailings such as circulars, booklets, and catalogs. Because there are several categories of third-class mail, consult your postmaster for information as to your specific needs.

Fourth-Class Mail (Parcel Post)

Packages weighing one pound or more fall into the category of fourth-class mail. It is mainly for domestic parcel post, and there are specific regulations as to pounds, length, and girth of the packages to be sent. Consult your post office to find out the latest regulations. If you are sending packages outside of the continental United States, consult the post office for the most current regulations.

There are special mailing rates in this class for books, manuscripts, records, catalogs, etc. Again, consult the nearest post office for current regulations.

Available Fast-Delivery Services

Such things as aerograms, express mail, special delivery, and mailgrams all are services offered by the post office. There are details such as return receipts, insurance of mail, C.O.D. service, money orders, and claims for damages. You will need a speaking acquaintance with these services. The post office is continually updating its available information, and you should have available the latest copy of their rates and fees.

In addition, check the yellow pages of the telephone book for other fast-delivery services, such as United Parcel Service, local messenger services, and Federal Armored Express. All these companies will be happy to supply you with information as to how their services work. Armed with this information, you, the secretary, can make good suggestions to your executive when delivery of letters or packages is of prime importance.

Writing a Report

Whether you are an executive secretary whose job requires you to write reports or a secretary who will only be helping your executive with his reports, you will do a better job if you understand what is involved. To put the report process in a nutshell, begin with research; end up with the finished form. Naturally, this is an over-simplification. There are many steps in between.

Style of Business Reports

The four basic styles of business reports are: the memorandum report, the letter report, the short report, and the formal report. The styling of each can vary from office to office, and it is up to the writer, either executive or secretary, to choose the style best suited to a particular report. The nature of what is to be written in the report will frequently dictate the proper style for that report.

The Memorandum Report

Information transferred from one person to another or from one department to another in an office is usually done by means of the memorandum report. This is an in-house report, generally routine, and may be of an informal nature.

Interoffice forms for departmental correspondence usually include "To, From, Date, and Subject" on them. Whether or not you have printed forms, it is important that this information is on all memoranda. The final draft of the memorandum report is usually single-spaced but may be altered to suit individual memos. Although memorandum reports may be signed, this is not usually the case, as the sender's name is at the top of the form.

The Letter Report

The letter report is generally directed to people or groups outside the company when more information is given than a normal letter would include. It is typed on company letterhead stationery, with plain bond paper for continuation sheets.

The body of the letter report may utilize headings to call attention to the most important aspects of the report. Subheadings also serve to emphasize and make reference easier.

The Short Business Report

The short business report may include a title page and a summary, as well as conclusions and recommendations. Such special parts as tables and graphs can be added easily to this report, and, since it is usually several pages in length, it may be unbound, side-bound, or top-bound.

The short business report may be either single- or double-spaced, but the style should be consistent throughout the report. The title page should include all pertinent information, such as title and address of the person to whom the report is submitted, as well as the name, title, and address of the preparer of the report. The date also should appear on the title page.

The Formal Report

The formal report will include a cover, title page, letter of authorization and/or transmittal, preface, table of contents, list of exhibits, summary, report body, footnotes, appendix, bibliography, and index.

All this is not as complicated as it may sound. The cover is simply the binder used to protect the report. The title page includes the report title, usually typed all in capital letters. A subtitle may also be included here, as well as other pertinent information, such as the name of the writer, department, and other necessary information about the report that may simplify its purpose for the recipient.

Letters of authorization and transmittal are not necessarily complicated. They tell who was authorized to write the study in the first case and sources of information and acknowledgements in the second. The writer of the report must decide which of these letters, or both, are to be included in the formal report.

The table of contents provides a breakdown of the contents of the report, with page numbers listed for easy location of specific material. The report may be prepared for many people, and each person will be interested in particular sections of the report as well as its entirety. An accurate table of contents is another way of outlining the final contents of the report.

The list of exhibits, such as illustrations, charts, and tables is another means of telling the recipient exactly where such things are in the body of the report. They are listed by page number.

The summary, synopsis, or abstract is the total report summed up in a few words. This allows a quick briefing before an actual in-depth study of the report is made.

The report body is the in-depth study of the subject matter with its conclusions.

Footnotes give credit to secondary sources used by the writer of the report. They may be placed at the bottom of the page on which the quoted material is used; however, an easier form is to number them where they appear and then include all footnotes at the end of the entire work.

The appendix should include clearly identified material such as details, documents, and summary tables not put into the body of the report.

The bibliography includes an alphabetical listing of the sources used by the writer to compile the report.

An index is not necessary in a short report but is of great help in long, detailed reports. The index serves as a cross-reference for the report and shows where specific material is located in the report.

Planning the Report

The most experienced of writers is well aware of the importance of planning the report. For anyone unfamiliar with writing reports, this is perhaps the most important phase of the work.

Be sure that the purpose of the report is clear in your own mind. Put that objective down on paper. If your report is to discuss the shortage control procedures, you will not need material about the selling requirements of the personnel. There may be some overlap, but you must zero in on the important points of the subject at hand.

The next step in planning the report is to collect the data you will need. This will include two types of material. The first is usually the most accessible, as it includes your own sources from the company for which you work. This will be all letters, documents such as previous reports on the subject, personal interviews and observations, as well as your own experience with the problem at hand. As you can see, you may not be able to gather this material in a few minutes. Particularly when observations and interviews are needed, this may take quite some time.

The second type of material needed is that which comes from other sources, such as periodicals, other reports on the same subject, and general research material that takes you out of the scope of your own company.

Organization

Now that you have clearly stated the purpose of the report and gathered as much material as you need, the organization of that material is your next step. Please note here that so far you have not written anything down on paper except the purpose of your report.

There are several methods of organizing a written report, although most do end up with a complete outline. Your particular report may best be outlined by lining up facts in the order of their appearance—in other words, by time. The dating of events as they occurred, what happened before and what happened after, as well as what is and what will be are all ways of clearly outlining a particular problem.

You may decide to outline in the order of the importance of the events described. You may prefer to outline from simple to complex facts or from the most important to the least important. Perhaps you prefer stating the best method first and working down to the least acceptable.

By giving careful attention to all phases of the outline, you are actually making the work of writing the report much simpler. A detailed outline may take time to work out, but it saves writing time in the long run. With the primary points of each section of your report carefully worked out in outline form, you are ready to fill in the details of a well-organized report.

A brief outline for this section of this book reads as follows:

I. Planning the Report
   A. Purpose of Report
   B. Collection of Data
   C. Organization

The principles applied to this small section of the outline apply to an outline for any long, detailed report. The fuller your outline is, the easier the report is to write.

Writing the Report

The language of a report should be specific and understandable to the recipient. Do not use a $1 word when a 25¢ word will do. Your object in writing the report is not to show how much of the dictionary you know. The object is clear communication of important ideas.

Objectivity should be maintained when writing a formal report. The report is not an expression of personal opinions or unsubstantiated conclusions. Rather, it is a formal study of a particular problem or problems from an impartial source. You, the writer, should not appear in the report. Eliminate such phrases as "I believe," and replace them with "Research shows that . . . ." There may be times when a person of authority does use the first person in a formal report, but as a general rule this is not done.

Use clear, concise sentences. In the event that a thought has developed into a lengthy sentence, break up the idea into a more understandable form.

Consider the recipient or recipients of the report. If the report concerns engineering and is going to engineers, the use of technical engineering terms will be most acceptable. However, if the report is not going to a particular technical group, do not let it confuse the reader with a lot of terms he will not understand.

Eliminate the verb "to be" where possible. A report that uses action verbs instead of "it is . . ." reads in a much more business-like manner.

Not — "It is the problem of the Board . . ."
But — "The Board's problem indicates . . ."

The writing of most formal reports includes a rough or first draft. When this is completed, the writer and/or you, the secretary, will revise and edit it. This is the time for correcting sentence structure and clarifying complicated material. Involved reports of importance may go through the stage of revision more than once before they are ready for the final finished form. Each of these stages offers an opportunity to improve the communication value of the report in making it as clear and concise and as informative as possible.

The Finished Form

No matter what care and attention was paid to writing the formal report, if it is not presented in a readable form, it will not be successful. Make preparation for the final typing of the report as carefully as you did for the report itself.

Your company may require a standard form as to the cover or binder of a report. If they do not, there are such covers available from the stationer. The purpose of the cover is to protect the report and to add to its attractiveness. A busy executive may push aside an unprofessional report, to be read later. He will undoubtedly at least look further if the presentation is clean and attractive.

The final report will include paragraphs of about 10 to 12 lines. Longer paragraphs tend to tire the reader. A varied length of paragraphs, some shorter than others, makes a more easily read report.

Margins for the finished report should measure 1 inch on the top, right side, and bottom. They should be 1½ inches at the left side, to allow space for the cover or binder.

Headings are usually typed in all capital letters; subtitles may use capitals and lower case.

Double-spacing is generally used in most formal reports. Such items as quoted material may be indented and single-spaced. This adds to the readability of the report.

All pages of the text of the report are usually numbered with Arabic numerals, while introductory material may use lower-case Roman numerals. Naturally, numbering the pages is one of the last things done in a formal report.

Conclusion

The best summation of the formal business report and its effectiveness may be the following questions about the report.

1. Does it accomplish and adhere to the purpose of the original plan?
2. Is it readable?
3. Is the information authentic and well documented?
4. Does the report include all the needed materials, such as charts and graphs?
5. Are all the pros and cons of the recommendations clearly stated?
6. Is the report technically correct as to sentence structure, spelling, and typographical errors?
7. Does this report include all the facts as the writer intended?

If the answers to these questions are positive and both you and your executive have checked and rechecked the formal report, chances are good that this a well-executed report — and worth the many hours of time and labor that created it.

Adjuncts to the Office

Certain books and materials provide great help in research for the secretary. Hopefully, this book is a start in the right direction. However, no single volume can hope to have all the answers needed. This is why it was suggested earlier to accumulate an office reference shelf that should be easily accessible to both the secretary and the executive. The list to follow will be small and compact, like this book, but it is a guide in the direction of gaining additional source material that should be in every office.

Cresci, Martha W.
Complete Book of Model Business Letters
Parker Publishing Company, Inc.
West Nyack, New York, 1976

Here is a book with over 275 actual letters that can help you find the right letter for your particular situation. The example letter may discuss an incorrect order of ceramic bowls. Your own mix-up may concern an incorrect order of stationery. You will easily adapt the ceramic-bowl letter to your own problem. The "Table of Contents" is detailed as to the many kinds of letters included, and the "Index" provides further help for specific letter problems.

Gavin, Ruth E., and Sabin, William A.
Reference Manual for Stenographers and Typists
Gregg Division/McGraw Hill Book Company
New York, 1970

While aimed for the use of the stenographer, this manual offers much help to the secretary as well. The "Table of Contents" ranges from grammar to resources, and the book is indexed fully, so that solutions to writing problems can be easily located as well as clearly understood. Both its compact size and wealth of information give this book a place on your office bookshelf of reference material.

Janis, J. Harold; Thompson, Margaret H.
New Standard Reference for Secretaries and Administrative Assistants
The Macmillan Company
New York, 1972

The authorities consulted in the preparation of this book offer the secretary in-depth research for specific business problems. Many accepted answers to problems are dealt with in the text itself. A thorough and comprehensive index as well as a quick reference table on the cover pages facilitate the use of this book.

Klein, A. E.
The New World Secretarial Handbook
Collins World Publishing Co., Inc.
Cleveland, Ohio 44111, 1968

In addition to carefully written chapters on the aspects of the secretary, written by experts in the field, this book offers a comprehensive list of words, spelled and syllabified. The complete appendix also includes such things as abbreviations, signs and symbols, and weights and measures.

Webster's Secretarial Handbook
G. & C. Merriam Company
Springfield, Massachusetts 01101, 1976

This combination of business facts includes such things as a guide to effective business English and career-path development, as well as section of suggestions for further reading. It is one of the most current (and therefore most up-to-date) of the enlarged secretarial handbooks available.

Before purchasing any of the above books for your office library, it is best to see and handle them yourself if possible. The above-listed books are available in many library systems. All are worthwhile and are well written as to accuracy and content.

Other Reference Material (listed alphabetically)

Area-Code Booklet

This is available all over the United States as a free service from the Telephone Company. It is of great help in expediting long-distance phoning.

Atlas

A comprehensive world atlas will be especially useful to the secretary whose work goes beyond the scope of a small local area. When letters or reports go out nationally or internationally, a good atlas comes into frequent use.

Dictionary

Every office bookshelf should include a good general dictionary. An unabridged version may not be required, but a good desk dictionary is important. In law or medical offices, the secretary should add a legal or medical dictionary.

Postage Rates

This information is usually available in pamphlet form at the post office. It lists postal regulations regarding all forms of mail, from first class to parcel post. Caution: Be sure the one you use is the latest one issued by the post office.

Telephone Directory

The local telephone book with its yellow pages should be accessible, if not kept with your reference material. This book can solve many local problems.

Zip-Code Directory

Local zip codes are usually available as a service of the post office. Comprehensive directories covering all 50 states of our country are available at a nominal cost from bookstores or stationers.

Use of the Local Library

Few secretarial positions do not include some research. A wise secretary will not wait until the executive gives a direct assignment to go to the nearest local library. Go before that assignment is issued, and familiarize yourself with the way the library is set up and what it has to offer.

Check the general library catalog. Books are listed in three ways—by author, by title, and by subject. The subject listing will also give you information that is available in periodicals.

Find out where government publications are listed and how they are available. The Federal government has written information on almost every subject, and the information is usually available from the Government Printing Office, Washington, D.C. 20402.

Take some time at the library to handle such books as *Who's Who In America, Bartlett's Familiar Quotations,* and *The Reader's Encyclopedia.* You may become interested and have a broadening experience at the same time.

Make a friend of the librarian. Ask the most efficient way to make telephone inquiries for information. Find out the regulations regarding borrowing of books (get a card for yourself, while you're there) and ascertain if the library has a copying machine. A quickly xeroxed page keeps reference material on your desk when you need it.

Never sell the library short. A good local library and full use of it may be one of the office's most useful accessories.

Tips for Secretarial Efficiency

Shortcuts become habit in handling secretarial work, and some of these time-savers are offered here as suggestions for you. They may seem obvious, or they may be real eye-openers, but they all work. Try them and see.

1. Start each day the day before. That may sound like a conundrum but it is a wise policy for efficiency. Before you leave the office at the end of the day, allow 15 or 20 minutes for planning. Check the calendar and memo pads, recording on them notes needed for the next day's work. Sort papers into their proper folders and files, and clear the desk. A well-ordered desk and a well-ordered mind will be ready to start work promptly the next morning.
2. When using carbon paper, be sure to alternate your carbons from top to bottom and from first carbon to last. This will give longer life to the carbons and ensure better copies.
3. Let a soft paint brush care for your typewriter. Daily maintenance of dusting with a soft brush will keep the exposed parts of your typewriter clean. The long handle will allow you to reach the corners. Your typewriter works hard for you. You owe it two minutes every day.
4. Tape a 3 by 5 card to your typewriter cover. List the needed minor repairs on this card as you notice them. In this way you will be ready for the serviceman when he comes; he, in turn, can do a better job for you by knowing exactly what you want.
5. In typing a two-page letter, put a light pencil mark at the left edge of your paper where you want the last line of typing to end on the first page. This will make it easier to keep the bottom margin one-inch deep. In typing a long report, mark each page in the same way with the light pencil mark. Then all pages will end at the same place. The marks can be easily erased after the page is typed.
6. Before you make an erasure on a letter in the typewriter, move the typewriter carriage to the extreme left or right. This will prevent pieces of the eraser from falling into the machine itself. Good care of your typewriter makes your work easier.
7. Erasers can and do get dirty and then they mark paper with smears. To make an ink-stained eraser work like new, rub it gently on a piece of sandpaper or an emery board. That will do the trick every time.
8. Keep a broken aspirin tablet handy to cover up erasures. A piece of white chalk rubbed on the erasure spot will do as well—but in a pinch, the broken aspirin works, too.
9. Develop a good rhythm when you type. Use a speed somewhat slower than your familiar easy letter com-

binations and let the less familiar catch up. A steady, moderate typing speed will improve your accuracy and save you nervous strain and fatigue.

10. To type a two-column page, newspaper style, make up a form before you begin typing. Use a dark pen (India ink is good) to draw a one-inch margin all around your guide page. This is for margins. Then draw a line down the center of the typing space. Place this guide sheet in back of your typing paper and you will have accurate margins for a two-column page.

11. If you have to make a change on a bound report, do not take the report apart. Insert a blank piece of paper into the typewriter so that an inch shows above the platen. Then insert the still-bound sheet between the platen and the plain sheet. Roll the platen backwards and you are ready to make your change.

12. To avoid tearing the contents of a letter when opening it, tap the unopened envelope on the edge of the desk. The contents will slip away from the top, and the envelope can be easily opened with a letter opener. In this way, the contents will be kept intact.

13. When making airline reservations for the executive, write down the name of the clerk making the original reservation. If changes or additions must be made later, time can be saved by not having to repeat that preliminary information.

14. If you are responsible for writing checks for your executive—either business or personal—fill out the check stub FIRST. You are then assured of never drawing a check without recording it. This helps in correct balancing of the checkbook.

15. Review your executive's appointment schedule with him at the beginning of each day. This will assure both of you that you and he have not made any conflicting dates.

16. If you must leave your desk and have no one who can cover in your absence, put a note in your typewriter stating where you have gone and when you expect to return. This thoughtfulness will tell your executive not only where you are but also that you care about his needs. Knowing when you will return will probably allow him to adjust his needs to your absence.

17. Color code your files. A small colored clip, available in most stationery stores, will allow you to keep an alphabetical file broken down into the specific needs of your office; i.e., a secretary of a company needing machine parts from three different suppliers can alphabetize her machine parts and easily identify them and the supplier by using colored clips. Screws are under S and the supplier is known by a blue clip on the screw file.

18. Any competent secretary is well aware of most of her executive's habits—both good and bad—as well as

many confidential facts that pass over his desk. Be sure the confidence placed in you by your executive is not misplaced. Learn to be a verbal football player. Carry your own ball efficiently but pass to your executive on confidential business.

19. When making long-distance calls, be aware of the time differences in different parts of the country. New York should not call California at 9:00 A.M. New York time. It is then only 6:00 o'clock in the morning in California. Check the time zones listed below before you place the call.

Eastern Time .... Noon
Central Time .... 11:00 A.M.
Mountain Time .... 10:00 A.M.
Pacific Time .... 9:00 A.M.

20. To make the rubber stamp you use easier to ink, store your stamp pad upside down when not in use. This will keep the ink at the top of the pad, ready to give you clear, sharp impressions of the stamp.

21. Open a new ream of paper on the unlabeled end. By keeping the label intact, you are assured of knowing what kind of paper is left in that ream for future use.

22. Telephone dials and receivers are dust-collectors. To keep them clean, use a cotton swab dipped in a liquid disinfectant. This is a small cleaning job that might be overlooked by the office custodian, but the telephone is one of the tools of the office trade and should be cleaned regularly.

23. Keep several paper clips attached to the side of the stenographic notebook for taking dictation. Use the clips to make any "rush" or special items that must be transcribed first. This is an easy way to mark these special items so that they can be located promptly without having to wade through all the given dictation.

24. If you need a brushup on shorthand symbols, use the slack periods of the day. Take a report from the files and practice your shorthand. It will improve your skill as well as your shorthand.

25. It you are interrupted in transcribing written notes, mark your last typed word with a colored pencil. In this way you will be able to find your place easily when you resume typing.

Forms of Address

Person	How to Address	Salutation
Alderman	Alderman John Doe The Honorable John Doe Alderman, City of Baltimore	Dear Alderman Doe: Dear Mr. Doe:
Ambassador	The Honorable John Doe United States Ambassador London, England	Dear Mr. Ambassador: My Dear Mr. Ambassador: My Dear Madam Ambassador:
Archbishop	The Most Reverend John Doe	Your Excellency: Most Reverend Sir: Dear Archbishop Doe:
Associate Justice of U. S. Supreme Court	Mr. Justice Doe The Supreme Court Washington, D. C. 20543	Sir: My dear Mr. Justice: Dear Mr. Justice Doe:
Bishop (Catholic)	The Most Reverend Bishop Doe	Your Excellency: Dear Bishop Doe:
Bishop (Protestant)	The Reverend Bishop Doe or The Right Reverend Bishop Doe	Most Reverend Sir: My dear Bishop Doe:
Cabinet Member, U. S. A.	The Honorable John Doe Secretary of State Washington, D. C. 20520	Sir: Dear Mr. Secretary: Dear Madam Secretary: Dear Mr. Doe:

Forms of Address *(continued)*

Cardinal, U. S. A.	His Eminence, John Cardinal Doe Archbishop of New York	Your Eminence: My dear Cardinal Doe:
Chaplain	Chaplain John Doe Captain, U. S. A.	My dear Chaplain: My dear Chaplain Doe:
Chief Justice of the United States	The Chief Justice The Supreme Court Washington, D. C. 20543	Sir: My dear Chief Justice:
	The Honorable John Doe Chief Justice of the United States	
City Attorney	Hon. (or Mr.) John Doe City Attorney	Dear Mr. Doe:
Commissioner, City	The Honorable John Doe Commissioner of the City of St. Louis	Dear Mr. Doe:
Congressman	The Honorable John Doe House of Representatives Washington, D. C. 20515	Dear Representative Doe: My dear Mr. Doe:
	The Honorable John Doe Representative in Congress 5214 Main Street Hometown, State 00000	My dear Mrs. Doe:

Forms of Address *(continued)*

Consul	Mr. John Doe American Consul London, England In South and Central America: Consul of the United States of America	Dear Mr. Doe:
County Supervisor	Hon. (or Mr.) John Doe Supervisor, Allegheny County	Dear Mr. Doe:
Dean of a School	Dean John Doe School of the Arts New York University	Dear Dean Doe:
	Dr. John Doe Assistant Dean, School of Law University of Maryland	Dear Dr. Doe:
District Attorney	The Honorable John Doe District Attorney, Dade County	Dear Mr. Doe:
Governor	The Honorable John Doe Governor of North Carolina Raleigh, North Carolina	Sir: Dear Governor Doe:
Judge	The Honorable John Doe Judge of the Circuit Court	Dear Judge Doe:

Forms of Address *(continued)*

Title	Address	Salutation
Lieutenant Governor	The Honorable John Doe Lieutenant Governor of Ohio Columbus, Ohio 00000	Sir: Dear Mr. Doe: My dear Governor Doe:
Mayor	The Honorable John Doe Mayor of Chicago Chicago, Illinois 00000	My dear Mayor Doe: Dear Mr. Mayor:
Minister	The Reverend John Doe The Reverend John Doe, D.D., Litt. D. The Very Reverend John Doe, D.D. Dean of St. Mary's Cathedral	Dear Mr. Doe: Dear Mr. Doe: Dear Dean Doe:
Mother Superior	The Reverend Mother Superior Convent of the Sacred Heart Mother Mary Jane, Superior Convent of the Sacred Heart	Reverend Mother: Dear Madam: Dear Mother Mary Jane:
Nun	Sister Mary Louise	Reverend Sister: Dear Sister Mary Louise:
Pope	His Holiness Pope Paul VI	Most Holy Father: Your Holiness:
President of a School	Dr. John Doe President, University of Texas	Dear Dr. Doe: Dear President Doe:

Forms of Address *(continued)*

President of State Senate	The Honorable John Doe, President The Senate of Arizona	Sir:
President of U.S. Senate	The Honorable John Doe President of the Senate Washington, D. C. 00000	Sir:
President of the United States	The President The White House Washington, D. C. 20500 The Honorable John Doe The White House Washington, D. C. 20500	Mr. President My dear Mr. President:
Priest	The Reverend John Doe The Reverend John Doe, Ph.D.	Dear Reverend Father: Dear Father Doe: Dear Dr. Doe:
Professor	Professor John Doe Dr. John Doe Associate Professor, Dept. of History	Dear Mr. Doe: Dear Dr. Doe: Dear Professor Doe:
Rabbi	Rabbi John Doe Dr. John Doe Rabbi John Doe, Ph.D.	My dear Rabbi Doe: My dear Dr. Doe:

Forms of Address *(continued)*

Secretary or Assistant to the President of the United States	The Honorable John Doe Secretary to the President The White House Washington, D. C. 20500	My dear Mr. Doe:
	General John Doe The Assistant to the President	My dear General Doe:
Senator, U. S. or State	The Honorable John Doe	My dear Senator Doe:
	Retired: The Honorable John Doe	My dear Mr. Doe:
Speaker of the House	The Honorable John Doe Speaker of the House of Representatives Washington, D. C. 20515	My dear Mr. Speaker:
State Legislator	The Honorable John Doe	Dear Senator Doe: Dear Mr. Doe:
State Officials	The Honorable John Doe Secretary of State of Iowa	Sir: My dear Mr. Secretary:
	The Honorable John Doe Director of Finance	Dear Mr. Doe:

Forms of Address *(continued)*

Undersecretary or Assistant Secretary (Federal Department)	The Honorable John Doe Undersecretary of State	My dear Mr. Doe:
	The Honorable John Doe Assistant Secretary of Labor	My dear Mr. Doe:
United Nations Officials	His Excellency John Doe Secretary General of the United Nations United Nations New York, New York 10021	My dear Secretary General:
	The Honorable John Doe Undersecretary of the United Nations	My dear Mr. Doe:
	His Excellency John Doe Representative of Great Britain to the United Nations	My dear Ambassador Doe:
	The Honorable John Doe United States Permanent Representative to the United Nations	My dear Ambassador Doe:
Vice President of the United States	The Vice President United States Senate Washington, D. C. 20510	Sir:
	The Honorable John Doe Vice President of the United States Washington, D. C. 20501	My dear Mr. Vice President:

Look-Alike Words With Different Meanings

Many words in the English language look and sound alike but do not mean the same thing. It is easy to confuse such words, especially in taking and transcribing dictation. Frequently only the meaning of the word as it is used in the sentence can tell you which word to use. The following list of words with their correct definitions is to help avoid this confusion.

accept	to take; to receive; to agree to
except	to leave out; to exclude
access	a way of approach; admission; entrance
excess	that which surpasses or goes beyond a definite limit
ad	colloquialism for advertisement
add	to join, unite to form one sum or whole
adapt	to make fit or suitable; to make to correspond
adopt	to select and accept as one's own
admittance	permission to enter
admission	the price paid for permission to enter
advice	opinion offered as to what one should do
advise	to give advice; to counsel
affect	to act on; to produce a change in
effect	that which is produced by an agent or cause; result; consequence
all ready	prepared in all respects
already	before this; previously to the time specified
all together	in a group
altogether	wholly; entirely
allusion	a passing or indirect reference; a hint or suggestion
illusion	an erroneous interpretation or unreal image presented to the bodily or mental vision
all ways	the whole way; every one of the ways
always	at all times; perpetually; invariably
ante	prefix meaning before
anti	prefix meaning against; opposite; instead of

any way	one particular way
anyway	in any way or manner; anyhow; carelessly
a piece	one thing or part
apiece	for each one; to each one
appraise	to put a price on; to fix the value of
apprise	to inform; to tell; to give notice
arraign	to call or set a prisoner at the bar; to call to account
arrange	to put into order; to settle terms; to prepare
assay	trial; test; examination
essay	a literary composition
assistance	help; aid
assistants	those persons who actually assist
baring	opening to view; exposing
barring	excepting; an exclusion of any kind
bearing	the manner in which a person acts or behaves
beside	at the side of; over and above; in addition to; apart or distinct from
besides	moreover
biannual	happening twice a year
biennial	happening once in two years.
born	to bring forth into being
borne	to carry
breath	the act of breathing freely; air expired by the lungs
breathe	to draw in and give out air from the lungs
breadth	distance from side to side; width
Britain	comprised of England, Northern Ireland, Wales, and Scotland; Great Britain
Briton	a native of Britain
calendar	a table of days, months, or seasons
calender	a hot press with rollers used to make cloth smooth and glossy
canvas	a coarse cloth made of hemp for sails, tents, etc.
canvass	to examine thoroughly; to solicit support

capital	first in importance
capitol	a state legislature building
Capitol	the building used by the U. S. Congress in Washington, D.C.
censor	to examine before publication for the purpose of changing or editing
censure	the act of finding fault; disapproval
click	a slight, short sound as of a latch in a door
clique	a narrow circle of persons with common interests
climactic	pertaining to the climax; the acme
climatic	referring to general atmospheric conditions
clothes	wearing apparel
cloths	any woven fabric or pieces of same
coarse	rough; rude; not refined
course	the act of passing from one point to another
complement	something completing a whole; that which supplies a deficiency
compliment	an expression of regard or admiration
compose	to form by uniting parts; to put in order
comprise	to include; to be composed of
comptroller	a person in charge of finance
controller	one who is in control or authority; power
confidant	a person in whom one can confide
confident	having assurance
contemptible	worthy of contempt; despicable
contemptuous	expressing contempt or disdain
correspon-dence	the exchange of letters; the letters themselves
correspon-dents	ones with whom intercourse is maintained by exchange of letters
council	an assembly summoned for consultation or advice
counsel	advice; opinion; deliberation together
consul	an officer appointed by a government to represent it in a foreign country

credible	worthy of belief
creditable	reliable; meriting credit
credulous	too prone to believe
credit	belief; trust; trustworthiness; the amount at a persons's disposal in a bank or account
accredit	to vouch for; to recommend
critic	one who expresses a reasoned judgement on any matter
critique	a criticism or review
cue	a signal, such as the last words of an actor's speech
queue	a line such as at the box office of a show
decent	fitting or becoming; modest or suitable
descent	the act of going down
dissent	to differ in opinion; to disagree
decree	an order made by a competent authority
degree	a step upward or downward
depository	a place to store for safekeeping
depositary	one with whom anything is left in trust
deprecate	to express disapproval of
depreciate	to lower in value
desert	a wide, sandy waste region; also, to abandon
dessert	a course served at the end of a meal
deserts	that which is deserved reward or punishment
device	that which is planned out or designed
devise	to invent; to contrive; to plan
die	to cease to live
die	a device for cutting in a press
dye	to give a new color to; to stain
disapprove	to form an unfavorable judgement of; to censure
disprove	to prove to be false; to refute

disassociate	to disunite; to separate
dissociate	to disclaim connection with
disburse	to pay out money to
disperse	to scatter here and there; to distribute
discomfit	to defeat; to foil; to baffle
discomfort	to impair the comfort of; to make uneasy
discreet	prudent; judicious; cautious in action and speech
discrete	separate; distinct
done	past participle of the verb "do"; completed; agreed
dun	to importune for payment of a debt
dual	consisting of two; denoting two persons or things
duel	a combat between two persons
egoist	a self-centered person (The term does not necessarily denote disapproval.)
egotist	one who talks or writes incessantly of himself
elder	one who is older, generally referring to members of the family
older	one who is more advanced in age or seniority
emigrate	to leave one's country to settle in another
immigrate	to migrate into a country
migrate	to remove one's residence from one place to another
eminent	prominent in rank, office, or public estimation
immanent	abiding in; inherent; innate
imminent	threatening immediately to fall or occur
enormity	quality of being enormous; great wickedness
enormousness	vast size; the quality of being huge
envelop	to cover by folding or wrapping; to surround

envelope	the cover of a letter
equable	a uniformity in action or intensity; of unruffled temperament
equitable	giving or disposed to give each his due; just
exceptional	outstanding; superior
exceptionable	objectionable
exercise	the use of the body for health purposes
exorcise	to free a person of evil spirits
exhausting	draining off completely; tiring
exhaustive	comprehensive; thorough
farther	to a greater distance; more remote
further	to help forward; to promote; referring to time, quantity, or degree
fete	a festival; a holiday
feat	an exploit or action of extraordinary strength
feet	plural of foot
flaunt	to display ostentatiously
flout	to mock; to disregard with contempt
forcefully	with strength and energy
forcibly	having force
forgo	to abstain from possession or enjoyment
forego	to precede; to go before
formally	being conventional or pedantically precise
formerly	preceding in time
forth	forward in place or time
fourth	next after third
guarantee	formal assurance given by way of security
guaranty	a pledge of committment; basis of security
healthy	having health; sound; vigorous; wholesome
healthful	promoting soundness of body

holy	belonging to or devoted to God
wholly	completely; entirely
hypocritical	insincere; simulation of goodness
hypercritical	critical beyond measure or reason
incidence	range of influence
incidents	events; occurrences
incredible	impossible to be believed
incredulous	not disposed to believe
ingenious	skilled in inventing or thinking out new ideas
ingenuous	frank; artless; innocent
interstate	between or among states of the Federal government
intrastate	within a state
isle	a tiny island
aisle	the passageway between rows
its	possessive of the pronoun "it"
it's	contraction for the verb "it is"
jibe	to be in harmony, agreement, or accord
gibe	to taunt; to sneer at
later	coming after; relating to time
latter	the second of two just mentioned
leased	contracted or rented
least	smallest; faintest; most minute
lessen	to make less; to diminish
lesson	a piece of instruction; something to be learned
liable	obliged in law or equity
libel	a defamatory writing or picture
loath	unwilling; reluctant; disinclined
loathe	to detest; to abominate
local	pertaining to a particular place
locale	the scene of an occurrence
lose	to mislay; to forfeit
loose	free; slack; unbound

luxuriant	in great abundance
luxurious	sumptuous; splendid; rich
material	the substance out of which something is fashioned
materiel	necessary tools, equipment, and supplies
moral	pertaining to right conduct or duties of man
morale	a disposition or mental state
motif	the dominent theme
motive	that which incites to action
ordinance	established rule or law
ordnance	a collective term for military weapons
past	gone by; time elapsed
passed	to have gone beyond or through
personal	peculiar to or done by a particular person
personnel	the persons employed in a business
perspective	drawn objects shown in relation to space
prospective	relating to the future; expected
plaintiff	the one who sues in a court of law
plaintive	expressing grief; mournful
postcard	a stamped card on which a message can be sent through the mail
postal card	a government-printed card with imprinted stamp
practical	workable and useful
practicable	capable of being accomplished or put into practice
precedence	priority in position, rank, or time
precedents	something done or said that may serve as an example in similar cases
prescribe	to set out rules for
proscribe	to put outside the protection of the law
presentiment	a previous notion or opinion
presentment	the act or state of representation

principal	chief in importance; first in rank
principle	a fundamental truth or law
prophecy	the foretelling of future events
prophesy	to foretell or predict
receipt	a written acknowledgement of something received
recipe	a prescription or formula usually used for cooking
residence	a place to dwell permanently
residents	those who live in a residence
respectfully	deferentially; politely
respectively	each of two or more things or people in the order named
rout	to defeat and throw into confusion
route	a course or way that is traveled to be followed
sight	one of the five senses; the act of seeing
site	a situation or location
cite	to summon; to bring forward as proof
sometime	at a time not definitely stated
some time	an indefinite time, usually in the future
sometimes	now and then; occasionally
stable	firmly fixed and established; steady
staple	a settled market; regularly produced or made for market
stationary	not moving; fixed; regular
stationery	writing materials
straight	without a bend; not crooked
strait	a narrow channel of water connecting two larger areas
suit	the act of suing, petition, or request; also, a set of clothes or a suit of cards
suite	a number of things used together such as furniture, rooms; also, an instrumental form
than	adverbial clause of comparison
then	at that time; immediately afterward

their	possessive of "they"
there	in that place; also, an introductory adverb
to	expressing motion toward
too	in addition; more than enough
two	the sum of one and one
use	to employ; to consume or expend
usage	long-established custom
waive	to give up claim to; to forgo
wave	a to-and-fro movement
weather	combination of atmospheric phenomena existing at one time in any particular place
whether	used to introduce the first of two alternative clauses
your	possessive form of you
you're	contraction for "you are"

Spelling and Word Division Guide

Webster's Spelling and Word-Division Guide is a convenient source for the essentials of spelling and word division. This dictionary, minus definitions, has been compiled as a quick reference aid for students, secretaries, typists, and anyone who deals with the written word.

For purposes of easier word flow and readability, the ideal would be the elimination of all word divisions, for it is preferable to preserve entire words rather than offer a series of split words. However, in typesetting, inflexible right-hand margins, line widths, and a limited number of spaces necessarily force the typesetter to divide words. To meet the need for uniform division practices, *Webster's Spelling and Word-Division Guide* attempts to lay down word break rules based on generally accepted orthographic principles, pronounceable parts, and also on customs derived from good printing practices.

Traditionally this publisher has accepted Webster's dictionaries as the prime source for word division and *Webster's Spelling and Word-Division Guide* has continued this policy. Webster's third unabridged (1961) adopted a new pattern of word breaks that caused changes in the division of many words. This book has adopted most of these changes but, because of a conflict with rule 5 (page 72), some changes were rejected. This decision has been justified by the general acceptance of users and the agreement of other dictionaries. Thus, where Webster's and this book differ, word breaks as listed here should be followed.

Webster's third is generally followed for word breaks in chemical terms. However, no spelling preferences are expressed, as we are interested only in correct word division and in the spelling of the particular term listed. Fine distinctions in chemical suffixes are reserved for those skilled in the art of chemistry.

Among the new words added in this here are the names and/or nationalities of most of the new countries that have come into being during the past decade. Where authorities differ in the English version of the pronunciation of certain names, preference has been given to the individual country's choice as expressed through its embassy.

Rules 2, 3, 4, 34, and 35 have been rewritten to reflect clarifying minor changes or to bring them in line with present practices. Although permissiveness is inferred by the use of the word "should" in many of these rules, adherence to all rules should be the general practice.

Careful consideration has been given not only to those words that might produce temporary uncertainty as to their correct division but also to their likelihood of use and usefulness. Obvious divisions have not been listed, but sufficient samples have been provided so that, for example, *es-ti-ma-tion* would serve as a guide for *es-ti-mate; gen-er-a-tor* for *gen-er-ate.*

For unlisted words, the application of the following rules, in addition to reference to analogous listed words, should assure reasonable coverage for most word divisions.

WORD-BREAK RULES

1. Division of words should be avoided when possible.

2. Except in narrow lines, word breaks should be avoided at the

ends of more than two lines. Similarly, no more than two consecutive lines should end with the same word, symbol, group of numbers, etc.

3. In two-line centerheads, the first line should be centered and be as full as possible, but it should not fill the line by unduly wide spacing. Word breaks should be avoided. Flush sideheads are typed full width; and word breaks are permitted if unavoidable.

4. The final word of a paragraph should not be divided.

5. Words should preferably be divided according to pronunciation; to avoid mispronunciation, they should be divided so that the part of the word left at the end of the line will suggest the whole word: *capac-ity*, not *capa-city*; *extraor-dinary*, not *extra-ordinary*; *Wednes-day*, not *Wed-nesday*; *physi-cal*, not *phys-ical*; *service-man*, not *serv-iceman*.

6. Although *Webster's Spelling and Word-Division Guide* lists beginning and ending one- letter syllables for pronunciation purposes, under no circumstances are words to be divided on a single letter (e.g., *usu-al-ly*, not *u-su-al-ly*; *imagi-nary*, not *i-mag-i-nar-y*).

7. Division of short words (of five or fewer letters) should be avoided. Two-letter divisions, including the carry-over of two-letter endings (*ed, el, en, er, es, et, fy, ic, in, le, ly, or,* and *ty*), should also be avoided. In narrow widths, however, a sounded suffix (e.g., paint-*ed;* not rained) or syllable of two letters may be carried over— only if unavoidable. (See rule 10.)

8. Words of two syllables are split at the end of the first syllable: *dis-pelled, con-quered;* words of three or more syllables, with a choice of division possible, divide preferably on the vowel: *particu-lar, sepa-rate.*

9. In words with short prefixes, divide on the prefix; *e.g., ac, co, de, dis, ex, in, non, on, pre, pro, re, un,* etc. (e.g., *non-essential,* not *nones-sential; pre-selected,* not *prese-lected*).

If possible, prefixes and combining forms of more than one syllable are preserved intact: *anti, infra, macro, micro, multi, over, retro, semi,* etc. (e.g., *anti-monopoly,* not *antimo-nopoly; over-optimistic,* not *overoptimistic*). (For chemical prefixes, see rule 29.)

10. *Words ending in* -er. Although two-letter carryovers are to be avoided (rule 7), many *-er* words that are derived from comparatives (*coarse, coarser; sharp, sharper*) have been listed to prevent a wrong word break; e.g., *coars-er,* not *coar-ser.*

Nouns ending in-*er* (*adviser, bracer, keeper, perceiver, reader*) derived from action verbs are also listed to prevent a wrong division; e.g., *perceiv-er,* not *percei-ver.*

Except in narrow lines and if unavoidable, the above *-er* words are not divided unless division can be made on a prefix; e.g., *per-ceiver.*

11. *Words ending in* -or. Generally, *-or* words with a consonant preceding are divided before the preceding consonant; e.g., *advi-sor* (legal), *fabrica-tor, guaran-tor, interve-nor, simula-tor, tai-lor;* but *bail-or, bargain-or, con-sign-or, grant-or.*

12. The following suffixes are not divided: *ceous, cial, cient, cion, cious, scious, geous, gion, gious, sial, tial, tion, tious,* and *sion.*

13. The suffixes *-able* and *-ible* are usually carried over intact; but when the stem word loses its original form, these suffixes are divided according to pronunciation: *comfort-able, corrupt-*

ible, manage-able; but *dura-ble, audi-ble.*

14. Words ending in *-ing*, with stress on the primary syllable, are preferably divided on the base word; e.g., *appoint-ing, combat-ing, danc-ing, engineer-ing, process-ing, program-ing, stencil-ing, trac-ing,* etc. However, present participles, such as *control-ling, forbid-ding, refer-ring,* with stress placed on the second syllable, divide between the doubled consonants (see also rule 16).

15. When the final consonant sound of a word belongs to a syllable ending with a silent vowel, the final consonant or consonants become part of the added suffix: *chuck-ling, han-dler, han-dling, crum-bling, twin-kled, twin-kling;* but *rollick-ing.*

16. When the addition of *-ed, -er, -est,* or of a similar ending, causes the doubling of a final consonant, the added consonant is carried over: *pit-ted, rob-ber, thin-nest, glad-den, control-lable, transmit-table;* but *bless-ed* (adj.), *dwell-er, gross-est.*

17. Words with doubled consonants are usually divided between these consonants: *clas-sic, ruf-fian, neces-sary, rebel-lion;* but *call-ing, mass-ing.*

18. If formation of a plural adds a syllable ending in an *s* sound, the plural ending should not be carried over by itself: *hor-ses, voices;* but *church-es, cross-es,* thus not breaking the base word (see also rule 7).

19. The digraphs *ai, ck, dg, gh, gn, ng, oa, ph, sh, tch,* and *th* are not split.

20. Do not divide contractions: *doesn't, haven't.*

21. Solid compounds are preferably divided preferably between the members: *bar-keeper, hand-*

kerchief, proof-reader, humming-bird.

22. Avoid a division that adds another hyphen to a hyphened compound: *court-martial,* not *court-mar-tial; tax-supported,* not *tax-sup-ported.*

23. A word of one syllable is not split: *tanned, shipped, quenched, through, chasm, prism.*

24. Two consonants preceded and followed by a vowel are divided on the first consonant: *abun-dant, advan-tage, struc-ture;* but *attend-ant, accept-ance, depend-ence.*

25. When two adjoining vowels are sounded separately, divide between them: *cre-ation, gene-alogy.*

26. In breaking homonyms, distinction should be given to their relative functions: *pro-ject* (v.), *proj-ect* (n.); *rec-ollect* (recall), *re-collect* (collect again).

27. *Words ending in* -meter. In the large group of words ending in *-meter,* distinction should be made between metric-system terms and terms indicating a measuring instrument. When it is necessary to divide metric terms, preserve the combining form *-meter;* e.g., *centi-meter, deca-meter, hecto-meter, kilo-meter.* However, measuring instruments divide after the *m:* altim-e-ter, ba- rom-e-ter, mi-crom-e-ter, mul-tim-e-ter, etc. Derivatives of these-*meter* terms follow the same form; e.g., *mul-tim-e-ter, mul-tim-e-try.*

For orthographic reasons, however, several measuring instruments do not lend themselves to the general rule; e.g., *flow- meter, flux-meter, gauss-meter, taxi-meter, torque-meter, volt-meter, water-meter, watt-meter,* etc.

28. *Chemical formulas.* In chemical formulas, the hyphen has an important function. If a

break is unavoidable in a formula, division is preferably made after an original hyphen to avoid the introduction of a misleading hyphen. If impractical to break on a hyphen, division may be made after an original comma, and no hyphen is added to indicate a runover. The following formula shows original hyphens and commas where division may be made. No letterspacing is used in a chemical formula, but to fill a line, a space is permitted on both sides of a hyphen.

1-(2,6,6-trimethylcyclohex-1-en-1-yl)-3,7,12,16

29. *Chemical combining forms, prefixes, and suffixes.* If possible and subject to rules of good spacing, it is desirable to preserve as a unit such combining forms as follows:

aceto, anhydro, benzo, bromo, chloro, chromo, cincho, cyclo, dehydro, diazo, flavo, fluoro, glyco, hydroxy, iso, keto, methyl, naphtho, phospho, poly, silico, tetra, triazo.

The following suffixes are used in chemical typing. For patent and narrow width composition, two-letter suffixes may be carried over.

al, an, ane, ase, ate, ene, ic, id, ide, in, ine, ite, ol, ole, on, one, ose, ous, oyl, yl, yne.

30. *Mineral elements.* When it is necessary tn break mineral constituents, division should preferably be made before a center period and beginning parenthesis and after inferior figures following a closing parenthesis; elements within parentheses are not separated. In cases of unavoidable breaks, a hyphen is not added to indicate a runover.

$Mg(UO_2)_2(SiO_3)_2(OH)_2 6H_2O$

31. The dash is not used at the beginning of any line unless it is required before a credit line or signature or in lieu of opening quotation marks in foreign languages.

32. Neither periods nor asterisks used as an ellipsis are overrun alone at the end of a paragraph. If necessary, run over enough preceding lines to provide a short word or part of a word to accompany the ellipsis. If a runback is possible, subject to rules of good spacing and word division, this method may be adopted.

33. Abbreviations and symbols should not be broken at the end of a line: *A.F. of L., A.T. & T., C. Cls. R., f.o.b., n.o.i.b.n., R. & D., r.p.m., WMAL.* Where unavoidable in narrow lines, long symbols may be broken after letters denoting a complete word. Use no hyphens. COM SUB A C LANT (Commander Submarine Allied Command Atlantic).

34. Figures of less than six digits, decimals, and closely connected combinations of figures and abbreviations should not be broken at the end of a line: *$15,000, 34,575, 0.31416 $10.25, 5,000 kw.-hr., A.D. 1952, 9 p.m., 18°F., NW.* If a break in six digits or over is unavoidable, divide on the comma or period, retain it, and use a hyphen.

35. Closely related abbreviations and initials in proper names and accompanying titles should not be separated, nor should titles, such as *Rev., Mr., Esq., Jr., 2d,* be separated from surnames.

36. Avoid dividing proper names, but, if inescapable, follow general rules for word division.

37. Divisional and subdivisional paragraph reference signs and figures, such as
18, section (a)(1), page 363(b), should not be divided, nor should such references be separated from the matter to which they pertain.

In case of an unavoidable break in a lengthy reference (e.g., *7(B)(1)(a)(i))*, division will be made after elements in parentheses, and no hyphen is used.

38. In dates, do not divide the month and day, but the year may be carried over.

39. In case of an unavoidable break in a land-description symbol group at the end of a line, use no hyphen and break after a fraction.

40. Avoid breaking longitude and latitude figures at the end of a line; space out the line instead. In case of an unavoidable break at the end of a line, use a hyphen.

A

Aar-on
Aa-ron-ic
ab-a-ca
ab-a-cus
ab-a-lo-ne
a-ban-don
a-ba-si-a
a-bat-a-ble
ab-a-tis
ab-at-toir
a-bet-ter
a-bet-tor (law)
ab-bre-vi-a-tor
ab-di-ca-tor
ab-do-men
ab-dom-i-nal
ab-dom-i-no-per-i-ne-al
ab-dom-i-nos-co-py
ab-duc-tor
a-be-ce-dar-i-an
A-bed-ne-go
ab-en-ter-ic
ab-er-om-e-ter
ab-er-ra-tion
a-bey-ance
ab-hor-rence
ab-hor-ri-ble
a-bid-ance
ab-i-ent
ab-i-e-tate
ab-i-et-ic
Ab-i-gail
Ab-i-lene
a-bil-i-ty
a-bi-ot-ic
a-bi-ot-ro-phy
ab-ju-ra-tion
ab-jur-a-to-ry
ab-la-tive
a-blep-si-a
ab-ne-ga-tor
ab-nor-mal-i-ty
ab-nor-mi-ty
a-bol-ish
ab-o-li-tion-ist
a-bom-i-na-ble
ab-o-rig-i-nes
a-bor-ti-cide

a-bort-in
a-bor-tive
ab-ra-ca-dab-ra
a-brad-ant
A-bra-ham
a-bran-chi-ate
ab-ra-si-om-e-ter
ab-ra-sion
ab-ra-sive
a-bridg-ment
ab-ro-ga-tive
ab-rupt
ab-scess
ab-scis-sa
ab-scis-sion
ab-scond
ab-sence
ab-sen-tee-ism
ab-sinthe
ab-sin-thin
ab-so-lu-tion
ab-so-lut-ism
ab-so-lu-tive
ab-so-lu-tize
ab-sol-u-to-ry
ab-sol-vent
ab-solv-er
ab-sorb-ate
ab-sorb-ent
ab-sorp-tance
ab-sorp-ti-om-e-ter
ab-ste-mi-ous
ab-sten-tious
ab-ster-gent
ab-sti-nence
ab-stract-er
ab-strac-tive
ab-struse
ab-surd-i-ty
a-bu-lo-ma-ni-a
a-bun-dance
a-bus-age
a-bu-sive
a-but-ting
a-bys-mal
a-byss-al
Ab-ys-sin-i-an
a-ca-cia

ac-a-dem-i-cal	ac-cres-cence
a-cad-e-mi-cian	ac-cre-tive
a-cad-e-my	ac-cul-tur-ate
a-camp-si-a	ac-cum-bent
ac-a-na-ceous	ac-cu-mu-la-tive
ac-an-tha-ceous	ac-cu-mu-la-tor
a-can-thoid	ac-cu-ra-cy
ac-an-tho-ma	ac-cursed (v.)
a-can-thus	ac-curs-ed (adj.)
a-cap-pel-la	ac-cus-a-ble
a-cap-su-lar	ac-cu-sa-tive
a-ca-pul-co	ac-cus-a-to-ry
a-car-dite	ac-cus-er
ac-a-ri-a-sis	ac-cus-tomed
a-car-i-cid-al	ac-e-naph-thy-lene
ac-a-roid	a-ceph-a-lous (adj.)
a-cau-date	a-ceph-a-lus (n.)
ac-ced-ence	ac-er-bate
ac-cel-er-ans	a-cer-bi-ty
ac-cel-er-a-tive	ac-er-ose
ac-cel-er-a-tor	ac-e-tab-u-lum
ac-cel-er-om-e-ter	ac-et-al-de-hyde
ac-cend-ible	a-cet-a-mide
ac-cen-tu-a-tor	ac-et-am-i-dine
ac-cept-a-ble	ac-et-a-mi-do-cin-nam-ic
ac-cept-ance	ac-et-an-i-lide
ac-cep-ta-tion	ac-et-ar-sone
ac-cept-er	ac-e-tate
ac-cep-tor (law)	ac-e-ta-to-so-da-lite
ac-ces-si-ble	a-ce-tic
ac-ces-so-ri-al	a-ce-ti-fy
ac-ciac-ca-tu-ra	ac-e-tin
ac-ci-den-tal	ac-e-to-ac-et-an-i-lide
ac-cla-ma-tion	a-cet-o-in
ac-clam-a-to-ry	ac-e-tol-y-sis
ac-cli-mate	ac-e-tom-e-ter
ac-cli-ma-ti-za-tion	ac-e-tom-e-try
ac-cliv-i-ty	ac-e-tone
ac-cli-vous	ac-e-ton-yl-i-dene
ac-co-lade	ac-e-to-phe-net-i-dide
ac-com-mo-dat-ing	ac-e-to-phe-none
ac-com-pa-ni-ment	ac-e-to-pro-pi-o-nate
ac-com-pa-nist	ac-e-to-pur-pu-rine
ac-com-plice	ac-e-tous
ac-com-plish	ac-e-tox-yl
ac-cord-ance	a-ce-tum
ac-cor-di-on-ist	ac-e-tyl-ac-e-tone
ac-couche-ment	a-cet-y-late
ac-cou-cheur	a-cet-y-la-tor
ac-count-a-ble	ac-e-tyl-cho-line
ac-count-an-cy	a-cet-y-lene
ac-cou-ter	a-cet-y-lide
ac-cred-i-ta-tion	ac-e-tyl-meth-yl-car-bi-nol

ac-e-tyl-phen-yl-hy-dra-zine
ac-e-tyl-sa-lic-y-late
ac-e-tyl-sal-i-cyl-ic
Ach-il-le-an
A-chil-les
a-chol-ic
ach-ro-mat-ic
ach-ro-ma-tic-i-ty
a-chro-ma-tin
a-chro-ma-tism
a-cic-u-lar
ac-i-dif-er-ous
ac-i-dim-e-ter
ac-i-dim-e-try
a-cid-i-ty
a-cid-o-phil
ac-i-doph-i-lus
ac-i-do-sis
a-cid-u-lous
ac-i-na-ceous
ac-knowl-edge-a-ble
ac-knowl-edg-ment
ac-o-lyte
a-con-ic
ac-o-nite
ac-o-nit-ic
a-con-i-tine
a-cou-me-ter
a-cou-me-try
a-con-ti-um
a-cous-tic
ac-ous-ti-cian
a-cous-ti-con
ac-quaint-ance
ac-quaint-ed
ac-qui-es-cence
ac-quire
ac-qui-si-tion
ac-quis-i-tive
ac-quit-tal
a-cre-age
ac-ri-bom-e-ter
ac-rid
ac-ri-dine
ac-ri-din-i-um
a-crid-i-ty
ac-ri-mo-ni-ous
ac-ro-bat-ic
ac-ro-gen
a-crog-e-nous
a-cro-le-in
ac-ro-lith
ac-ro-nym
a-crop-e-tal
ac-ro-pho-bi-a
a-croph-o-ny
a-crop-o-lis
a-cros-tic

a-crot-ic
ac-ryl-am-ide
ac-ry-late
a-cryl-ic
ac-ry-lo-ni-trile
a-cryl-o-yl
ac-ry-lyl
ac-tin-ic
ac-tin-ism
ac-tin-i-um
ac-ti-no-bac-il-lo-sis
ac-ti-noid
ac-tin-o-lite
ac-ti-nom-e-ter
ac-ti-no-my-cin
ac-ti-no-my-co-sis
ac-ti-nos-co-py
ac-tion-om-e-ter
ac-ti-va-ble
ac-ti-va-tor
ac-tiv-ism
ac-tiv-ist
ac-tiv-i-ty
ac-to-my-o-sin
ac-tor
ac-tress
ac-tu-al-i-ty
ac-tu-ar-y
ac-tu-a-tor
a-cu-i-ty
a-cu-men
a-cu-mi-nate
a-cute-ness
a-cy-clic
ac-yl-ate
ad ab-sur-dum
ad-age
a-da-gio
ad-a-mant
ad-a-man-tine
A-dam-si-a
ad-ams-ite
Ad-am-son
a-dapt-a-ble
a-dapt-a-bil-i-ty
ad-ap-ta-tion
a-dapt-er
a-dapt-ive
ad-ap-tom-e-ter
a-dap-tor
ad-ax-i-al
add-a-ble
add-ed
ad-den-da
add-er (one who adds)
ad-der (snake)
ad-dict-ed
ad-dic-tion

ad-dit-a-ment
ad-di-tion
ad-di-tive
ad-di-to-ry
ad-dress-ee
ad-dress-er
Ad-dres-so-graph
ad-dres-sor (law)
ad-du-cent
ad-duc-i-ble
ad-duc-tor
Ad-e-la
Ad-e-laide
Ad-el-bert
ad-e-nase
a-de-ni-a
a-den-i-form
ad-e-nine
ad-e-ni-tis
ad-e-no-car-ci-no-ma
ad-e-no-fi-bro-ma
ad-e-noi-dal
ad-e-no-ma
ad-e-nom-a-tous
ad-e-nop-a-thy
a-den-o-sine
ad-e-not-o-my
ad-e-nyl
ad-ept
a-dept-ness
ad-e-qua-cy
a-der-min
ad-her-ence
ad-her-ent
ad-he-res-cent
ad-he-sion
ad-he-sive
ad-i-a-bat-ic
ad in-fi-ni-tum
ad-i-nole
a-dip-a-mide
ad-i-pate
a-dip-ic
ad-i-po-ni-trile
ad-i-po-sis
ad-i-pos-i-ty
ad-i-po-so-gen-i-tal
ad-i-po-yl
ad-ja-cent
ad-jec-ti-val
ad-jec-tive
ad-ju-di-cate
ad-junc-tive
ad-ju-ra-tion
ad-jur-er
ad-just-a-ble
ad-just-er
ad-jus-tor (zoology)

ad-ju-tage
ad-ju-tant
ad-ju-vant
Ad-le-ri-an
ad lib-i-tum
ad-min-is-tra-tor
ad-min-is-tra-trix
ad-mi-ra-ble
ad-mi-ral-ty
ad-mi-ra-tion
ad-mir-er
ad-mis-si-ble
ad-mit-tance
ad-mon-ish
ad-mo-ni-tion
ad-mon-i-to-ry
ad nau-se-am
a-do-be
ad-o-les-cent
Ad-olph
A-do-nis
a-dopt-er
a-dop-tive
a-dor-a-ble
ad-o-ra-tion
a-dor-er
a-dorn-ment
ad-re-nal
A-dren-a-lin
a-dren-er-gen
ad-re-ner-gic
a-dre-no-chrome
a-dre-no-cor-ti-co-troph-ic
A-dri-an
A-dri-at-ic
a-droit-ness
ad-sorb-ate
ad-sorb-ent
ad-sorp-tive
ad-u-la-tion
a-dul-ter-a-tor
a-dult-i-cide
ad-um-brate
ad va-lo-rem
ad-vanc-er
ad-van-ta-geous
ad-vec-tive
ad-ven-ience
Ad-vent-ist
ad-ven-ti-tious
ad-ven-tur-er
ad-verb-i-al
ad-ver-sar-y
ad-ver-si-ty
ad-vert-ence
ad-ver-tise-ment
ad-ver-tis-er
ad-vis-a-ble

ad-vis-er	Ag-as-siz
ad-vi-sor (law)	ag-ate
ad-vi-so-ry	Ag-a-thin
ad-vo-ca-cy	a-ga-ve
ad-voc-a-to-ry	a-gen-cy
Ae-ge-an	a-gen-da
ae-o-li-an	a-gen-ti-val
aer-ate	a-geu-si-a
aer-a-tor	ag-er-a-tum
aer-i-al	ag-glom-er-ate
ae-rie	ag-glu-ti-nant
aer-if-er-ous	ag-glu-ti-noid
aer-i-fi-ca-tion	ag-gran-dize
aer-o-bac-ter	ag-gra-vate
aer-o-bat-ics	ag-gre-gate
aer-o-bic	ag-gres-sive
aer-o-dy-nam-ic	ag-gres-sor
aer-ol-o-gy	ag-griev-ance
aer-om-e-ter	ag-ile
aer-o-mo-tor	a-gil-i-ty
aer-o-nau-tics	ag-i-ta-tive
aer-on-o-my	ag-i-ta-tor
aer-o-scope	ag-it-prop
aer-os-co-py	a-glo-mer-u-lar
ae-rose	ag-no-si-a
aer-o-sol	ag-nos-te-rol
aer-o-stat	ag-nos-ti-cism
Aes-chy-le-an	ag-o-niz-ing
af-fa-ble	ag-o-ra-pho-bi-a
af-fec-ta-tion	a-grar-i-an
af-fect-er	ag-ri-cul-tur-al
af-fect-i-ble	ag-ri-mo-ny
af-fec-tion-ate	ag-ro-nom-ic
af-fer-ent	a-gron-o-mist
af-fi-anced	a-gron-o-my
af-fi-da-vit	ag-ros-tol-o-gy
af-fil-i-ate	ag-ryp-not-ic
af-fin-i-ty	a-gu-ish
af-firm-ance	aide me-moire
af-fir-ma-tion	ai-grette
af-firm-a-tive	ai-le-ron
af-fla-tus	ai-lu-ro-phobe
af-flict-ive	air-i-ness
af-flu-ent	air-om-e-ter
Af-ghan-i-stan	Ak-ti-en-ge-sell-schaft
a-fi-ci-o-na-do	Al-a-bam-i-an
a-for-ti-o-ri	al-a-bas-ter
Af-ri-can-ize	a-lac-ri-ty
af-ter	al-a-me-da
a-gam-ic	al-a-mo
ag-a-ric	a-la-mode
a-gar-i-cin-ic	al-a-nine
ag-a-rin-ic	al-a-nyl

a-larm-ist
A-las-kan
Al-ba-ni-an
al-ba-tross
al-be-dom-e-ter
al-be-rene
al-bes-cent
al-bin-ic
al-bi-nism
al-bi-nos
al-bo-lite
Al-bu-quer-que
al-bu-men (egg
al-bu-min (chemical)
al-bu-mi-nate
al-bu-mi-nom-e-ter
al-bu-mi-no-sis
al-bu-mi-nu-ri-a
al-bur-num
al-ca-mine
al-chem-ic
al-che-mist
al-che-my
al-co-hol-ism
al-co-hol-om-e-ter
al-co-hol-om-e-try
al-co-hol-y-sis
Al-deb-a-ran
al-de-hyd-ic
al-de-hy-drol
al-der-man
Al-der-ney
Al-dine
al-do-fu-ran-o-side
al-dol-ase
al-don-ic
a-le-a-to-ry
a-lem-bi-cate
a-lep-ric
a-lert-ness
al-eu-drin
al-eu-rit-ic
al-eu-rom-e-ter
al-eu-rone
A-leu-tian
a-lex-i-a
a-lex-in
al-ge-bra-i-cal
al-ge-fa-cient
Al-ge-ri-an
al-ge-si-a
al-ge-sim-e-ter
al-gi-nate

al-gin-ic
al-gol-o-gy
al-gom-e-ter
Al-go-rab
al-go-rism
al-gra-phy
a-li-as
al-i-bi
al-i-cy-clic
al-i-dade
al-ien-ate
al-ien-ist
a-lif-er-ous
al-i-men-ta-ry
al-i-mo-ny
a-line-ment
a-lin-er
al-i-phat-ic
al-i-quot
al-i-vin-cu-lar
a-liz-a-rin
al-ka-li
al-ka-lim-e-ter
al-ka-lin-i-ty
al-ka-loi-dal
al-ke-nyl
alk-ox-ide
alk-ox-yl-ate
al-kyl-ate
al-kyl-ene
al-kyl-ic
al-kyl-ize
al-lan-to-in-ase
al-le-ga-tion
Al-le-ghe-ni-an
Al-le-ghe-ny
al-le-giance
al-le-gor-i-cal
al-le-go-ry
al-le-gro
al-ler-gen-ic
al-ler-gic
al-le-vi-ate
al-le-vi-a-tor
al-li-a-ceous
al-li-ga-tor
al-lit-er-a-tive
al-lo-ca-ble
al-lo-ca-tor
al-log-a-my
al-lom-er-ism
al-lom-e-try
al-lo-path

al-lop-a-thy
al-loph-a-nate
al-lo-se-mat-ic
al-lo-troph-ic
al-lot-ro-py
al-lot-ted
al-lot-tee
al-lot-ting
al-lur-ing
al-lu-sive
al-lu-vi-al
al-lu-vi-um
al-lyl-a-mine
al-lyl-ic
al-ma-nac
al-might-y
al-mond
al-mon-er
a-lo-di-um
al-o-et-ic
al-o-gism
al-o-in
al-o-pe-ci-a
Al-o-ys-i-us
al-pac-a
al-pha-bet-i-cal
al-pha-bet-ize
al-pha-mer-ic
al-pha-tron
Al-pine
Al-pin-ism
al-read-y
al-sike
al-tar
al-ter
al-ter-na-tive
al-ter-na-tor
al-tim-e-ter
al-tim-e-try
al-ti-tu-di-nar-i-an
al-to-geth-er
al-trose
a-lu-mi-na
al-u-min-i-um
a-lu-mi-nize
a-lu-mi-nous
a-lu-mi-num
a-lum-nus
a-lun-dum
al-u-nite
al-ve-o-lar
Al-ve-o-li-tes
a-lys-sum
a-mal-ga-mate
a-mal-ga-ma-tor
a-man-u-en-sis
am-a-ranth
am-a-ran-thine

am-a-roid
am-a-ryl-lis
am-a-teur-ish
am-a-tol
am-a-to-ry
a-maze-ment
Am-a-zo-ni-an
am-bas-sa-do-ri-al
am-ber-gris
am-ber-oid
am-bi-dex-trous
am-bi-ent
am-bi-gu-i-ty
am-big-u-ous
am-bip-a-rous
am-bi-tious
am-biv-a-lence
am-bling
am-blys-to-ma
am-bro-si-a
am-bu-lance
am-bu-la-to-ry
am-bus-cad-er
a-me-ba
a-me-bi-a-sis
a-me-bic
A-mel-ia
a-me-lio-ra-tive
am-e-lo-blas-to-ma
a-me-na-ble
a-mend-a-to-ry
a-men-i-ty
a-men-or-rhe-a
am-ent (botany)
am-en-ta-ceous
A-mer-i-can-a
A-mer-i-can-ism
am-er-i-ci-um
ames-ite
am-e-thyst
a-mi-a-ble
am-i-ca-ble
a-mi-cus cu-ri-ae
am-i-dase
am-ide
a-mid-ic
a-mi-do
a-mi-do-gen
am-i-dol
am-i-dox-ime
a-mi-go
am-i-nate
a-mine
a-mi-no
a-mi-no-ben-zo-ic
am-i-nol-y-sis
am-i-nop-ter-in
a-mi-no-sal-i-cyl-ic

am-me-ter	A-nac-re-on
am-mo-ni-a	a-nad-ro-mous
am-mo-ni-ate	an-aer-o-bi-a
am-mo-nite	an-aer-o-bic
Am-mon-ites (Biblical tribe)	a-nag-ly-phy
am-mo-ni-um	an-a-glyp-tics
am-mu-ni-tion	an-a-gog-ic
am-ne-sia	a-nal-cite
am-nes-ty	an-a-lep-tic
a-mo-le	an-al-ge-si-a
am-o-rous	an-al-ge-sic
a-mor-phism	an-a-log-i-cal
am-or-ti-za-tion	a-nal-o-gous
A-moy-ese	a-nal-o-gy
am-per-age	a-nal-y-sis
am-pere-me-ter	an-a-lyst
am-per-o-met-ric	an-a-lyt-i-cal
am-per-om-e-try	an-a-lyz-er
am-per-sand	an-a-mor-pho-sis
am-phet-a-mine	An-a-ni-as
am-phib-i-an	an-a-phy-lax-is
am-phib-i-ol-o-gy	an-ar-chism
am-phib-i-ous	an-ar-chis-tic
am-phi-bol-ic	an-ar-chy
am-phib-o-lite	a-nas-to-mo-sis
am-phib-o-lous	a-nas-to-mot-ic
am-phi-dip-loi-dy	an-a-tase
am-phi-ge-net-ic	a-nath-e-ma
am-phig-e-nous	an-a-tom-i-cal
am-phi-kar-y-on	a-nat-o-mist
Am-phip-o-da	a-nat-o-my
am-pho-ter-ic	an-ces-tral
am-phot-er-ism	an-chor-age
am-pli-fi-er	an-cho-rite (hermit)
am-pli-tude	an-chor-ite (rock)
am-poule	an-cho-vy
am-pu-ta-tor	an-cient
Am-ster-dam	an-cil-lar-y
am-u-let	an-cy-lo-sto-mi-a-sis
a-mu-si-a	An-da-lu-sian
a-mus-ing	an-da-lu-site
a-myg-da-la-ce-ae	An-da-man
a-myg-da-lin	an-de-site
a-myg-da-loi-dal	and-i-ron
am-y-la-ceous	An-dor-ran
am-y-lase	an-dor-ite
am-yl-ene	An-do-ver
am-y-loi-dal	an-dro-gen-ic-i-ty
am-y-loi-do-sis	an-drog-y-nous
am-y-lol-y-sis	An-drom-e-da
am-y-lo-pec-tin	An-dro-mede
am-y-lose	an-dro-sin
a-nab-a-sine	an-dro-stane
an-a-bi-o-sis	an-dros-te-rone
an-a-bol-ic	.an-ec-dot-al
a-nab-o-lism	a-ne-mi-a
a-nach-ro-nism	a-ne-mic
an-a-con-da	a-nem-o-gram

an-e-mom-e-ter
a-nem-o-ne
a-nem-o-scope
an-er-oid
an-es-the-sia
an-es-the-sim-e-ter
an-es-the-si-ol-o-gy
an-es-thet-ic
an-es-the-tist
a-neu-ri-a
an-eu-rin
an-eu-rysm
an-ga-ry
an-gel-ic
an-ger
an-gi-i-tis
an-gi-na pec-to-ris
an-gi-o-car-di-og-ra-phy
an-gi-o-cyst
an-gi-om-e-ter
an-gi-op-a-thy
an-gi-o-sis
an-gi-os-to-my
an-gi-o-to-nin
an-gler
An-gli-can
an-gli-cize
An-go-lese
An-go-ra
an-gos-tu-ra
an-gry
ang-strom
an-guish
an-gu-lar-i-ty
an-he-dral
an-hi-dro-sis
an-hi-drot-ic
an-hy-dride
an-hy-dro-bi-o-sis
an-hy-drous
an-i-lide
an-i-line
a-nil-i-ty
an-i-mad-ver-sion
an-i-mal-cule
an-i-mal-ism
an-i-ma-tion
an-i-mism
an-i-mos-i-ty
an-i-on-ic
an-i-on-ot-ro-py
an-is-ate
an-ise

an-i-seed
an-is-ette
a-nis-ic
a-nis-i-dine
an-i-sot-ro-py
an-klet
an-ky-lo-sis
an-ky-los-to-ma
an-nal-ist
An-nam-ese
an-neal-er
an-ni-hi-late
an-ni-ver-sa-ry
an-no-ta-tor
an-nounc-er
an-nu-al
an-nu-i-tant
an-nu-lar
an-nu-let
an-nun-ci-a-to-ry
an-ode
an-od-ic
an-od-ize
an-o-dyne
a-noint-ment
a-nom-a-lis-tic
a-nom-a-lous
a-nom-a-ly
an-o-nym-i-ty
a-non-y-mous
an-o-op-si-a
A-noph-e-les
an-ox-i-a
an-ser-ine
an-swer
ant-ac-id
an-tag-o-nism
Ant-arc-tic
An-tar-es
an-te-ced-ent
an-te-di-lu-vi-an
an-te-lope
an-te-pe-nul-ti-mate
an-te-ri-or
ant-he-lion
ant-hel-min-tic
an-them
an-ther-al
an-tho-cy-an-i-din
an-thog-e-nous
an-tho-log-i-cal
an-thol-o-gy
An-tho-ny

an-thra-cene	a-part-heid
an-thra-cif-er-ous	ap-as-tron
an-thra-cite	ap-a-thet-ic
an-thra-co-sil-i-co-sis	ap-a-thy
an-thra-nil-ic	ap-a-tite
an-thran-o-yl	Ap-en-nine
an-thra-pur-pu-rin	a-pe-ri-ent
an-thra-qui-no-nyl	a-pe-ri-od-ic
an-thrax	a-per-i-tif
an-thro-poi-dal	ap-er-tom-e-ter
an-thro-po-log-i-cal	ap-er-tur-al
an-thro-pol-o-gy	aph-a-nite
an-thro-pom-e-ter	aph-a-nit-ic
an-thro-po-met-ric	a-pha-sia
an-thro-poph-a-gy	a-phe-lion
an-ti-bi-ot-ic	aph-i-cide
an-ti-cal	aph-o-rism
an-tic-i-pa-to-ry	a-phra-si-a
an-ti-cli-nal	aph-ro-dis-i-ac
an-ti-dot-al	Aph-ro-di-te
an-ti-gen-ic	a-pi-a-rist
an-ti-ge-nic-i-ty	a-pi-ar-y
An-tig-o-ne	ap-i-cal
An-ti-guan	a-pi-ose
an-ti-his-ta-min-ic	ap-ish
An-til-le-an	a-piv-o-rous
an-til-o-gism	ap-neu-sis
an-ti-mo-ny	a-poc-a-lyp-tic
an-ti-pas-to	a-poc-o-pe
an-ti-pa-thet-ic	a-poc-ry-phal
an-tip-a-thy	Ap-o-des
an-tiph-o-nal	ap-o-dic-tic
an-tip-o-dal	a-pog-a-my
an-ti-pode	ap-o-ge-an
an-tip-o-de-an	ap-o-gee
an-tip-o-des	a-pog-e-ny
an-ti-quar-i-an	A-pol-li-nar-is
an-ti-quate	A-pol-lo
an-tique	a-pol-o-get-ic
an-tiq-ui-ty	ap-o-lo-gi-a
an-ti-sep-tic	a-pol-o-gist
an-tith-e-sis	ap-o-pho-rom-e-ter
an-ti-thet-i-cal	ap-o-phyl-lite
ant-ler	ap-o-plec-tic
an-to-nym	ap-o-plex-y
Ant-werp	a-pos-ta-sy
an-u-re-sis	a-pos-tate
anx-i-e-ty	a-pos-ta-tize
anx-ious	a pos-te-ri-o-ri
a-or-tic	a-pos-tle
a-pache (Paris thug)	a-pos-to-late
A-pach-e (Indian tribe)	ap-os-tol-ic
a-pa-re-jo	a-pos-tro-phe

ap-os-troph-ic
a-poth-e-car-y
a-poth-e-o-sis
Ap-pa-lach-ian
ap-pall-ing
ap-pa-nage
ap-pa-ra-tus
ap-par-eled
ap-par-ent
ap-pa-ri-tion
ap-pear-ance
ap-pel-lant
ap-pel-la-tion
ap-pend-age
ap-pend-ant
ap-pen-dec-to-my
ap-pen-di-cal
ap-pen-di-ci-tis
ap-pen-dix
ap-per-cep-tion
ap-pet-i-ble
ap-pe-tiz-er
ap-pe-tiz-ing
ap-pli-ca-ble
ap-pli-ca-tor
ap-pli-ca-to-ry
ap-pli-que
ap-pog-gia-tu-ra
ap-point-ee
ap-point-ive
ap-po-site
ap-pos-i-tive
ap-prais-al
ap-pre-ci-a-tive
ap-pre-hen-si-ble
ap-pre-hen-sive
ap-pren-tice
ap-proach-ing
ap-pro-ba-tion
ap-pro-pri-a-tive
ap-prov-al
ap-prox-i-mate
ap-pui
ap-pur-te-nance
a-pri-cot
A-pril
a pri-o-ri
ap-ro-pos
ap-sis
ap-te-ri-um
ap-ter-ous
ap-ti-tude
aq-ua-plane

aq-ua-relle
a-quar-i-um
A-quar-i-us
a-quat-ic
aq-ua-tint
aq-ua-vit
aq-ue-duct
a-que-ous
aq-ui-fer
aq-ui-line
ar-a-besque
A-ra-bi-an
Ar-a-bic
a-rab-i-nose
Ar-ab-ize
ar-a-ble
A-rach-ni-da
ar-ach-noi-dal
Ar-a-go-nese
a-rag-o-nite
ar-al-kox-y
ar-al-kyl-ate
Ar-a-ma-ic
A-rap-a-ho
A-rau-ca-ni-an
ar-bi-ter
ar-bi-tra-ble
ar-bi-trag-er
ar-bit-ra-ment
ar-bi-trar-y
ar-bi-tra-tor
ar-bo-re-al
ar-bo-res-cent
ar-bo-re-tum
ar-bo-ri-cul-tur-al
ar-bo-rize
ar-bor-vi-tae
ar-bu-tus
ar-cade
Ar-ca-di-an
ar-ca-num
ar-cha-ic
ar-che-o-log-i-cal
ar-che-ol-o-gy
arch-er-y
ar-che-typ-al
ar-che-us
Ar-chi-bald
ar-chi-e-pis-co-pa-cy
Ar-chi-me-de-an
ar-chi-pel-a-go
ar-chi-tec-tur-al
ar-chi-trave

ar-chives
ar-chi-vist
Arc-tic
Arc-tu-rus
ar-cu-ate
ar-dent
ar-dor
ar-du-ous
ar-e-al
a-re-na
ar-e-na-ceous
a-re-o-la
ar-gen-tal
ar-gen-te-ous
ar-gen-tif-er-ous
Ar-gen-ti-na
ar-gen-tite
ar-gen-tous
ar-gen-tum
ar-gil-la-ceous
ar-gil-lif-er-ous
ar-gel-lite
ar-gi-nine
ar-gol
ar-gon
Ar-go-naut
ar-go-sy
ar-gu-men-ta-tive
Ar-gy-rol
a-rid-i-ty
Ar-i-el
A-ri-es
A-ri-on
a-ris-tate
ar-is-toc-ra-cy
a-ris-to-crat-ic
Ar-is-to-te-li-an
Ar-is-tot-le
ar-ith-met-ic (adj.)
a-rith-me-tic (n.)
ar-ith-met-i-cal
ar-ith-mom-e-ter
Ar-i-zo-nan
Ar-kan-san
ark-ite (mineral)
ar-ma-da
ar-ma-dil-los
Ar-ma-ged-don
ar-ma-ment
ar-ma-men-tar-i-um
ar-ma-ture
Ar-me-ni-an
ar-mi-stice

ar-mor-er
ar-mo-ri-al
ar-mo-ry
ar-ni-ca
a-ro-ma
ar-o-mat-ic
ar-o-ma-ti-za-tion
a-rous-al
a-rous-ing
ar-raign
ar-range-ments
ar-rear-age
ar-rest-er
ar-res-tive
ar-rhyth-mi-a
ar-riv-al
ar-ro-gant
ar-ron-disse-ment
ar-roy-o
ar-se-nal
ar-se-nate
ar-se-nic (n.)
ar-sen-ic (adj.)
ar-sen-i-cal
ar-se-nide
ar-se-ni-ous
ar-se-ni-o-sid-er-ite
ar-se-no-ben-zene
ar-sine
ar-son-ist
ar-so-ni-um
ars-phen-a-mine
ar-te-ri-al
ar-te-ri-og-ra-phy
ar-te-ri-o-lar
ar-te-ri-o-scle-ro-sis
ar-te-ri-ot-omy
ar-te-ri-tis
ar-ter-y
ar-te-sian
ar-thrit-ic
ar-thri-tis
ar-thro-dese
ar-throd-e-sis
ar-throg-e-nous
ar-throg-ra-phy
ar-throm-e-ter
ar-throp-a-thy
ar-thro-pod
Ar-throp-o-da
ar-ti-choke
ar-ti-cle
ar-tic-u-la-tor

ar-ti-fact
ar-ti-fice
ar-tif-i-cer
ar-ti-fi-cial
ar-til-ler-y
ar-ti-nite
ar-ti-san
art-ist
ar-tiste
ar-tis-ti-cal
ar-tist-ry
A-run-del (Maryland)
Ar-y-an-ize
ar-yl-am-ine
ar-yl-ate
ar-yl-ene
as-a-fet-i-da
as-bes-to-sis
as-ca-ri-a-sis
as-car-i-dole
as-cend-an-cy
as-cend-ant
as-cend-er
as-cer-tain
as-cet-i-cism
as-cid-i-an
as-ci-tes
a-scor-bic
as-cribe
a-sep-sis
a-sep-tic
Ash-ke-na-zi
A-si-at-ic
as-i-nin-i-ty
a-skance
a-skew
as-pa-rag-i-nase
as-par-a-gine
as-par-a-gus
as-par-tic
as-pect
as-pen
as-per-ate
as-perge
as-per-gil-lus
as-per-i-ty
as-per-sion
as-phal-tene
as-phal-tic
as-phyx-i-ate
As-pi-dis-tra
as-pi-rant
as-pi-ra-tor

as-pir-a-to-ry
as-pi-rin
As-ple-ni-um
as-sail-ant
As-sam-ese
as-sas-si-nate
as-sem-bla-ble
as-sem-bler
as-sem-bly
as-sen-tor
as-sert-i-ble
as-ser-tive
as-sess-ee
as-ses-sor
as-ses-so-ri-al
as-sev-er-ate
as-si-du-i-ty
as-sid-u-ous
as-si-ette
as-sign-a-ble
as-sig-nat
as-sig-na-tion
as-sign-ee
as-sign-or
as-sim-i-la-ble
as-sist-ant
as-so-ci-a-ble
as-so-ci-ate
as-so-nance
as-suage
as-sump-sit
as-sur-ance
As-syr-i-an
as-ta-tine
as-ter
as-te-ri-al
as-ter-isk
as-ter-oid
as-ter-oi-dal
as-the-ni-a
as-then-ic
asth-mat-ic
as-tig-mat-ic
a-stig-ma-tism
as-tig-mom-e-ter
as-ton-ish
as-tound-ing
as-tra-gal
as-trag-a-lus
as-tra-khan
as-tral
as-tric-tion
as-trin-gent

as-tri-on-ics
as-tro-ga-tor
as-trog-o-ny
as-troid
as-tro-labe
as-trol-o-ger
as-tro-log-i-cal
as-trol-o-gy
as-trom-e-try
as-tro-naut
as-tro-nau-tics
as-tron-o-mer
as-tro-nom-i-cal
as-tron-o-my
as-tro-sphere
As-tu-ri-an
as-tute
a-sun-der
a-sy-lum
a-sym-met-ri-cal
as-ymp-tote
as-ymp-tot-ic
a-syn-ap-sis
a-sys-to-le
At-a-brine
at-a-rac-tic
at-a-vism
at-a-vis-tic
a-tax-i-a
at-e-lier
a-the-is-ti-cal
ath-e-ne-um
A-the-ni-an
Ath-ens
ath-er-o-ma
ath-er-om-a-tous
ath-er-o-scle-ro-sis
ath-let-i-cal-ly
a-threp-si-a
ath-ro-cyte
ath-ro-gen-ic
At-lan-tic
at-lan-tite
at-mol-y-sis
at-mom-e-ter
at-mos-pher-i-cal
at-oll
a-tom-ic
a-tom-i-cal
at-o-mic-i-ty
at-om-ism
at-om-is-tic
at-om-iz-er

a-ton-al
a-tone-ment
at-o-ny
at-o-py
a-tre-si-a
a-tri-o-ven-tric-u-lar
a-tri-um
a-tro-cious
a-troc-i-ty
a-troph-ic
at-ro-phy
at-ro-pine
at-ro-pin-ize
at-ta-ché
at-tain-der
at-tem-per-a-tor
at-tend-ant
at-ten-tive
at-ten-u-a-tor
at-test-ant
at-tes-ta-tion
at-test-er
at-ti-tu-di-nize
at-tor-ney
at-tract-ant
at-trac-tive
at-trac-tor
at-trib-ut-a-ble
at-tri-bute (n.)
at-trib-ute (v.)
at-trib-u-tive
at-tri-tus
auc-tion-eer
auc-to-ri-al
au-da-cious
au-dac-i-ty
au-di-ble
au-di-ence
au-di-o-gen-ic
au-di-om-e-ter
au-di-om-e-try
au-di-to-ri-um
au-di-to-ry
Au-du-bon
au-gan-ite
au-ger
au-gite
au-gi-tite
aug-men-ta-tion
aug-ment-a-tive
aug-men-tor
au-gu-ry
au-gust

Au·gus·tin·i·an
au·ral
au·ra·mine
au·re·ate
au·re·li·an
au·re·ole
Au·re·o·my·cin
au·ri·cle
au·ric·u·lar
au·ric·u·lo·pa·ri·e·tal
au·ro·ra bo·re·al·is
au·rum
aus·cul·tate
aus·pic·es
aus·pi·cious
aus·ten·it·ic
aus·ter·i·ty
Aus·tra·la·sian
Aus·tra·lian
Aus·tri·an
au·tar·chic
au·tar·chy
au·then·ti·cal·ly
au·then·ti·ca·tor
au·then·tic·i·ty
au·thor·i·tar·i·an
au·thor·i·ta·tive
au·thor·i·za·tion
au·thor·iz·er
au·tism
au·toc·ra·cy
au·to·crat
au·to·ge·net·ic
au·to·gen·ic
au·tog·e·nous
au·to·gi·ro
au·to·graph
au·tog·ra·pher
au·tol·y·sate
au·to·mat·i·cal
au·to·ma·tic·i·ty
au·tom·a·tin
au·to·ma·tion
au·tom·a·tism
au·tom·a·tist
au·tom·a·ti·za·tion
au·tom·a·ton
au·tom·a·tous
au·tom·ne·si·a
au·to·net·ics
au·to·nom·ic
au·ton·o·mous
au·toph·a·gous

au·toph·o·ny
au·top·sy
au·tos·co·py
au·tot·o·my
au·tox·i·diz·a·ble
au·tum·nal
aux·a·nom·e·ter
aux·il·ia·ry
aux·in
aux·o·chrom·ic
aux·om·e·ter
av·a·lanche
av·a·ri·cious
av·a·tar
av·e·nue
av·er·age
a·ver·sion
a·vert·i·ble
a·vi·an·ize
av·i·a·rist
a·vi·ar·y
a·vi·a·tor
a·vi·a·trix
av·i·din
a·vid·i·ty
A·vi·gnon·ese
a·vi·on·ics
av·o·ca·dos
av·o·ca·tion
a·voc·a·to·ry
a·void·ance
av·oir·du·pois
a·vow·al
a·vun·cu·lar
a·wak·en
awk·ward
awn·ing (n., v.)
ax·i·al·ly
ax·il·lar·y
ax·i·o·mat·ic
Ax·min·ster
ax·o·lotl
ax·om·e·ter
a·za·lea
az·e·la·ic
a·ze·o·trop·ic
a·ze·ot·ro·py
Az·er·bai·ja·ni
az·ide
az·i·do·a·ce·tic
az·i·mi·no
az·i·muth·al
az·ine

az-o-im-ide
az-ole
az-o-meth-ane
a-zo-ni-um
A-zo-to-bac-ter
az-o-tom-e-ter
az-ox-y-ben-zene

Az-tec-an
az-u-lene
az-ure
az-u-rin
az-ur-ite
az-y-gous

B

ba-bas-su
bab-bitt
bab-bling
Ba-bel
bab-i-ru-sa
ba-boon
ba-bush-ka
Bab-y-lo-ni-an
bac-ca-lau-re-ate
bac-cha-na-lian
bac-chant
bac-cif-er-ous
bach-e-lor
bac-il-lar-y
ba-cil-li
ba-cil-lus
bac-i-tra-cin
ba-con
Ba-co-ni-an
bac-te-ri-a
bac-te-ri-cid-al
bac-te-ri-cid-in
bac-ter-id
bac-te-ri-o-log-i-cal
bac-te-ri-ol-o-gy
bac-te-ri-ol-y-sis
bac-te-ri-o-lyt-ic
bac-te-ri-os-co-py
bac-te-ri-um
bac-te-roi-dal
badg-er
bad-i-nage
Bae-de-ker
baf-fling
ba-gasse
bag-a-telle
ba-gel
ba-guette

Ba-ha-i
Ba-ha-ma
bail-ee
bail-er
Bai-ley
bail-iff
bail-i-wick
ba-ke-lite
bak-er-y
bak-sheesh
Ba-la-kla-va
bal-a-lai-ka
bal-anc-er
ba-la-ta
bal-brig-gan
bal-co-ny
bal-der-dash
bal-dric
Bal-e-ar-ic
ba-leen
Ba-li-nese
Bal-kan
balk-y
bal-lad-eer
bal-le-ri-na
bal-lis-tics
bal-lo-net
bal-loon-ist
bal-ma-caan
balm-i-ness
Bal-mor-al
bal-ne-al
ba-lo-ney
bal-sam
Bal-tic
Bal-ti-mor-e-an
bal-us-trade
bam-bi-no

bam-boo-zle	Bar-kis
ba-nal (commonplace)	bark-om-e-ter
ban-al (governor)	Bar-na-bas
ba-nal-i-ty	bar-na-cle
ba-nan-a	bar-o-graph
Ban-bury	ba-rom-e-ter
ban-dag-er	bar-o-met-ric
ban-dan-na	bar-o-met-ro-graph
ban-deau	bar-o-me-trog-ra-phy
band-er	ba-rom-e-try
ban-dit-ry	bar-on-ess
ban-do-leer	bar-on-et
band-dy-ing	ba-ro-ni-al
ban-ga-lore	ba-roque
ban-gle	bar-o-scope
ban-ish	ba-rouche
ban-is-ter	bar-ra-cu-da
bank-er	bar-rage
bank-rupt-cy	bar-ra-try
ban-quet-er	bar-reled
ban-shee	bar-ren
ban-tam	bar-rette
ban-ter	bar-ri-cade
bant-ling	bar-ring
ban-zai	bar-ris-ter
bap-tis-mal	bar-ter
bap-tis-ter-y	Bart-lett
bap-tiz-er	bar-y-lite
Bar-ab-bas	ba-ry-ta
Bá-rá-ny	ba-ryt-ic
bar-a-the-a	bar-y-tron
Bar-ba-dos	ba-sal
bar-bar-i-an	ba-salt
bar-bar-ic	ba-sal-tic
bar-ba-rism	ba-sic
bar-ba-rous	ba-si-cal-ly
Bar-ba-ry	ba-sic-i-ty
bar-be-cue	ba-sid-i-um
bar-ber	bas-il
bar-bette	ba-sil-i-ca
bar-bi-tal	bas-i-lisk
bar-bi-tu-rate	ba-sin
bar-bi-tu-ric	ba-sis
bar-gain-er	Bas-ker-ville
bar-gain-or (law)	bas-ket-ry
bar-ing	bas-si-net
bar-ite	bas-tar-dy
bar-i-tone	bas-tille
bar-i-to-sis	bas-ti-na-do
bar-i-um	Ba-ta-vi-an
bar-ken-tine	ba-teau
bark-er	bath-o-lith-ic
Bark-hau-sen	ba-thom-e-ter

ba-thos
ba-thym-e-ter
bath-y-met-ric
ba-thym-e-try
bath-y-scaphe
ba-thys-mal
ba-tik
ba-tiste
ba-ton (n.)
bat-on (v.)
ba-tra-chi-um
bat-tal-ion
bau-ble
Bau-mé
baux-ite
baux-it-ic
Ba-var-i-an
bay-ard
bay-o-net
Ba-yonne
bay-ou
ba-zoo-ka
bdel-li-um
bea-con
bead-er
bea-dle
bea-gle
beak-er
bé-ar-naise
beat-er
be-a-tif-ic
be-at-i-fy
be-at-i-tude
Be-a-trice
beau-sé-ant
beau-te-ous
bea-ver
be-bee-rine
Bech-u-a-na-land
beck-on
Bec-que-rel
be-di-zen
Bed-ou-in
Be-el-ze-bub
Be-er-she-ba
Bee-tho-ven
bee-tle
beg-gar-y
be-gin-ning
beg-ohm
be-go-nia
be-hav-ior-al
be-he-moth

be-hold-en
bei-del-lite
be-lat-ed
be-lea-guered
bel-fry
Bel-gian
be-liev-er
bel-la-don-na
bel-li-cos-i-ty
bel-lig-er-ent
Be-na-res
ben-e-fac-tor
be-nef-i-cent
ben-e-fi-cial
ben-e-fi-ci-ar-y
ben-e-fi-ci-ate
ben-e-fit-ed
be-nev-o-lence
be-nign
be-nig-nant
be-ni-to-ite
Ben-ja-min
ben-ton-ite
benz-al-de-hyde
ben-zald-ox-ime
benz-am-ide
Ben-ze-drine
ben-zene-di-a-zo-ni-um
ben-ze-noid
ben-zil-ic
benz-im-id-a-zole
ben-zo-ate
ben-zo-fla-vine
ben-zo-ic
ben-zo-in
ben-zo-i-nat-ed
ben-zo-phe-none
ben-zo-sul-fi-mide
benz-ox-y-a-ce-tic
ben-zo-yl-ate
ben-zyl-ate
ben-zyl-ox-y
ber-ba-mine
ber-ber-ine
be-ret
ber-ga-mot
berg-schrund
ber-i-ber-i
Ber-ing
Berke-ley
berke-li-um
Ber-mu-da
Bern-ese

Ber-noul-li
Ber-tha
berth-ing
Ber-tram
be-ryl-li-um
ber-yl-loid
Bes-sa-ra-bi-an
Bes-se-mer
bes-tial
bes-ti-al-i-ty
be-stride
be-ta-cism
be-ta-ine
be-ta-tron
be-tel
Be-tel-geuse
Be-thes-da
be-troth-al
Beu-lah
bev-a-tron
bev-eled
bev-er-age
be-wil-der
bez-el
Bhu-ta-nese
Bi-a-fra
bi-ased
bi-be-lot
Bi-ble
Bib-li-cal
bib-li-o-graph-ic
bib-li-og-ra-phy
bib-li-o-phile
bib-u-lous
bi-car-bon-ate
bi-ceph-a-lous
bi-chlo-ride
bi-chro-mate
bick-er-ing
bi-cus-pid
bi-cy-clist
bi-cy-clo-al-kane
bi-fur-cat-ed
big-a-mous
big-ot-ry
bi-gua-nide
Bi-ki-ni
bil-i-ar-y
bil-i-cy-a-nin
bil-i-fi-ca-tion
bil-ious
bil-i-ru-bin
bil-i-ru-bi-ne-mi-a

bil-liards
bi-loc-u-lar
bi-met-al-lism
bi-na-ry
bin-au-ral
bind-er-y
bin-na-cle
bin-oc-u-lar
bi-no-mi-al
bi-og-e-ny
bi-o-graph-i-cal
bi-og-ra-phy
bi-o-log-i-cal
bi-ol-o-gist
bi-ol-y-sis
bi-om-e-ter
bi-o-met-ric
bi-om-e-try
bi-on-o-my
bi-op-sy
bi-os-co-py
bi-os-o-phy
bi-os-ter-ol
bi-ot-ic
bi-o-tin
bi-o-tite
bi-o-vu-lar
bip-a-rous
bi-par-ti-ble
bi-par-ti-ent
bi-par-tite
Bir-ming-ham
bis-cuit
bish-op-ric
bis-muth-ate
bis-muth-yl
bi-son
bit-er
bi-tu-men
bi-tu-mi-nous
bi-u-ret
bi-va-lent
biv-ouacked
bi-zarre
black-ened
blad-ed
blam-a-ble
Blan-chard
blanch-er
blan-dish
blan-ket
blar-ney
blas-phe-mous

blas-te-ma
blast-er
blas-tog-e-ny
Blas-to-my-ce-tes
blas-to-my-co-sis
blas-tu-la
bla-tant
blath-er-ing
blaz-er
bla-zon
blem-ish
blend-er
bleph-a-ral
bless-ed (adj.)
blessed (v.)
blind-er
blink-er
blis-ter
bloat-er
block-ade
blon-dine
bloom-er
bloop-er
blu-cher
bludg-eon
bluff-ing
blu-ing
blun-der-er
blus-ter
boat-swain
bob-bi-net
bo-cac-cio
bo-dhi-satt-va
bod-ice
bod-i-ly
bo-gey (golf term)
bo-gie (cart)
bo-gy (specter)
Bo-he-mi-an
boil-er
bois-ter-ous
bo-le-ro
bo-le-tus
Bo-liv-i-an
Bo-lo-gna
bo-lom-e-ter
Bol-she-vi-ki
bol-she-vism
Bol-she-vist
bol-ster
bom-bard-ier
bom-bas-ti-cal
bom-ba-zine

bom-bi-nate
bo-na fi-de
bo-nan-za
Bo-na-parte
bond-age
Bond-er-ize
bo-ni-to
bo-nus
boo-by
boo-dler
Bool-e-an
boo-mer-ang
boor-ish
boost-er
boo-tee
boo-ty
booz-er
bo-rac-ic
bo-ra-cite
bo-rat-ed
bo-rax
Bor-deaux
bor-der
bo-re-al
Bor-ghe-se
bo-ric
bo-ride
Bor-ne-an
bor-ne-ol
born-ite
bor-nyl
bo-ron
bor-ough
Bor-zoi
bos-om
Bos-po-rus
boss-ism
Bos-to-ni-an
bo-tan-i-cal
bot-a-nist
bot-a-ny
both-er-a-tion
bo-tog-e-nin
bot-ry-oi-dal
Bot-swa-na
bot-u-lin-ic
bot-u-lism
bou-cle
bou-doir
Bou-gain-vil-le-a
bouil-la-baisse
bouil-lon
boul-der

bou-le-vard
bound-a-ry
boun-te-ous
bou-quet
Bour-bon-ism
bour-geois
bour-geoi-sie
bou-ton-niere
bo-vine
bowd-ler-ize
bow-ie
boy-sen-ber-ry
bra-ce-ro
brach-i-al
bra-chi-o-la
Brach-i-op-o-da
brach-y-ceph-a-lous
bra-chyp-ter-ous
brach-ysm
bra-chyt-ic
brac-ing
brack-et
brack-ish
brac-te-al
brag-ga-do-ci-o
Brah-man-ism
bram-ble
bran-chi-al
bran-chif-er-ous
Bran-chi-op-o-da
brand-er
bran-dish
bra-se-ro
Bra-sí-lia
bra-sid-ic
bras-siere
bra-va-do
brav-er-y
bra-vo
bra-vu-ra
bray-er
bra-zen
bra-zier
braz-il (mining term)
bra-zil (wood, nut)
Bra-zil
Bra-zil-ian
breath-er
brec-ci-a
breez-i-ness
Bre-men
brems-strah-lung
brem-sung

brenn-schluss
breth-ren
Bret-on
bre-vet
bre-vi-ar-y
bre-vier
brev-i-ty
brew-er-y
Brew-ster
brib-er-y
brid-al
bri-dle
bri-dling
bri-er
bri-gade
brig-a-dier
brig-and-age
brig-an-tine
Brigh-ton
bril-liant
brin-dle
Bri-nell
bri-quet-ted
bri-sance
brisk-en
bris-ket
bris-tle
bris-tly
Brit-ain
Bri-tan-ni-a
Brit-ish
broad-cast-er
bro-cade
broc-co-li
bro-chure
broil-er
bro-ken
bro-ker-age
brom-ar-gy-rite
bro-mate
bro-me-lin
bro-mide
bro-mid-ic
bro-mi-dro-sis
bro-min-ate
bro-mi-na-tion
bro-mine
bro-mo-cre-sol
bro-mo-i-o-dide
bro-mo-met-ric
bro-mom-e-try
bron-chi-al
bron-chi-tis

bron-chop-o-ny
bron-chos-co-py
bron-co
bron-tom-e-ter
brood-er
broth-el
broth-er
brows-er
bru-cel-lo-sis
bruc-ine
bruc-ite
bruis-er
bru-tal-ize
brut-ish
bu-bon-ic
buc-ca-neer
buc-ci-na-tor
Bu-chan-an
Bu-cha-rest
buck-et-ful
buck-ler
buck-ling
bu-col-ic
Bu-da-pest
Bud-dha
budg-er-i-gar
budg-et-ar-y
budg-et-eer
Bue-nos Ai-res
buf-fa-lo
buff-er
buf-fet
buff-ing
buf-foon-er-y
bu-gle
bul-ba-ceous
bul-bar
bul-bo-cap-nine
bul-bous
Bul-gar-i-an
bulg-er
bulk-er
bul-late
bull-doz-er
bul-le-tin
bul-lion
bull-ish
bul-lock
bul-ly-ing
bul-rush
bum-bling
bump-er
bump-i-ness

bump-om-e-ter
bump-tious
bun-combe
Bun-des-rat
bun-dler
bun-ga-low
bun-gee
bun-gler
bun-ion
bun-ker-age
bun-kum
bunt-ing (v.)
bun-ting (bird, flag)
buoy-ant
bur-bled
bur-den
bu-reau
bu-reauc-ra-cy
bu-reau-crat-ic
bu-ret
bur-gee
bur-geon
bur-gess
bur-gher
bur-glar-ize
bur-gla-ry
bur-go-mas-ter
Bur-gun-di-an
bur-i-al
bur-ied
bur-lesque
bur-ley
Bur-mese
burn-ers
bur-nish-er
bur-sar
bur-si-tis
Bu-run-di-an
bur-y-ing
bus-es
bush-el
bus-i-ly
busi-ness
bus-kin
bust-er
bus-tling
bu-ta-di-ene
bu-tal-de-hyde
bu-tane
bu-ta-no-ic
bu-ta-nol
butch-er
bu-te-nyl

bu-tox-yl
but-tress
bu-tyl-a-mine
bu-tyl-ene
bu-tyr-a-ceous
bu-tyr-ate
bu-tyr-ic
bu-tyr-in-ase
bu-tyr-o-lac-tone

bu-tyr-om-e-ter
bu-tyr-yl
bux-om
buz-zard
buzz-er
Byel-o-rus-sia
By-ron-ic
bys-si-no-sis
Byz-an-tine

C

ca-bal
cab-a-la
cab-a-lis-ti-cal
ca-ban-a
ca-bane
cab-a-ret
cab-bage
ca-ber-net
cab-e-zon
cab-i-net
ca-bling
cab-o-chon
ca-boose
cab-o-tage
cab-ri-o-let
ca-bu-ya
ca-ca-o
cach-a-lot
ca-chec-tic
ca-chet
cach-in-na-tion
ca-chou
ca-cique
cack-ling
cac-o-dyl-ic
ca-cog-ra-phy
cac-o-mis-tle
ca-coph-o-ny
cad-a-lene
ca-das-tral
ca-dav-er-ous
ca-delle
ca-dence
ca-den-za
ca-det
cad-i-nene
Ca-diz

cad-mi-um
cad-re
ca-du-ca-ry
ca-du-ce-us
Cae-sar
cae-si-ous
caf-e-te-ri-a
caf-feine
Ca-ga-yan
cais-son
ca-jol-er-y
ca-la-di-um
cal-a-mine
ca-lam-i-tous
ca-lan-dri-a
ca-lash
cal-a-ver-ite
cal-car-e-ous
cal-cif-er-ol
cal-cif-er-ous
cal-ci-fi-ca-tion
cal-cim-e-ter
cal-ci-mine
cal-ci-na-tion
cal-cite
cal-ci-um
cal-cu-la-ble
cal-cu-la-tor
cal-cu-la-to-ry
cal-cu-lus
cal-dron
cal-e-fa-cient
cal-en-dar
cal-en-der
ca-len-du-lin
ca-les-cent
cal-i-ber

cal-i-brat-er
cal-i-bra-tor
ca-li-che
Cal-i-for-ni-an
cal-i-for-ni-um
ca-lig-i-nous
cal-i-per
ca-liph
cal-is-then-ics
calk-er
cal-li-graph-ic
cal-lig-ra-phy
cal-li-o-pe
cal-lous (adj.)
cal-lus (n.)
cal-lus-es
cal-o-mel
cal-o-res-cence
ca-lor-ic
cal-o-rie
ca-lor-i-fa-cient
cal-o-rif-ic
cal-o-rim-e-ter
cal-o-ri-met-ri-cal
cal-o-rize
ca-lum-ni-ate
cal-um-ny
Cal-va-ry
Cal-vin-ism
ca-ly-coid
ca-lyp-so
cal-lyp-tra
ca-lyx
ca-ma-ra-de-rie
cam-a-ril-la
ca-ma-ta
cam-ber
cam-bi-um
Cam-bo-di-an
cam-bric
cam-el-eer
ca-mel-o-pard
Cam-em-bert
cam-e-o
cam-er-a
Cam-e-roon
ca-mion
cam-i-sole
cam-o-mile
Ca-mor-ra
cam-ou-flage
cam-pa-ni-le
camp-er

cam-pha-nyl
cam-phoid
cam-pho-len-ic
cam-pho-ra-ceous
cam-phor-ene
cam-phor-ic
cam-pim-e-ter
cam-pus
Ca-naan
Can-a-da
Ca-na-di-an
ca-nai-gre
ca-naille
ca-nal-i-za-tion
ca-na-pe
ca-nard
ca-nar-y
ca-nas-ta
Ca-nav-er-al
can-celed
can-cel-ing
can-cel-la-tion
can-cer-ous
can-croid
can-de-la
can-de-la-brum
can-de-li-lla
can-did
can-di-date
can-died
can-dling
can-dor
ca-nes-cent
ca-nic-o-la
ca-nine
can-is-ter
can-ker
can-na-bi-nol
can-na-bis
can-ner-y
can-ni-bal-ize
can-non-ade
can-nu-lar
ca-noe-ist
can-on
ca-ñon (Spanish form for
    canyon)
can-on-ess
can-non-i-cal
can-on-i-za-tion
Ca-no-pus
can-o-py
can-ta-bi-le

can-ta-loupe
can-tan-ker-ous
can-ta-ta
can-ter (v.)
cant-er (n.)
can-thar-i-des
can-tha-ris
can-thus
can-ti-cle
can-ti-le-ver
can-ton-ment
Ca-nuck
can-vassed
can-vass-er
caou-tchouc
ca-pa-ble
ca-pa-cious
ca-pac-i-tance
ca-pac-i-tor
ca-par-i-son
cap-e-lin
ca-per
ca-pi-as
cap-il-la-ros-co-py
cap-il-lar-y
cap-i-tal-ist
cap-i-tal-i-za-tion
ca-pi-tan
ca-pit-u-la-tor
cap-no-di-um
ca-pon-ette
ca-pote
cap-ric
ca-pric-cio
ca-price
ca-pri-cious
Cap-ri-cor-nis
cap-ro-ate
ca-pro-ic
cap-ry-late
ca-pryl-ic
cap-ry-lyl
cap-sa-i-cin
cap-si-cum
cap-stan
cap-su-lar
cap-ti-va-tor
cap-u-chin
cap-y-bar-a
car-a-bao
car-a-bi-neer
Ca-ra-cas
car-a-cul

ca-rafe
car-a-mel
car-a-pace
car-at
car-a-van-sa-ry
car-a-way
carb-ac-i-dom-e-ter
carb-alk-ox-yl
car-ba-mate
car-bam-ic
car-bam-ide
carb-am-i-do-hy-dan-to-in
car-ba-mine
carb-am-i-no
car-bam-o-yl
car-ba-nil-ic
car-ba-nil-ide
car-bar-sone
car-baz-ic
car-ba-zole
car-beth-ox-yl
car-bine
car-bi-nol
car-bo-cy-a-nine
car-bo-cy-clic
car-bo-di-i-mide
car-bol-ic
car-bo-lize
Car-bo-loy
car-bo-na-ceous
car-bon-ate
car-bon-ic
car-bon-if-er-ous
car-bo-ni-um
car-bon-ize
car-bon-yl
car-bon-y-late
Car-bo-run-dum
car-box-yl-ase
car-box-yl-ic
car-bun-cle
car-bu-rant
car-bu-ret-ed
car-bu-ret-or
car-bu-riz-er
car-byl-a-mine
car-cass
car-cin-o-gen
car-ci-no-gen-ic
car-ci-noid
car-ci-no-ma
car-ci-no-ma-to-sis
car-ci-nom-a-tous

car-ci-no-sis
car-da-mom
car-di-ac
Car-di-a-zol
car-di-nal
card-ing
car-di-o-gen-ic
car-di-og-ra-phy
car-di-oid
car-di-ol-o-gy
car-di-om-e-ter
car-di-ot-o-my
car-di-tis
ca-reen
ca-reer
ca-ress-ive
car-et
Car-ib-be-an
car-i-bou
car-i-ca-tur-al
car-ies
car-il-lon-neur
ca-ri-na
car-i-nate
car-i-ous
Car-list
Car-mel-ite
car-min-a-tive
car-min-ic
car-nage
car-nal-i-ty
car-nau-ba
Car-ne-gie
car-ne-lian
car-ni-tine
car-ni-val
car-niv-o-rous
car-no-tite
car-oled
Car-o-lin-i-an
car-om
car-o-tene
ca-rot-e-noid
ca-rot-id
ca-rous-al
Car-pa-thi-an
car-pel
car-pen-try
carp-er
car-pho-lite
car-pho-sid-er-ite
car-po-go-ni-um
car-riage

car-ri-on
car-ron-ade
car-rou-sel
cart-age
car-tel-ize
car-ti-lag-i-nous
car-tog-ra-phy
car-ton
car-toon-ist
car-touche
car-tridge
car-un-cle
car-vene
carv-er
Car-ver
car-y-at-id
car-y-op-sis
ca-sa-ba
Ca-sa-blan-ca
cas-car-a
ca-sein-ate
ca-se-ous
cash-ew
cash-ier
cas-ing
ca-si-no
cas-ket
cas-se-role
cas-si-mere
Cas-si-o-pe-ian
cas-sit-er-ite
cas-ta-net
cas-tel-late
cast-er
cas-ti-ga-tor
cas-tile
Cas-til-ian
cas-tle
cas-tor-ite
cas-tra-tive
cas-u-al-ty
cas-u-ist-ry
ca-sus bel-li
cat-a-bol-ic
ca-tab-o-lism
cat-a-clys-mic
cat-a-di-op-tric
cat-a-falque
cat-a-lase
cat-a-lec-tic
cat-a-lep-tic
cat-a-loged
cat-a-log-ing

ca-tal-y-sis
cat-a-lyst
cat-a-lyt-i-cal-ly
cat-a-lyz-er
cat-a-ma-ran
cat-a-me-ni-al
cat-a-pult
cat-a-ract
ca-tarrh-al
ca-tas-tro-phe
cat-a-stroph-ic
Ca-taw-ba
cat-e-che-sis
cat-e-chet-i-cal
cat-e-chism
cat-e-chu-men-al
cat-e-chol
ca-te-na
cat-e-gor-i-cal
cat-e-go-rize
cat-e-nar-y
cat-e-noid
ca-ter-er
cat-er-pil-lar
cat-er-waul
ca-thar-sis
ca-thar-tic
Ca-thar-ti-dae
ca-thec-tic
ca-the-dral
ca-thep-sin
cath-e-ter-i-za-tion
cath-e-tom-e-ter
cath-ode
ca-thod-ic
cath-o-lic-i-ty
ca-thol-i-cism
cat-i-on-ic
Cau-ca-sian
cau-cus
cau-dal
cau-di-llo
cau-li-flow-er
caus-al
cau-sal-i-ty
cau-sa-tion
caus-a-tive
cause ce-le-bre
cau-se-rie
caus-tic-i-ty
cau-ter-i-za-tion
cav-al-cade
cav-a-lier

cav-al-ry
cav-a-ti-na
ca-ve-at
cav-ern-ous
cav-i-ar
cav-iled
cav-il-er
cav-i-ta-tion
Ca-vi-te
cav-i-ty
ca-vort
cay-enne
Ca-yu-ga
Cay-use
ce-cum
ce-dar
ce-drat
ce-drol
ce-du-la
ceil-om-e-ter
Cel-an-ese
Cel-e-bes
cel-e-brate
ce-leb-ri-ty
ce-ler-i-ty
cel-er-y
ce-les-tial
cel-es-tite
ce-li-ac
cel-i-ba-cy
ce-li-ot-o-my
ce-lite
cel-lif-er-ous
cel-lo-phane
cel-lu-lar
cel-lu-loid
cel-lu-lose
cel-lu-los-ic
Cel-si-us
Celt-ic
cel-ti-um
ce-men-ta-tion
ce-ment-er
ce-ment-ite
ce-men-ti-tious
cem-e-ter-y
ce-no-bi-an
cen-o-bite
Ce-no-zo-ic
cen-so-ri-ous
Cen-tau-rus
cen-ta-vo
cen-te-nar-i-an

cen-te-nar-y
cen-ten-ni-al
cen-tes-i-mal
cen-te-si-mo
cent-ge-ner
cen-ti-me-ter
cen-ti-pede
cen-tral-ize
cen-trif-u-gal
cen-tri-fuge
cen-trip-e-tal
cen-troi-dal
cen-tu-ry
ce-phal-ic
ceph-a-lin
ceph-a-lo-di-um
ceph-a-lom-e-ter
ceph-a-lom-e-try
Ceph-e-id
ce-ram-ic
ce-ram-ist
ce-ram-i-um
ce-ra-ti-um
cer-a-to-sau-rus
Cer-ber-us
ce-re-al
cer-e-bel-lo-ru-bral
cer-e-bel-lum
cer-e-bral
cer-e-brate
cer-e-bro-side
cer-e-bro-spi-nal
cer-e-brum
cere-ment
cer-e-mo-ni-al
Ce-ren-kov
Ce-res
cer-e-sin
ce-rise
ce-rite
ce-ri-um
ce-ro-graph
ce-rog-ra-phy
ce-roid
ce-ro-lite
ce-rot-ic
cer-tain-ly
cer-tif-i-cate
cer-ti-fi-ca-tion
cer-ti-o-ra-ri
cer-ti-tude
ce-ru-le-an
ce-ru-men

ce-russ-ite
cer-van-tite
cer-vi-cal
ce-sar-e-an
ce-si-um
ces-sa-tion
Ce-ta-ce-a
ce-tane
ce-tene
ce-tyl
Cha-blis
Chad-i-an
chaf-er
chaff-er (one who chaffs
    or banters)
chaf-fer (trade term—buying
    and selling)
Cha-gres
cha-grin
chair-maned
chaise longue
chal-ced-o-ny
chal-ce-don-yx
chal-co-py-rite
chal-dron
cha-let
chal-ice
chal-i-co-sis
cha-lyb-e-ate
cham-ber-lain
cham-bray
cha-me-le-on
cham-fer
cham-ois
cham-pi-gnon
cham-pi-on
chan-cel-ler-y
chan-cel-lor
chan-cer-y
chan-cre
chan-croi-dal
chan-de-lier
chan-delle
chan-dler
change-a-ble
chang-er
chan-neled
chan-teur
chan-ti-cleer
cha-ot-ic
chap-ar-ral
cha-peau
chap-el

chap-er-on
chap-lain
char-a-banc
char-ac-ter-is-tic
cha-rade
charge-a-ble
char-gé d'af-faires
charg-er
char-i-ly
char-i-ness
char-i-ot-eer
cha-ris-ma
char-is-mat-ic
char-i-ta-ble
cha-ri-va-ri
Char-ley
Char-lotte
charm-er
char-nel
char-ter
char-treuse
Cha-ryb-dis
chas-er
chas-sis
chas-ten
chas-tis-er
chas-ti-ty
cha-teau
cha-te-laine
Chat-ham
cha-toy-an-cy
Chau-ce-ri-an
chau-tau-qua
chau-vin-ism
check-ered
chedd-ite
Che-ha-lis
chei-li-tis
Che-ka
che-la-tion
chel-i-do-ni-um
che-li-form
che-lo-ne
Chel-ten-ham
chem-i-at-ric
chem-i-cal
che-mig-ra-phy
che-mise
chem-i-sette
chem-is-try
chem-o-sphere
chem-o-ther-a-py
che-mot-ro-pism

che-mur-gic
chem-ur-gy
che-nille
Che-no-po-di-um
cher-ish
cher-no-zem
Cher-o-kee
che-root
cher-ub
che-ru-bic
cher-u-bim
Chesh-ire
Ches-ter
chev-a-lier
chev-i-ot
chev-ron
Chey-enne
chi-a-ro-scu-ro
chi-ca-ner-y
chick-en
chi-cle
chic-o-ry
chif-fon
chif-fo-nier
chi-gnon
chil-dren
Chil-e-an
chi-me-ra
chi-mer-i-cal
chim-pan-zee
Chi-nese
chi-noi-se-rie
Chi-nook
chin-qua-pin
Chi-ri-qui
chi-ro-graph
chi-rog-ra-pher
chi-ro-man-cy
chi-rop-o-dy
chi-ro-prac-tor
chi-rur-gi-cal
chis-eled
chis-el-ing
chi-tin-oid
chiv-al-rous
chlo-ral
chlor-al-um
chlor-a-lu-mi-nite
chlor-am-ide
chlor-am-ine
chlor-am-phen-i-col
chlo-rate
chlor-az-ide

chlor-co-sane
Chlo-rel-la
chlor-e-mi-a
chlor-en-chy-ma
Chlo-re-tone
chlo-ric
chlo-ride
chlo-ri-dize
chlor-im-ide
chlo-ri-nate (v.)
chlo-rin-ate (n.)
chlo-rine
chlo-rit-ic
chlo-ro-form
chlo-ro-gen-ic
chlo-rom-e-ter
chlo-rom-e-try
Chlo-ro-my-ce-tin
chlo-ro-phyll
chlo-ro-prene
chlo-ro-sis
chlo-ro-then
chlo-rous
choc-o-late
choic-est
chok-er
cho-lan-ic
chol-an-threne
cho-le-ate
cho-le-cal-cif-er-ol
cho-le-cys-tec-to-my
cho-le-cys-ti-sis
cho-le-cys-tog-ra-phy
cho-le-cys-to-ki-nin
cho-le-cys-tos-to-my
cho-le-ic
cho-le-mi-a
chol-er
chol-er-a
cho-le-ret-ic
chol-er-ic
cho-les-tane
cho-les-ta-nol
cho-les-ter-ic
cho-les-ter-ol
cho-lic
cho-lin-er-gic
cho-lin-es-ter-ase
chol-o-ge-net-ic
cho-los-co-py
chon-dri-o-som-al
chon-dri-o-some
chon-drit-ic

chon-dro-dite
chon-dro-dit-ic
chon-dro-ma
chon-drom-a-tous
chon-drot-o-my
chon-drule
cho-ral
cho-rale
chord-al
chor-date
chor-di-tis
chor-dot-o-my
cho-re-a
cho-re-og-ra-pher
cho-ri-o-men-in-gi-tis
cho-ri-sis
cho-ris-ter
cho-roi-dal
cho-roid-i-tis
cho-rol-o-gy
chor-tle
cho-rus
cho-sen
chow-der
chres-tom-a-thy
chris-ten
Chris-tian
Chris-ti-an-i-ty
chro-ma-mom-e-ter
chro-mate
chro-mat-ic
chro-ma-tic-i-ty
chro-ma-tin
chro-mat-o-gram
chro-ma-tog-ra-phy
chro-ma-tol-y-sis
chro-mat-o-lyt-ic
chro-mat-o-scope
chro-ma-to-sis
chro-mic
chro-mif-er-ous
chro-mi-nance
chro-mite
chro-mi-um
chro-mo-gen-ic
chro-mo-i-so-mer-ic
chro-mom-e-ter
chro-mos-co-py
chro-mo-som-al
chro-mo-trop-ic
chro-mous
chron-i-cler
chron-o-graph

chro-nog-ra-pher
chro-nol-o-ger
chron-o-log-i-cal-ly
chro-nol-o-gy
chro-nom-e-ter
chron-o-met-ri-cal
chro-nom-e-try
chron-o-scope
chro-nos-co-py
chrys-a-lis
chrys-a-loid
chrys-an-the-mum
chrys-a-ro-bin
chrys-a-zin
chry-sene
chrys-o-er-i-ol
chrys-o-graph
chry-sog-ra-phy
chry-so-i-dine
chrys-o-lite
chrys-o-phyll
chuck-ling
Church-ill
churl-ish
chut-ist
chy-la-ceous
chy-lo-sis
chy-mi-fy
chy-mo-tryp-sin
ci-ca-da
cic-a-tri-sive
cic-a-trix
cic-a-trize
cic-e-ro-ne (n.)
cic-e-rone (v.)
ci-der
ci-gar
cig-a-rette
cil-i-ar-y
cil-i-um
ci-mi-cid
cim-o-lite
cin-cho-loi-pon
cin-cho-me-ron-ic
cin-cho-na
cin-chon-a-mine
cin-cho-nine
cin-cho-phen
cinc-ture
Cin-der-el-la
cin-e-ma
cin-e-mat-o-graph
cin-e-ma-tog-ra-pher

cin-e-ole
cin-e-rar-i-a
ci-ne-re-ous
cin-na-bar
cin-nam-ic
cin-nam-o-yl
ci-pher
ci-pho-ny
cir-ci-nate
cir-clet
cir-cling
circ-o-var-i-an
cir-cuit-al
cir-cuit-er
cir-cu-i-tous
cir-cuit-ry
cir-cu-lar-ize
cir-cu-la-to-ry
cir-cum-e-ter
cir-cum-fer-en-tial
cir-cum-lo-cu-tion
cir-cum-loc-u-to-ry
cir-cum-scrib-a-ble
cir-cum-stan-tial
cir-rho-sis
cis-tern
cit-a-ble
ci-ta-to-ry
cit-i-fy
cit-i-zen
cit-ral
cit-rate
cit-ric
cit-ri-nin
cit-ron
cit-ron-el-la
cit-rus
civ-et
civ-il
ci-vil-ian
civ-i-li-za-tion
claim-ant
clam-or-ous
clan-des-tine
clang-or
cla-queur
Clar-ence
clar-et
clar-i-fi-ca-tion
clar-i-net
clar-i-on
clas-si-cal
clas-si-fy

clas-tic
claus-tro-pho-bi-a
clav-a-cin
clav-i-cle
cla-vic-u-lar
cleans-er
cleans-ing
clear-ance
cleav-age
Clem-a-tis
clem-en-cy
Clem-en-tine
Cle-o-pat-ra
cler-gy-man
cler-i-cal
clev-er
clev-is
cli-an-thus
click-er
cli-ent-age
cli-en-tele
cli-mac-ter-ic
cli-mac-tic
cli-mat-ic
cli-ma-tize
cli-ma-to-log-i-cal
cli-ma-tol-o-gy
cli-ma-tom-e-ter
cli-max
climb-er
clin-i-cal
cli-ni-cian
clin-i-co-path-o-log-ic
clin-i-co-pa-thol-o-gy
clink-er
cli-no-he-dral
cli-nom-e-ter
cli-quish
clit-o-ris
cloi-son-ne
clois-ter
Clo-rox
Clos-trid-i-um
clo-sure
cloth-ier
clo-ture
clo-ven
clo-ver
clown-ish
clum-si-ness
clus-ter
cne-mi-al
co-ad-ju-tor

co-ag-u-la-tor
co-ag-u-lom-e-ter
co-a-les-cence
co-a-lite (v.)
Coal-ite (n.)
co-a-li-tion
co-arc-ta-tion
coast-al
coast-er
co-bal-a-min
co-bal-tic
co-balt-if-er-ous
co-bal-ti-ni-trite
co-bal-to-cal-cite
co-bal-tom-e-nite
co-bal-tous
cob-bler
co-bra
co-caine
coc-cid-i-oi-dal
coc-cid-i-oi-din
coc-cid-i-o-sis
coc-cin-ic
coc-ci-nite
coc-cyg-e-al
co-chin
coch-i-neal
coch-le-ar
cock-ade
cock-er-el
cock-le-bur
co-coa
co-co-nut
co-coon
co-deine
codg-er
cod-i-cil
cod-i-fy
co-di-mer
cod-ling
co-erc-i-ble
co-er-cive
co-e-val
co-gen-cy
cog-i-ta-tive
co-gnac
cog-na-tus
cog-ni-tive
cog-ni-za-ble
cog-no-men
co-gno-scen-ti
cog-nos-ci-ble
co-her-ence

co-he-si-ble
co-he-sive
co-in-ci-den-tal
col-an-der
col-chi-cine
Col-chi-cum
co-lec-ti-vo
col-ec-to-my
Co-le-op-te-ra
col-ick-y
col-i-se-um
co-li-tis
col-lab-o-ra-tor
col-la-gen-ase
col-lag-e-nous
col-laps-i-ble
col-lat-er-al
col-la-tor
col-league
col-lect-a-ble
col-lec-ta-ne-a
col-lec-tive
col-lec-tor
col-le-gi-ate
col-lier
col-li-ma-tor
col-li-sion
col-lo-di-on
col-loi-dal
col-lo-qui-al-ism
col-lo-quy
col-lu-sive
col-lu-vi-um
co-logne
Co-lom-bi-an
co-lo-met-ric
co-lom-e-try
co-lon
colo-nel
co-lo-ni-al
co-lon-ic
col-o-nize
col-on-nade
col-o-ny
col-o-phon
col-o-pho-ny
col-or
Col-o-rad-an
Col-o-ra-do
col-or-a-tu-ra
col-or-im-e-ter
col-or-i-met-ric
col-or-im-e-try

co-los-sal
Col-os-se-um
co-los-sus
co-los-to-my
co-los-trum
col-por-teur
Co-lum-bi-a
col-um-bif-er-ous
col-um-bine
co-lum-bite
co-lum-bi-um
col-umn
co-lum-nar
col-um-nist
co-lure
Co-man-che
co-ma-tose
co-mat-u-la
com-bat-ant
com-bat-ed
com-bat-ing
com-bat-ive-ness
com-ba-tiv-i-ty
comb-er
com-bin-a-ble
com-bi-na-tive
com-bu-rim-e-ter
com-bus-ti-ble
com-bus-tor
co-me-di-an
com-e-dy
co-mes-ti-ble
com-e-tar-y
co-met-ic
com-fort-a-ble
com-fort-er
com-i-cal
Com-in-form
com-ing
co-mique
com-i-ty
com-man-dant
com-man-deer
com-mand-er
com-man-do
com-mem-o-ra-tor
com-mend-a-ble
com-men-da-tion
com-mend-a-to-ry
com-men-su-ra-ble
com-men-tar-y
com-men-ta-tor
com-mer-cial

com-mi-na-to-ry
com-min-gle
com-mi-nute
com-mis-er-ate
com-mis-sar-i-at
com-mis-sar-y
com-mis-sion
com-mis-sur-al
com-mis-sur-ot-o-my
com-mit-ta-ble
com-mit-tee
com-mo-di-ous
com-mod-i-ty
com-mon-er
com-mon-sen-si-ble
com-mo-rant
com-mu-nal
com-mu-ni-ca-tive
com-mu-ni-ca-tor
com-mun-ion
com-mu-ni-que
com-mu-nism
Com-mu-nist
com-mu-nis-tic
com-mu-ni-ty
com-mut-a-ble
com-mu-ta-tion
com-mu-ta-tor
com-mut-er
com-pact-er
com-pact-i-ble
com-pac-tor
com-pan-ion
com-pa-ny
com-pa-ra-ble
com-par-a-tive
com-par-a-tor
com-par-i-son
com-par-o-scope
com-part-men-tal-ize
com-pat-i-ble
com-pel-ling
com-pen-di-um
com-pen-sa-ble
com-pen-sat-ing
com-pen-sa-to-ry
com-pe-tent
com-pe-ti-tion
com-pet-i-tor
com-pi-la-tion
com-pil-er
com-pla-cent
com-plain-ant

com-plai-sance
com-ple-men-tal
com-ple-men-ta-ry
com-ple-tive
com-plex-ion
com-pli-cate
com-plic-i-ty
com-pli-men-ta-ry
com-po-nent
com-pos-er
com-pos-ite
com-po-si-tion
com-pos-i-tor
com-po-sure
com-pound-er
com-pre-hend-i-ble
com-pre-hen-si-ble
com-press-i-ble
com-press-ing
com-pres-sive
com-pres-som-e-ter
com-pres-sor
com-pris-al
com-pro-mise
Comp-tom-e-ter
comp-trol-ler
com-pul-so-ry
com-put-er
com-put-ist
co-nal
co-na-tion
con-cat-e-na-tion
con-cav-er
con-ciev-a-ble
con-cen-tra-tor
con-cen-tri-cal
con-cen-tric-i-ty
con-cep-tu-al
con-cer-ti-na
con-cert-ize
con-ces-sion-aire
con-chi-form
con-choi-dal
con-cho-log-i-cal
con-chol-o-gy
con-chyl-i-um
con-cil-i-a-to-ry
con-clu-sive
con-coct-er
con-com-i-tant
con-cord-ance
con-cord-ant
con-cres-cence

con-cret-er
con-cu-bi-nage
con-cu-pis-cence
con-cu-pis-ci-ble
con-dem-na-to-ry
con-den-sa-ble
con-den-sa-tion
con-dens-er
con-dens-ing
con-de-scen-sion
con-di-ment
con-do-lence
con-do-min-i-um
con-don-ance
con-duc-i-ble
con-du-cive
con-duct-ance
con-duct-ed
con-duct-i-ble
con-duc-tiv-i-ty
con-duc-tom-e-ter
con-duc-tor
con-duit
con-du-ran-gin
con-dy-loid
con-el-rad
Con-es-to-ga
con-fec-tion-er-y
con-fed-er-a-tion
con-fes-sor
con-fi-dant (n.)
con-fi-dent (adj.)
con-fig-u-ra-tion
con-fin-er
con-firm-a-ble
con-fir-ma-tion
con-firm-a-to-ry
con-firm-er
con-fis-ca-to-ry
con-fla-gra-tion
con-flic-tive
con-flux-i-ble
con-form-a-ble
con-for-ma-tion
con-form-i-ty
Con-fu-cian-ism
con-fus-a-ble
con-fut-a-ble
con-fu-ta-tion
con-ge-la-tive
con-gel-i-fract
con-ge-ner
con-ge-nial

con-ge-ni-al-i-ty
con-gen-i-tal
con-ge-ries
con-gest-i-ble
con-glom-er-at-ic
Con-go-lese
con-grat-u-la-to-ry
con-gre-ga-tor
con-gres-sion-al
con-gru-i-ty
con-i-cal
co-nic-e-ine
co-nid-i-um
con-i-fer
co-nif-er-ous
Co-ni-oph-o-ra
co-ni-um
con-jec-tur-al
con-ju-gal
con-ju-gate
con-junc-ti-vi-tis
con-ju-ra-tion
con-jur-er
con-nect-a-ble
con-nect-er
Con-nect-i-cut-er
con-nec-tive
con-niv-ance
con-nois-seur
con-nu-bi-al
co-noi-dal
co-no-phor
con-quer-or
con-quin-a-mine
con-san-guin-e-ous
con-sci-en-tious
con-scion-a-ble
con-scious
con-se-cra-tor
con-sec-u-tive
con-se-nes-cence
con-sen-sus
con-se-quen-tial
con-ser-va-tion
con-serv-a-tive
con-ser-va-tor
con-serv-a-to-ry
con-sid-er-ate
con-sig-na-tion
con-sign-ee
con-sign-or
con-sist-ent
con-sis-to-ry

con-so-la-tion
con-sol-i-date
con-som-me
con-so-nant
con-sor-ti-um
con-spi-cu-i-ty
con-spic-u-ous
con-spir-a-cy
con-spi-ra-tion
con-sta-ble
con-stab-u-lar-y
con-stan-cy
con-stant-an
con-ster-na-tion
con-sti-pa-tion
con-stit-u-ent
con-sti-tu-tive
con-stric-tor
con-struc-tor
con-sul-ar
con-sul-ate
con-sult-ant
con-sul-ta-tion
con-sult-a-tive
con-sult-er
con-sum-er
con-sum-mate
con-sum-ma-to-ry
con-sump-ti-ble
con-tac-tor
con-ta-gious
con-tam-i-na-tor
con-tem-pla-tor
con-tem-po-ra-ne-ous
con-tempt-i-ble
con-temp-tu-ous
con-tend-er
con-ten-tious
con-test-ant
con-tes-ta-tion
con-tex-tur-al
con-ti-gu-i-ty
con-tig-u-ous
con-ti-nence
con-ti-nen-tal
con-tin-gen-cy
con-ti-nu-i-ty
con-tin-u-ous
con-tin-u-um
con-tor-tive
con-tra-band
con-tract-a-ble
con-tract-ile

con-trac-tor
con-tra-dict-er
con-tra-dic-tor
con-tra-dic-to-ry
con-trail
con-tra-ri-e-ty
con-trar-i-wise
con-tras-tive
con-trib-ut-ing
con-tri-bu-tion
con-trib-u-tor
con-triv-ance
con-triv-er
con-trol-la-ble
con-trolled
con-tro-ver-sy
con-tro-vert-i-ble
con-tu-ma-cious
con-tu-me-li-ous
con-tu-me-ly
con-tu-sion
co-nun-drum
co-nus
con-va-les-cence
con-vec-tor
con-ven-ience
con-ven-ien-cy
con-ver-gent
con-verg-ing
con-vers-a-ble
con-ver-sant
con-ver-sive
con-vert-er
con-vert-i-ble
con-vey-or
con-vic-tive
con-vin-ci-ble
con-vinc-ing
con-viv-i-al
con-vo-lute
con-vul-sive
con-y-rine
cool-ant
cool-er
Coo-lidge
coo-lie
coop-er-age
co-op-er-a-tive
co-or-di-na-tor
coot-ie
co-pai-ba
co-pal-ite
Co-pen-ha-gen

Co-per-ni-cus
cop-ies
co-pi-ous
co-pla-nar
co-pol-y-mer
co-po-lym-er-ize
co-pra
cop-ro-por-phy-rin
cop-ro-stane
co-pros-ta-nol
co-pros-ter-ol
cop-u-la-tive
co-quet-ry
co-quet-tish
co-qui-na
cor-al
Cor-a-mine
cord-age
cor-date
cor-dial
cor-dial-i-ty
cor-dil-le-ra
cord-ite
Cor-do-ba
cor-don
cor-do-van
cor-du-roy
cor-dyl-ite
co-re-op-sis
co-re-spond-ent
co-ri-a-ceous
co-ri-an-der
Cor-i-ci-din
Cor-inth
Co-rin-thi-an
cor-i-o-lis
cor-mo-rant
cor-mus
cor-ne-al
cor-nered
cor-net-ist
cor-nice
cor-nif-ic
Cor-nish
cor-nu-co-pi-a
co-rol-la
cor-ol-lar-y
co-ro-na
cor-o-nal
cor-o-nar-y
cor-o-na-tion
cor-o-nene
cor-o-ner

cor-o-net
co-ro-ni-um
cor-po-ral
cor-po-ra-tive
cor-po-re-al
cor-pu-lent
cor-pus-cle
cor-pus-cu-lar
cor-rect-a-ble
cor-rect-ant
cor-rec-tive
cor-rec-tor
cor-re-late
cor-rel-a-tive
cor-re-spon-dence
cor-ri-dor
cor-ri-gen-dum
cor-ri-gi-ble
cor-rob-o-ra-to-ry
cor-rod-i-ble
cor-ro-si-ble
cor-ro-sive
cor-ru-ga-tor
cor-rupt-i-ble
cor-rup-tive
cor-sage
corse-let
cor-tege
cor-ti-cate
cor-ti-cip-e-tal
cor-ti-ci-um
cor-ti-co-ad-re-nal-o-trop-ic
cor-ti-cos-ter-one
cor-ti-sone
co-run-dum
co-rus-cant
cor-us-ca-tion
cor-vus-ite
co-ryd-a-line
cor-ym-bose
cor-y-phee
co-ry-za
co-sa-lite
co-se-cant
co-sine
cos-me-col-o-gy
cos-met-i-cal
cos-me-ti-cian
cos-me-tol-o-gy
cos-mi-cal-i-ty
cos-mism
cos-mo-gon-ic
cos-mog-o-ny

cos-mog-ra-pher
cos-mo-graph-ic
Cos-mo-line
cos-mol-o-gy
cos-mo-naut
cos-mo-pol-i-tan
cos-mop-o-lite
cos-mo-ra-ma
cos-mo-ram-ic
cos-mos-o-phy
cos-mo-tron
Cos-ta Ri-can
cos-tive
cos-tum-er
co-tar-nine
co-te-rie
co-ter-mi-nous
co-til-lion
co-to-ne-as-ter
cot-tag-er
cot-y-le-don
couch-ant
cou-lomb
cou-lom-e-ter
cou-ma-rin
cou-ma-rone
coun-cil-or
coun-seled
coun-sel-or
coun-te-nance
count-er (who counts)
coun-ter (other meanings)
coun-ter-feit
count-ess
coun-try
coun-ty
cou-pler
cou-plet
cou-pling
cou-pon
cour-age
cou-ra-geous
cou-rant
cou-ri-er
cours-er
cour-te-ous
cour-te-san
cour-te-sy
cour-tier
cous-in
cou-tu-ri-er
cou-vert
cov-e-nant-er

cov-e-nan-tor (law)
Cov-en-try
cov-er-age
cov-ert-ly
cov-et-ous
cov-ey
cox-i-tis
Cox-sack-ie
cow-ard-ice
cowl-ing
coy-ote
coz-en
co-zi-ness
crack-ers
crack-ling
cra-dling
cra-nid-i-um
cra-ni-ec-to-my
cra-ni-o-graph
cra-ni-og-ra-pher
cra-ni-ol-o-gy
cra-ni-om-e-ter
cra-ni-os-co-py
cra-ni-um
cra-ter-i-form
cra-tic-u-lar
cra-vat
Cra-ven-ette
crawl-er
cray-on
cra-zy
cream-er-y
creas-er
cre-at-ic
cre-a-tine
cre-at-i-nine
cre-a-tiv-i-ty
crea-ture
cre-den-tial
cre-den-za
cred-i-ble
cred-it-a-ble
cred-i-tor
cre-do
cre-du-li-ty
cred-u-lous
creed-ite
creep-er
cre-ma-to-ry
Cre-mo-na
cre-nate
cren-a-ture
cren-eled

cren-el-lat-ed	cro-ny-ism
cre-nit-ic	cro-qui-gnole
cren-u-lat-ed	cro-ta-lar-i-o-sis
cre-oph-a-gous	crotch-et-y
cre-o-sol	cro-ton-ate
cre-o-sote	cro-ton-o-yl
crep-i-tant	crou-pi-er
cre-pus-cu-lar	croup-ous
cre-scen-do	crou-ton
cres-cen-tic	cru-cial
cre-sol	cru-ci-ble
cre-sor-ci-nol	cru-ci-fix
cre-sot-ic	cru-ci-form
cres-o-tine	cru-di-ty
cres-yl-ate	cruis-er
cre-syl-ic	crul-ler
cre-ta-ceous	crum-bling
cre-tin-ism	crum-ple
cre-tonne	cru-ral
cre-vasse	cru-sad-er
crev-ice	crus-ta-ceous
cre-vic-u-lar	crust-al
crib-el-late	crus-tose
cri-bel-lum	cry-o-gen-ics
cri-ce-tus	cry-om-e-ter
crick-et-er	cry-o-phil-ic
cri-coid	cry-oph-o-rus
Cri-me-an	cry-os-co-py
crim-i-nal-i-ty	crypt-a-nal-y-sis
crim-i-no-log-ic	cryp-ta-rithm
crim-i-nol-o-gy	cryp-ti-cal
crim-i-not-ic	cryp-to-gram-mic
cring-er	cryp-tog-ra-pher
crin-kle	cryp-to-graph-ic
cri-noi-dal	cryp-tom-e-ter
crin-o-line	crys-taled
cri-nos-i-ty	crys-tal-lin-i-ty
crip-pling	crys-tal-lite
cris-pate	crys-tal-li-za-tion
crisp-er	crys-tal-liz-er
cris-tate	crys-tal-log-ra-phy
cri-te-ri-a	crys-tal-loi-dal
crit-i-cal	cten-o-phore
crit-i-cism	cte-tol-o-gy
cri-tique	cu-bi-cal
croak-er	cu-bic-u-lum
cro-ce-tin	cub-ism
cro-cheted	cub-ist
cro-chet-ing	cu-bi-tal
cro-cid-o-lite	cu-bi-tus
croc-o-dile	cu-boi-dal
croc-o-ite	cuck-old
cro-con-ic	cuck-oo

cudg-eled
cui-rass
cui-sine
cul-i-nar-y
cull-ing
cul-mi-na-tion
cu-lotte
cul-pa-ble
cul-prit
cult-ism
cul-ti-va-tor
cul-tur-al
cu-mal-de-hyde
cum-ber-some
cum-brous
cu-mene
cu-me-nyl
cu-mic
cu-mi-dine
cum-in
cu-min-o-in
cu-mi-nol
cu-mi-nyl
cu-mo-yl
cu-mu-la-tive
cu-mu-lene
cu-mu-lo-nim-bus
cu-mu-lus
cu-ne-ate
cu-ne-i-form
cu-no-ni-a-ceous
cu-pid-i-ty
cu-po-la
cu-pram-mo-ni-um
cu-pre-ine
cu-pre-ous
cu-pric
cu-prif-er-ous
cu-prite
cu-pro-cy-a-nide
cu-proid
cu-pro-ri-va-ite
cu-prous
cur-a-ble
Cu-ra-cao
cu-ra-re
cu-rate
cu-ra-tive
cu-ra-tor
cur-cu-min
cur-dle
cu-rette
cur-few

cu-rie
cu-rine
cu-ri-os-i-ty
cu-ri-o-so
cu-ri-ous
cu-rite
cu-ri-um
curl-i-cue
curl-i-ness
cur-mudg-eon
cur-ric-u-lums
cur-sive
cur-so-ry
cur-tain
cur-te-sy
cur-va-ceous
cur-va-ture
cur-vet-ted
cur-vi-lin-e-ar
cur-vom-e-ter
cush-ioned
cus-pa-rine
cus-pi-dal
cus-pi-dor
cuss-ed-ness
cus-tard
cus-to-di-an
cus-tom-ar-i-ly
cus-tom-ar-y
cus-tom-er
cu-ta-ne-ous
cu-ti-cle
cu-tic-u-lar
cy-an-a-mide
cy-a-nate
cy-an-e-ous
cy-an-ic
cy-a-ni-da-tion
cy-a-nide
cy-an-i-din
cy-a-nite
cy-an-o-gen
cy-a-no-ge-net-ic
cy-a-no-gua-ni-dine
cy-a-no-hy-drin
cy-a-nom-e-ter
cy-a-no-met-ric
cy-a-nope
cy-a-no-phy-cin
cy-a-no-sis
cy-a-nu-ric
cy-aph-e-nine
cy-ber-net-ics

cyc-la-mate
cy-cli-cal
cy-clic-i-ty
cy-cling
cy-clist
cy-cli-tis
cy-cli-za-tion
cy-clo-hex-i-mide
cy-clo-hex-yl-a-mine
cy-cloi-dal
cy-clol-y-sis
cy-clom-e-ter
cy-clon-ic
cy-clo-nite
Cy-clo-pe-an
cy-clo-ra-ma
cy-clo-ser-ine
cy-clot-o-my
cy-clo-tron
cyl-in-der
cyl-in-dra-ceous
cy-lin-dri-cal
cyl-in-dric-i-ty
cyl-in-drite
cy-mene
cy-mo-graph
cy-mose
cyn-i-cal
cyn-i-cism
cyn-o-don-tin
cy-no-sure
Cyn-thi-a

cy-press
Cyp-ri-an
Cyp-ri-ot (native of Cyprus)
Cy-prus
Cyr-e-na-ic
Cy-ril-lic
cys-tec-to-my
cys-te-ic
cys-teine
cys-tine
cys-ti-tis
cys-toid
cys-to-ma
cys-tom-e-ter
cys-to-scope
cys-tos-co-py
cy-tase
cyt-i-dine
cyt-i-dyl-ic
cyt-i-sine
cy-toc-i-dal
cy-to-ge-net-ics
cy-tog-e-nous
cy-tol-o-gy
cy-tol-y-sin
cy-tol-y-zate
cy-to-lyze
cy-tom-e-ter
cy-to-sine
czar-ism
Czech-o-slo-vak

D

dachs-hund
Da-cron
dac-tyl-ic
dac-tyl-o-graph
dac-ty-log-ra-phy
dac-ty-loid
dac-ty-lol-o-gy
dac-ty-los-co-py
dac-ty-lus
Dae-da-li-an
daf-fo-dil
da-guerre-o-type
dahl-ia
Da-ho-me-an
dain-ti-ness
Dai-qui-ri

dair-y
dai-sy
Da-kar
Da-kin
Dal-e-car-li-an
dal-li-ance
Dal-ma-tian
dam-a-scene
Da-mas-cus
dam-ask
dam-na-ble
damn-ing
Dam-o-cles
Da-mon
damp-en-er
damp-er

damp-ish
dam-son
danc-ing
dan-de-li-on
dan-druff
dan-ger-ous
dan-gling
Dan-ish
dan-seuse
dark-en
dar-ling
da-sheen
das-tard
da-sym-e-ter
da-tive
da-tum
da-tu-ric
daub-er
daugh-ter
dau-phin
Da-vi-son-ite
da-vit
daw-dler
daz-zling
dea-con-ess
deaf-en-ing
deal-er
de-ba-cle
de-bar-ka-tion
de-bat-a-ble
deb-au-chee
de-bauch-er-y
de-ben-ture
deb-ile
de-bil-i-tate
deb-it
deb-o-nair
de-bris
debt-or
de-but
deb-u-tante
dec-ade
dec-a-dence
dec-a-dent
dec-a-he-dral
dec-a-lage
de-cal-co-ma-ni-a
de-ca-les-cence
Dec-a-lin
dec-a-li-ter
dec-a-log
de-cam-e-ter (verse)
dec-a-me-ter (measure)

dec-a-me-tho-ni-um
de-ca-nal (adj.)
dec-a-nal (n.)
dec-ane
dec-a-no-ic
dec-a-no-yl
De-cap-o-da
de-cap-i-ta-tor
de-cant-er
dec-are
de-cath-lon
de-ce-dent
de-ceiv-er
de-cel-er-a-tor
de-cel-er-om-e-ter
de-cel-er-on
De-cem-ber
de-cen-cy
dec-ene
de-cen-na-ry
de-cen-ni-al
dec-e-nyl
de-cep-tive
dec-i-bel
de-cid-u-ous
dec-ile
dec-i-mal
dec-i-ma-tion
dec-i-me-ter
de-ci-pher
de-ci-sion
de-ci-sive
deck-led
dec-la-ma-tion
de-clam-a-to-ry
de-clar-ant
dec-la-ra-tion
de-clar-a-tive
de-clar-a-to-ry
de-clin-a-ble
dec-li-na-tion
de-clin-a-to-ry
dec-li-nom-e-ter
de-cli-vate
de-cliv-i-ty
de-cli-vous
de-coct-i-ble
de-coc-tive
de-cod-er
de-col-le-te
dec-o-ra-tive
dec-o-rous
de-co-rum

dec-re-ment
de-crem-e-ter
de-crep-i-tude
de-cre-tive
dec-re-to-ry
dec-yl-ene
de-cyl-ic
ded-i-ca-to-ry
de-duc-i-ble
de-duct-i-ble
de-fal-ca-tion
def-a-ma-tion
de-fam-a-to-ry
de-fat-i-ga-ble
de-fea-si-ble
def-e-ca-tor
de-fec-ti-bil-i-ty
de-fec-tive
de-fec-tor
de-fend-ant
de-fend-er
de-fen-si-ble
de-fen-sive
de-fer
def-er-ence
de-fer-ra-ble
de-fer-ves-cence
de-fi-bra-tor
de-fi-cient
def-i-cit
def-i-lade
de-file
de-fin-a-ble
def-i-ni-tion
de-fin-i-tive
def-la-gra-tion
de-fla-tion
de-flec-tive
de-flec-tom-e-ter
de-flec-tor
def-lo-ra-tion
def-lu-ent
de-fo-li-ate
de-form-a-ble
de-for-ma-tion
de-form-a-tive
de-for-me-ter
de-form-i-ty
de-frau-da-tion
de-frost-er
de-gen-er-a-tive
de-glu-ti-tion
deg-ra-da-tion

de-grade
de-guel-in
de-his-cent
de-hy-dra-tor
de-hy-dro-cho-late
de-hy-dro-cho-les-ter-ol
de-hy-dro-gen-ase
de-i-fi-ca-tion
de-is-tic
de-jeu-ner
Del-a-war-e-an
de-lec-ta-ble
del-e-gate
del-e-te-ri-ous
de-le-tion
de-lib-er-a-tive
del-i-ble
del-i-ca-cy
del-i-ca-tes-sen
de-li-cious
De-li-lah
de-lin-e-a-tor
de-lin-quen-cy
del-i-ques-cence
de-lir-i-ous
de-lir-i-um
de-lo-mor-phous
del-phi-nin
del-phin-i-um
Del-sar-ti-an
del-toi-dal
del-uge
de-lu-so-ry
dem-a-gog
dem-a-gog-ic
dem-a-gogu-er-y
de-mand-ant
de-mar-ca-tion
de-mean-or
de-men-tia
de-mer-it
de-mesne
dem-i-monde
de-mise
dem-i-tasse
de-mo-bi-li-za-tion
de-moc-ra-cy
dem-o-crat
de-moc-ra-tize
de-mog-ra-pher
de-mo-graph-ic
dem-oi-selle
de-mol-ish

dem-o-li-tion
de-mon-e-tize
de-mo-ni-a-cal
de-mon-ic
de-mon-stra-ble
dem-on-stra-tion
de-mon-stra-tive
dem-on-stra-tor
de-mor-al-ize
de-mul-cent
de-mur-rage
de-nar-i-us
de-na-ry
den-drit-ic
den-dro-lite
den-drol-o-gy
den-drom-e-ter
Den-eb
de-ner-vate
den-gue
de-ni-er (one who denies)
de-nier (coin; silk)
den-i-gra-to-ry
den-im
den-i-zen
de-nom-i-na-tive
de-nom-i-na-tor
de-noue-ment
den-sim-e-ter
den-si-tom-e-ter
den-si-ty
den-tal
den-ti-cle
den-tic-u-lar
den-ti-frice
den-tig-er-ous
den-tist-ry
de-nu-da-tion
de-nun-ci-a-tive
de-nun-ci-a-to-ry
de-o-dor-ant
de-o-dor-iz-er
de-ox-y-ri-bose
de-part-men-tal-ize
de-par-ture
de-pend-a-ble
de-pend-en-cy
de-pend-ent
de-perm-ing
de-phleg-ma-to-ry
dep-i-late
de-pil-a-to-ry
de-plor-a-ble

dep-lo-ra-tion
de-po-nent
de-por-ta-tion
de-port-ee
de-pos-al
de-pos-er
de-pos-i-tar-y
de-pos-it-ed
dep-o-si-tion
de-pos-i-to-ry
de-pot
dep-ra-va-tion
de-prav-i-ty
dep-re-ca-to-ry
de-pre-ci-ate
dep-re-da-tion
dep-re-da-to-ry
de-pres-sant
de-press-i-ble
de-pres-sor
de-priv-al
dep-ri-va-tion
depth-om-e-ter
dep-u-ra-tor
dep-u-tize
de-rac-i-nate
de-re-cho
der-e-lict
de-ri-gueur
de-ri-sive
der-i-va-tion
de-riv-a-tive
der-ma-ti-tis
der-mat-o-graph
der-ma-tol-o-gy
der-ma-to-sis
der-moi-dal
der-nier
der-o-gate
de-rog-a-to-ry
der-vish
des-cant
de-scend-ant
de-scend-er
de-scend-i-ble
de-scrib-a-ble
de-scrip-tive
des-cry
des-e-crat-er
des-e-de-ri-um
Des-er-et
de-sert (n., that which is de-
    served)

des-ert (n., adj., barren tract)
de-sert (v.)
de-sert-er
des-ic-cate
des-ic-ca-tor
de-sid-er-a-tum
des-ig-na-ble
des-ig-nat-a-ble
des-ig-na-tive
des-ig-na-tor
de-sign-ed-ly
des-ig-nee
de-sign-er
de-sip-i-ent
de-sir-a-ble
de-sist-ance
des-mo-di-um
des-mo-lase
des-mol-y-sis
des-mo-trop-ic
des-mot-ro-pism
des-o-la-tion
des-ox-y-cho-lic
des-ox-y-ri-bo-nu-cle-ase
de-spair
des-per-a-do
des-per-ate
des-pi-ca-ble
de-spis-a-ble
de-spis-er
de-spite
de-spoil
de-spo-li-a-tion
de-spond-ence
de-spond-ent
des-pot-i-cal
des-pot-ism
des-pu-ma-tion
des-qua-ma-tion
des-sert
des-ti-na-tion
des-ti-ny
des-ti-tute
de-stroy-er
de-struct-i-ble
de-struc-tive
de-struc-tor
des-ue-tude
des-ul-to-ry
des-yl
de-syn-ap-sis
de-tect-a-ble
de-tec-tive

de-tec-tor
de-ten-tive
de-ter-gent
de-te-ri-o-ra-tive
de-ter-mi-na-ble
de-ter-mi-nant
de-ter-min-er
de-ter-rence
de-test-a-ble
det-o-nant
det-o-na-tor
de-trac-tor
det-ri-men-tal
de-tri-tal
de-tri-tus
deu-ter-ide
deu-te-ri-um
deu-ter-on
Deu-ter-o-nom-ic
Deu-ter-on-o-my
deut-sche
dev-as-ta-tor
de-vel-op-men-tal
de-vi-a-tor
de-vice
dev-il-ish
dev-il-try
de-vi-ous
dev-i-see
de-vis-er
dev-i-sor (legal)
De-vo-ni-an
dev-o-tee
Dew-ar
dex-ter-i-ty
dex-tral-i-ty
dex-trin-ate
dex-trin-o-gen-ic
dex-tro-car-di-a
dex-tro-pi-mar-ic
dex-trorse
dex-trose
dex-trous
di-a-ban-tite
di-a-be-tes
di-a-bet-ic
di-a-bol-i-cal
di-ab-o-lism
di-ac-e-tyl
di-a-dem
di-ag-no-sis
di-ag-nos-ti-cian
di-ag-o-nal

di-a-gramed
di-a-gram-mat-i-cal
di-a-lec-tic
di-a-lec-tol-o-gy
di-a-log
di-a-lu-ric
di-al-y-sis
di-a-lyt-ic
di-a-lyz-er
di-a-man-tine
di-am-e-ter
di-a-met-ri-cal
di-am-i-no-gen
di-a-mond
Di-an-a
di-a-nite
di-a-pa-son
di-a-per
di-aph-a-nom-e-ter
di-aph-a-nous
di-a-phon-ic
di-aph-o-re-sis
di-a-phragm
di-a-phrag-mat-ic
di-ar-rhe-a
di-a-ry
di-as-po-ra
di-a-spore
di-a-stase
di-as-ta-sis
di-a-stat-ic
di-a-stim-e-ter
di-as-to-le
di-a-stol-ic
di-a-sto-mat-ic
di-as-tro-phe
di-a-stroph-ic
di-ath-e-sis
di-a-ther-my
di-a-thet-ic
di-a-tom
di-a-to-ma-ceous
di-at-o-mite
di-at-ro-pism
di-a-zine
di-a-zo-ic
di-az-o-im-ide
di-a-zole
di-az-o-meth-ane
di-a-zo-ni-um
di-az-o-tize
di-az-o-type
di-ba-sic

di-bro-mo-a-ce-tic
di-bu-caine
di-ce-tyl
di-chlone
di-chlo-ro-di-flu-o-ro-meth-ane
di-cho-tom-ic
di-chot-o-mous
di-chot-o-my
di-chro-mat-ic
di-con-dyl-ic
di-cot-y-le-don
di-cou-ma-rol
di-crot-ic
Dic-ta-phone
dic-ta-tor
dic-ta-to-ri-al
dic-tion-ar-y
Dic-to-graph
di-dac-tic
di-dym-i-um
di-er-e-sis
di-e-ret-ic
die-sel-ize
di-e-tar-y
di-e-tet-ic
di-e-ti-tian
dif-fer-en-tial
dif-fi-dence
dif-flu-ent
dif-frac-tion
dif-frac-tom-e-ter
dif-fran-gi-ble
dif-fus-er
dif-fus-i-ble
dif-fu-sive
di-gest-er
di-gest-i-ble
di-ges-tive
dig-i-tal
dig-i-tal-is
dig-i-tal-i-za-tion
dig-i-tal-ose
dig-i-ti-ner-vate
dig-it-iz-er
dig-i-to-gen-in
dig-i-to-nin
dig-ni-tar-y
di-he-dral
di-hy-dro-er-go-cor-nine
di-hy-dro-er-got-a-mine
di-hy-drox-y-a-ce-tic
di-lap-i-dat-ed
di-lat-ant

dil-a-ta-tion
di-la-tion
dil-a-tom-e-ter
di-la-tor
dil-a-to-ry
di-lem-ma
dil-et-tan-te
dil-u-ent
di-lut-ant
di-lut-er
di-me-don
di-men-hy-dri-nate
di-men-si-ble
di-mer-cap-rol
di-mer-ic
di-meth-yl
di-mid-i-ate
di-min-ish
dim-i-nu-tion
di-min-u-tive
dim-i-ty
di-mor-phous
din-ghy
di-ni-tro-tol-u-ene
di-no-saur
di-oc-e-san
di-o-cese
Di-og-e-nes
di-op-side
di-op-ter
di-op-tom-e-ter
di-o-ra-ma
di-o-ram-ic
di-o-rite
di-par-tite
di-phen-yl
diph-the-ri-a
diph-the-rit-ic
diph-the-roid
diph-thong-al
di-pic-o-lin-ic
di-ple-gi-a
di-plex-er
dip-loi-dal
dip-loid-ize
di-plo-ma-cy
dip-lo-mat
di-plo-ma-tist
di-plo-sis
dip-o-dy
dip-so-ma-ni-a
dip-ter-al
di-rec-tiv-i-ty

di-rec-tor-ate
di-rec-to-ri-al
dir-i-gi-ble
dirn-dl
dirt-i-ness
dis-ap-peared
dis-ap-point-ed
dis-as-ter
dis-as-trous
dis-az-o
dis-burs-al
dis-burs-er
dis-cern-i-ble
dis-cerp-ti-ble
dis-ci-ple
dis-ci-pli-nar-i-an
dis-ci-pli-nar-y
dis-ci-plin-er
dis-clo-sure
dis-coi-dal
dis-com-fi-ture
dis-con-so-late
dis-cord-ant
dis-co-theque
dis-cour-sive
dis-crep-an-cy
dis-crete
dis-cre-tion-ar-y
dis-crim-i-na-ble
dis-crim-i-na-tor
dis-cur-sive
dis-cus
dis-cuss-ant
dis-cuss-i-ble
dis-cus-sion
dis-eas-es
di-seuse
dis-ha-bille
di-shev-eled
dis-in-fect-ant
dis-in-te-grate
dis-man-tle
dis-mis-sal
dis-par-ag-er
dis-par-ate
dis-par-i-ty
dis-patch-er
dis-pens-a-ble
dis-pen-sa-ry
dis-pens-er
dis-per-sal
dis-pers-ant
dis-pers-er

dis-pers-i-ble
dis-per-sive
dis-per-soid
dis-pir-it
dis-pos-al
dis-put-a-ble
dis-pu-tant
dis-pu-ta-tious
dis-pu-ta-tive
dis-put-er
dis-qui-si-tion
dis-quis-i-tive
dis-rep-u-ta-ble
dis-re-pute
dis-rupt-er
dis-sat-is-fied
dis-sect-i-ble
dis-sec-tor
dis-sem-i-na-tive
dis-sen-sion
dis-sent-er
dis-sim-i-la-tive
dis-si-pat-er
dis-sol-u-ble
dis-so-lute
dis-solv-a-ble
dis-sol-vent
dis-so-nance
dis-suad-er
dis-sua-sive
dis-sym-me-try
dis-taff
dis-tant
dis-tem-per
dis-ten-si-ble
dis-ten-tion
dis-til-la-tion
dis-tilled
dis-till-er-y
dis-till-ing
dis-tinc-tive
dis-tin-guished
dis-to-ma-ta
di-sto-ma-to-sis
di-stom-a-tous
dis-tor-tive
dis-tract-er
dis-tract-i-ble
dis-trac-tive
dis-tress-ing
dis-trib-ut-a-ble
dis-trib-u-tar-y
dis-trib-ute

dis-trib-u-tee
dis-tri-bu-tion
dis-trib-u-tive
dis-trib-u-tor
dis-turb-ance
dis-turb-er
di-thi-o-nate
di-thi-o-nous
di-thi-zone
dith-y-ram-bic
di-tol-yl
di-u-re-sis
di-u-ret-ic
di-ur-nal
di-va-ga-tion
di-van
div-er
di-ver-gent
di-vers (several)
di-ver-si-ty
di-vert-er
di-vert-i-ble
di-ver-tic-u-lec-to-my
di-ver-tic-u-lo-sis
di-ver-tic-u-lum
di-ver-tise-ment
di-ver-tisse-ment
di-ver-tive
di-ver-tor (electricity)
di-vest-i-ble
di-ves-ti-ture
di-vid-ed
div-i-dend
di-vid-er
div-i-na-tion
di-vin-a-to-ry
di-vin-i-ty
di-vis-i-ble
di-vi-sion
di-vi-so-ry
di-vor-cee
di-vul-gence
do-blon
do-cent
doc-i-ble
doc-ile
do-cil-i-ty
dock-et
doc-o-sane
doc-tor-al
doc-tor-ate
doc-tri-naire
doc-tri-nal

doc-u-ment-a-ble
doc-u-men-ta-ry
do-de-cane
do-dec-a-no-ic
Do-dec-a-nese
do-dec-ant
do-de-cyl-ene
dodg-er
dog-ger-el
dog-mat-ic
dog-ma-tism
dog-ma-tize
dol-drum
dol-er-ite
dol-i-cho-ce-phal-ic
do-lo-mite
do-lo-rous
dol-phin
do-main
do-mes-ti-cate
do-mes-tic-i-ty
dom-i-cil-i-ar-y
dom-i-nant
dom-i-na-tor
dom-i-neer
Dom-i-ni-ca
do-min-i-cal
Do-min-i-can
dom-i-nie
do-min-ion
dom-i-no
do-na-ble
do-nee
don-keys
do-nor
doo-dle
Dopp-ler
Do-ri-an
Dor-ic
Dor-is
dor-mant
dor-mer
dor-mi-to-ry
Dor-o-the-a
dor-sal
dor-sa-lis
dos-age
do-sim-e-ter
do-sim-e-try
dos-sier
dot-age
dot-ard
dot-ing

dot-ish
dou-ble
dou-blet
dou-bling
dou-bloon
dou-bly
dough-ty
dou-rine
dow-a-ger
dow-eled
down-i-ness
dox-o-log-i-cal
dox-ol-o-gy
doy-en
doz-en
drag-on
dra-goon
drain-age
dra-ma
Dram-a-mine
dra-mat-ic
dra-ma-tis per-so-nae
dram-a-tize
drap-er-y
dream-i-ness
drear-i-ness
dredg-er
dredg-ing
dress-er
dri-er
drift-age
drift-er
drill-ing
drink-om-e-ter
driv-el-er
driv-en
driv-er
droll-er-y
drom-e-dar-y
drop-si-cal
drop-sonde
dro-som-e-ter
dro-ver
drows-i-ness
drudg-er-y
drunk-ard
drunk-en-ness
dru-pa-ceous
du-al-ism
du-ar-chy
du-bi-e-ty
du-bi-ous
du-bi-ta-ble

du-cal
duc-at
duch-ess
du-chesse
duc-ti-ble
duc-tile
dudg-eon
duf-fel bag
duff-er
du-fre-nite
dul-ci-mer
dul-ci-tol
dul-lard
dull-er
dum-found
dump-er
dump-ling
dump-y
dun-ga-ree
Dun-ge-ness
dun-geon
du-nite
Dun-kard
Dun-stan
du-o-dec-i-mos
du-o-de-nal
du-o-de-ni-tis
du-o-de-nos-co-py
du-o-de-num
du-op-o-ly
du-op-so-ny
du-plex-er
du-pli-ca-tive
du-pli-ca-tor
du-plic-i-ty
du-ra-bil-i-ty
du-ral-u-min

dur-ance
du-ra-tion
du-rene
du-ress
du-rom-e-ter
dur-yl
dusk-i-ness
dust-er
du-te-ous
du-ti-ful
du-ve-tyn
dwarf-ish
dwell-ing
dwin-dling
Dy-cril
dy-nam-e-ter
dy-nam-i-cal
dy-nam-ics
dy-na-mit-er
dy-na-mi-za-tion
dy-na-mom-e-ter
dy-na-mo-met-ric
dy-na-mom-e-try
dy-na-mos
dy-na-mo-tor
Dy-na-Soar
dy-nas-tic
dy-na-tron
Dy-nel
dy-node
dys-cra-site
dys-en-ter-y
dys-pep-si-a
dys-pho-ri-a
dysp-ne-a
dys-pro-si-um

E

ea-ger
ea-glet
ear-li-er
earn-er
ear-nest
earth-en-ware
ea-sel
eas-i-ly
Eas-ter

east-er (storm)
east-ern-er
eb-on-ite
eb-on-y
e-bul-lient
e-bul-li-om-e-ter
e-bul-li-o-scop-ic
e-bul-li-os-co-py
eb-ul-li-tion

ec-cen-tric-i-ty
ec-cle-si-as-ti-cal
ec-dys-i-al
ec-go-nine
ech-e-lon
e-chi-noid
e-chi-nus
ech-o-me-ter
ec-lamp-si-a
ec-lec-ti-cal
e-clip-tic
e-clo-sion
ec-o-log-i-cal
e-col-o-gy
e-con-o-met-ric (adj.)
e-con-o-me-trics (n.)
ec-o-nom-i-cal
ec-o-nom-ics
e-con-o-mist
e-con-o-mize
ec-o-sphere
ec-sta-sy
ec-stat-ic
ec-to-der-moi-dal
ec-tog-e-nous
ec-to-pi-a
ec-top-ic
ec-to-plasm
ec-typ-al
Ec-ua-dor-an
ec-u-men-i-cal
ec-ze-ma
ec-zem-a-tous
e-del-weiss
e-de-ma
ed-i-ble
ed-i-fi-ca-tion
ed-i-fice
e-di-tion
ed-i-to-ri-al-ize
ed-u-ca-ble
ed-u-ca-tor
e-duc-i-ble
e-duc-tor
ee-ri-ly
ef-fac-ing
ef-fect-i-ble
ef-fec-tive
ef-fec-tu-al
ef-fem-i-nate
ef-fer-ves-cence
ef-fer-ves-ci-ble
ef-fi-ca-cious

ef-fi-ca-cy
ef-fi-cien-cy
ef-fi-cient
ef-fi-gy
ef-flo-res-cence
ef-flu-vi-um
ef-fron-ter-y
ef-ful-gence
ef-fu-si-om-e-ter
ef-fu-sive
e-gal-i-tar-i-an
e-go-cen-trism
e-go-ism
e-go-is-ti-cal
e-go-tism
e-go-tis-ti-cal
e-gre-gious
E-gyp-tol-o-gy
ei-co-sane
ei-der
ei-gen
eight-een
eight-i-eth
ei-ko-nom-e-ter
ein-stein-i-um
eis-e-ge-sis
Ei-sen-how-er
ei-ther
e-jac-u-la-to-ry
e-jec-tive
e-jec-tor
e-lab-o-ra-tive
e-las-tic-i-ty
e-las-to-mer
e-las-tom-e-ter
e-las-to-sis
e-lat-er-in
el-a-te-ri-um
el-der
el-e-cam-pane
e-lec-tion-eer
e-lec-tive
e-lec-tor-al
e-lec-tor-ate
e-lec-tri-cal
e-lec-tric-i-ty
e-lec-tri-fi-ca-tion
e-lec-tro-car-di-o-gram
e-lec-tro-cute
e-lec-trode
e-lec-tro-graph-ic
e-lec-trog-ra-phy
e-lec-trol-y-sis

e-lec-tro-lyte
e-lec-tro-lyt-i-cal
e-lec-trom-e-ter
e-lec-tron-i-cal-ly
e-lec-tron-ics
e-lec-troph-o-rus
e-lec-trot-o-nus
el-ee-mos-y-nar-y
el-e-gant
el-e-gi-ac
el-e-gy
el-e-men-tar-i-ly
el-e-men-ta-ry
el-e-phan-ti-a-sis
el-e-va-tor
e-lev-enth
el-e-von
elf-in
e-lic-it
el-i-gi-ble
e-lim-i-nant
e-lim-i-na-tor
e-lix-ir
E-liz-a-be-than
el-lip-soi-dal
el-lip-som-e-ter
el-lip-ti-cal
el-lip-tic-i-ty
e-lo-gi-um
e-lon-ga-tion
el-o-quent
e-lu-ci-date
e-lud-i-ble
e-lu-so-ry
e-lu-tri-ate
e-lu-vi-um
E-lyr-i-a
E-ly-sian
E-ly-si-um
e-ma-ci-ate
em-a-nate
e-man-ci-pate
em-a-nom-e-ter
e-mar-gi-nate
e-mas-cu-late
em-ba-cle
em-bar-go
em-bar-ka-tion
em-bar-ras (n.)
em-bar-rass (v.)
em-bed-ded
em-bla-zon
em-blem-at-i-cal

em-bod-i-ment
em-bold-en
em-bol-ic
em-bo-lism
em-bo-lus
em-boss-er
em-bou-chure
em-brac-er
em-bra-sure
em-broi-der-y
em-bry-ol-o-gy
em-bry-on-ic
e-mend-a-ble
e-men-da-tion
e-mend-a-to-ry
em-er-al-dine
e-mer-gen-cy
e-mer-i-tus
e-mer-sion
em-er-y
e-met-ic
em-e-tine
em-i-grant
em-i-gree
em-i-nence
em-is-sar-y
e-mis-siv-i-ty
e-mit-ter
em-o-din
e-mol-lient
e-mol-u-ment
e-mot-er
e-mo-tion-al-ize
em-path-ic
em-pa-thy
em-pen-nage
em-per-or
em-pha-sis
em-phat-ic
em-phy-se-ma
em-pir-i-cal
em-pi-ris-tic
em-ploy-ee
em-po-ri-um
em-press
emp-ti-ness
em-py-e-ma
em-py-re-an
em-py-reu-ma
em-u-la-tive
em-u-la-to-ry
em-u-lous
e-mul-si-fi-er

e-mul-sive
e-mul-soi-dal
en-a-bling
en-am-el-er
en-am-o-ra-to
en-am-ored
e-nan-thic
en-ar-gite
en-ar-thro-sis
en-cap-su-late
en-caus-tic
en-ceinte
en-ce-phal-ic
en-ceph-a-li-tis
en-ceph-a-lo-cele
en-ceph-a-lo-gram
en-ceph-a-lo-graph-ic
en-ceph-a-log-ra-phy
en-ceph-a-loid
en-chi-la-da
en-chym-a-tous
en-clos-er
en-clo-sure
en-coi-gnure
en-co-mi-ast
en-co-mi-um
en-coun-ter
en-cour-age
en-cri-nal
en-crin-ic
en-cum-ber
en-cum-brance
en-cyc-li-cal
en-cy-clo-pe-di-a
en-cys-ta-tion
end-ar-te-ri-tis
en-deav-ored
en-de-mi-al
en-dem-i-cal-ly
en-de-mic-i-ty
en-de-mi-ol-o-gy
En-der-by
end-er-gon-ic
en-dive
en-do-car-di-tis
en-do-cri-nal
en-do-crine
en-do-crin-o-log-ic
en-do-cri-nol-o-gy
en-do-cri-no-path-ic
en-do-cri-nop-a-thy
en-doc-ri-nous
en-do-ge-net-ic

en-do-ge-nic-i-ty
en-dog-e-nous
en-do-me-tri-tis
en-do-plas-ma
en-dors-a-ble
en-dors-ee
en-dors-er
en-dos-co-py
en-drin
en-dur-a-ble
en-dur-ance
ene-di-ol
en-e-ma
en-er-get-i-cal-ly
en-er-giz-er
en-er-vate
en-fi-lade
en-force-a-ble
en-fran-chise
en-gen-der
en-gi-neer-ing
en-gine-ry
Eng-land
Eng-lish
en-grav-er
e-nig-mat-ic
e-nig-ma-tize
en-join-der
en-liv-en
en-mi-ty
en-nui
e-nor-mi-ty
e-nor-mous
en-rolled
en-roll-ee
en-sem-ble
en-sign
en-si-lage
en-ter-ic
en-ter-i-tis
en-ter-o-cri-nin
en-ter-os-to-my
en-thal-py
en-thu-si-asm
en-thu-si-as-tic
en-tire-ty
en-ti-ty
en-to-mo-log-i-cal
en-to-mol-o-gy
en-tou-rage
en-trails
en-trance
en-tree

en-tre-pre-neur-i-al
en-tro-py
e-nu-cle-ate
e-nu-mer-ate
e-nun-ci-a-tive
en-vel-op (v.)
en-ve-lope (n.)
en-vel-op-ment
en-vi-a-ble
en-vi-ous
en-vi-ron
en-vis-age
en-zy-mat-ic
en-zy-mol-o-gy
e-o-sin-o-phil
e-os-pho-rite
ep-a-go-ge
ep-au-let
ep-en-dy-ma
e-phed-rine
e-phem-er-al
e-phem-er-is
E-phra-im
Eph-ra-ta
ep-i-cal
ep-i-cu-re-an
ep-i-dem-i-cal
ep-i-de-mi-o-log-i-cal
ep-i-de-mi-ol-o-gy
ep-i-der-mis
ep-i-der-moi-dal
ep-i-dote
ep-i-du-ral
ep-i-ge-al
e-pig-e-nous
ep-i-glot-tis
e-pig-ra-pher
ep-i-la-tor
ep-i-lep-tic
ep-i-log
ep-i-mer-i-za-tion
ep-i-neph-rine
Ep-i-nine
E-piph-a-ny
e-piph-y-sis
ep-i-pter-ic
E-pi-rus
E-pis-co-pa-lian
ep-i-sco-tis-ter
ep-i-sod-ic
e-pis-ta-sis
ep-i-stat-ic
e-pis-te-mol-o-gy

e-pis-tle
e-pis-to-lar-y
ep-i-stome
ep-i-taph
ep-i-the-li-um
e-pith-e-sis
ep-i-thet
e-pit-o-me
ep-i-tom-i-cal
e-pit-ro-phy
ep-och-al
ep-ox-y
ep-si-lon
eq-ua-ble
e-qualed
e-qual-iz-er
e-qua-nim-i-ty
e-quat-ive
e-qua-to-ri-al
eq-uer-ry
e-ques-tri-an
e-qui-dis-tant
e-qui-lat-er-al
eq-ui-len-in
e-quil-i-bra-tion
e-qui-lib-rist
e-qui-lib-ri-stat
e-qui-lib-ri-um
e-qui-noc-tial
e-qui-nox
eq-ui-page
eq-ui-poise
e-quipped
eq-ui-ta-ble
eq-ui-ty
e-quiv-a-lent
e-quiv-o-cal
e-quiv-o-ca-tor
e-rad-i-ca-tor
e-ras-er
e-ra-sure
er-bi-um
Er-e-bus
e-rec-tile
e-rec-tor
er-e-ma-cau-sis
er-ga-tive
er-god-ic
er-go-gen-ic
er-gom-e-ter
er-go-no-vine
er-gos-ter-ol
er-got

er-got-a-mine
er-got-ic
er-go-tize
e-rin-e-um
er-in-ite
er-i-nose
er-i-o-dic-ty-ol
er-i-om-e-ter
Er-len-mey-er
er-mine
e-rod-i-ble
e-ro-sive
e-rot-i-cism
err-a-bil-i-ty
er-ra-ta
er-rat-ic
er-ro-ne-ous
er-u-bes-cent
e-ru-cic
e-ruc-ta-tion
er-u-di-tion
e-rup-tiv-i-ty
er-y-sip-e-las
er-y-the-ma
er-y-them-a-tous
er-y-thrine
er-y-thrite
e-ryth-ri-tol
e-ryth-ro-cyte
e-ryth-ro-cy-tom-e-ter
er-y-thro-i-dine
er-y-thro-pi-a
e-ryth-ro-scope
er-y-throse
e-ryth-ro-sin
er-y-thro-sis
e-ryth-ru-lose
es-ca-drille
es-ca-la-tor
es-cal-loped
es-cap-a-ble
es-ca-pade
es-cap-ee
es-cap-ism
es-cap-ist
es-ca-role
es-carp-ment
es-cha-tol-o-gy
es-chy-nite
es-cri-toire
es-crow
es-cu-dos
es-cu-lent

es-cutch-eon
es-er-o-line
Es-ki-mos
e-soph-a-ge-al
e-soph-a-gi-tis
e-soph-a-go-scope
e-soph-a-gos-co-pist
e-soph-a-gus
es-o-ter-ic
es-pal-ier
es-pe-cial
Es-pe-ran-to
es-pi-o-nage
es-pla-nade
es-pous-al
es-pous-er
es-tab-lish
es-ter-ase
es-ter-ize
es-thet-ic
es-ti-ma-ble
es-ti-ma-tor
es-ti-va-tor
Es-to-nian
es-top-pel
es-to-vers
es-tra-di-ol
es-trange
es-tray
es-tro-gen-ic
es-tu-a-rine
es-tu-ar-y
e-ter-ni-ty
eth-ane
eth-a-nol-a-mine
eth-a-nol-y-sis
eth-e-nyl
e-the-re-al
e-the-re-ous
e-ther-ize
eth-i-cal
eth-i-on-ic
e-thi-o-nine
E-thi-o-pi-an
eth-moi-dal
eth-moid-i-tis
eth-ni-cal
eth-nog-e-ny
eth-no-graph-ic
eth-nog-ra-phy
eth-no-log-i-cal
eth-nol-o-gy
eth-ox-y-line

eth-yl-a-mine
eth-yl-ate
ethy-yl-ene-di-a-mine
eth-yl-e-nic
eth-yl-e-phed-rine
eth-yl-i-dine
eth-y-nyl-a-tion
e-ti-o-late
e-ti-o-log-i-cal
e-ti-ol-o-gy
e-ti-o-phyl-lin
et-i-quette
et-y-mo-log-i-cal
et-y-mol-o-gy
eu-ca-lyp-tus
Eu-cha-rist
eu-chred
eu-chro-ite
eu-clase
Eu-clid-e-an
eu-da-lene
eu-di-om-e-ter
Eu-ge-nia
eu-gen-ic
eu-gen-ist
eu-ge-nol
eu-lo-gis-ti-cal
eu-lo-gize
eu-lo-gy
eu-nuch
eu-pa-to-rin
eu-pav-er-ine
eu-phe-mism
eu-pho-ni-um
eu-pho-ny
eu-pho-ri-a
Eur-a-sian
eu-re-ka
Eu-ro-pe-an
eu-ro-pi-um
eu-ryth-mics
Eu-sta-chi-an
eu-tha-na-si-a
eu-then-ics
eux-e-nite
e-vac-u-ate
e-vag-i-nate
ev-a-nes-cence
e-van-gel-i-cal
e-van-ge-list
e-van-ge-lize
e-vap-o-ra-tor
e-vap-o-rim-e-ter

e-va-si-ble
e-va-sive
e-ven-ing (making level)
eve-ning (close of day)
e-ven-tu-al-i-ty
e-ver-si-ble
ev-er-y
e-vic-tor
ev-i-denc-ing
ev-i-den-tial
e-vinc-i-ble
e-vis-cer-a-tor
ev-i-ta-ble
e-voc-a-to-ry
ev-o-lu-tion-ar-y
ev-o-lu-tion-ist
ex-ac-er-bat-ing
ex-ac-ti-tude
ex-ag-ger-ate
ex-al-ta-tion
ex-am-i-na-tion
ex-am-in-er
ex-as-per-ate
ex-ca-va-tor
ex-cel-len-cy
ex-cel-si-or
ex-cept-a-ble
ex-cerpt-er
ex-cerpt-i-ble
ex-ces-sive
ex-cheq-uer
ex-cip-i-ent
ex-cit-a-ble
ex-cit-ant
ex-cit-a-tive
ex-cit-er
ex-cla-ma-tion
ex-clam-a-to-ry
ex-clud-a-ble
ex-clu-so-ry
ex-co-ri-a-tion
ex-cre-ment
ex-cres-cence
ex-cre-to-ry
ex-cru-ci-ate
ex-cul-pa-to-ry
ex-cus-a-ble
ex-e-cra-to-ry
ex-ec-u-tant
ex-e-cut-ed
ex-ec-u-tive
ex-ec-u-to-ry
ex-e-ge-sis

ex-e-get-ic
ex-em-pla-ry
ex-empt-i-ble
ex-emp-tive
ex-e-qua-tur
ex-er-cis-er
ex-er-e-sis
ex-ert-ive
ex-hal-ant
ex-ha-la-tion
ex-haust-ed
ex-haust-i-ble
ex-haus-tive
ex-hib-it
ex-hi-bi-tion
ex-hib-i-tive
ex-hib-i-to-ry
ex-hil-a-ra-tive
ex-hor-ta-tion
ex-hort-a-to-ry
ex-hu-ma-tion
ex-i-gen-cy
ex-i-gi-ble
ex-i-gu-i-ty
ex-ig-u-ous
ex-ist-ence
ex-is-ten-tial-ism
ex li-bris
ex-o-don-ti-a
ex-o-dus
ex-og-e-nous
ex-on-er-ate
ex-o-pep-ti-dase
ex-or-bi-tant
ex-or-di-um
ex-o-ter-ic
ex-o-ther-mic-i-ty
ex-ot-ic
ex-pand-a-ble
ex-pand-er
ex-pan-si-ble
ex-pan-sive
ex-pa-ti-ate
ex-pa-tri-ate
ex-pect-an-cy
ex-pect-ant
ex-pec-ta-tion
ex-pect-a-tive
ex-pec-to-ra-tor
ex-pe-di-en-cy
ex-pe-dit-er
ex-pe-di-tious
ex-pel-lee

ex-pel-ling
ex-pend-i-ture
ex-pen-sive
ex-pe-ri-ence
ex-per-i-men-tal
ex-per-i-ment-er
ex-per-tise (n.)
ex-pert-ize (v.)
ex-pi-a-to-ry
ex-pi-ra-tion
ex-pir-a-to-ry
ex-pla-na-tion
ex-plan-a-to-ry
ex-ple-tive
ex-pli-ca-ble
ex-pli-ca-tive
ex-pli-ca-tor
ex-plic-a-to-ry
ex-plic-it-ly
ex-plod-er
ex-ploi-ta-tion
ex-ploit-a-tive
ex-ploit-er
ex-plo-ra-tion
ex-plor-a-to-ry
ex-plo-si-ble
ex-plo-sim-e-ter
ex-plo-sive
ex-po-nen-tial
ex-port-a-ble
ex-por-ta-tion
ex-pose (v.)
ex-po-sé (n.)
ex-po-si-tion
ex-pos-i-to-ry
ex-pos-tu-late
ex-po-sure
ex-press-age
ex-press-er
ex-press-i-ble
ex-pres-sive
ex-pres-sor
ex-pug-na-to-ry
ex-pul-sive
ex-pur-ga-to-ry
ex-quis-ite
ex-sic-cate
ex-tem-po-ra-ne-i-ty
ex-tem-po-re
ex-tem-po-rize
ex-tend-a-ble
ex-tend-er
ex-ten-si-ble

ex-ten-som-e-ter
ex-ten-sor
ex-ten-u-a-tor
ex-te-ri-or-ize
ex-ter-mi-na-tor
ex-ter-nal-i-ty
ex-tinc-tive
ex-tin-guish-er
ex-tir-pa-tor
ex-tract-a-ble
ex-tract-ant
ex-trac-tive
ex-trac-tor
ex-tra-dit-a-ble
ex-tral-i-ty
ex-tra-ne-ous
ex-traor-di-nar-i-ly
ex-trap-o-lat-ed
ex-trap-o-la-to-ry
ex-tra-sen-so-ry

ex-trav-a-gance
ex-trav-a-sa-tion
ex-tre-mism
ex-trem-ist
ex-trem-i-ty
ex-tri-cate
ex-trin-sic
ex-tro-vert-ish
ex-tro-ver-tive
ex-trud-er
ex-tru-si-ble
ex-tu-ber-ance
ex-u-ber-ant
ex-u-da-tion
ex-ult-ant
ex-ul-ta-tion
ex-ur-bi-a
eye-le-teer
ey-ing

F

fa-ba-ceous
Fa-bi-an
fa-bled
fab-ri-ca-tor
Fab-ri-koid
fab-u-lous
fa-cade
face-a-ble
fac-er
fac-et-ed
fa-ce-tious
fa-cial
fa-cient
fa-ci-es
fac-ile
fa-cil-i-ty
fac-ing
fa-con-ne
fac-sim-i-le
fac-tic-i-ty
fac-tious
fac-ti-tious
fac-tor
fac-to-ri-al
fac-to-ry
fac-to-tum

fac-u-la
fac-ul-ty
fa-cun-di-ty
fade-om-e-ter
fad-er
fa-gine
fag-ot
Fahr-en-heit
fa-ience
fail-ure
fai-naigue
fair-y-like
fak-er (one who fakes)
fa-kir (dervish)
Fa-lan-gist
fal-cip-a-rum
fal-con-er
fal-la-cious
fal-la-cy
fall-en
fal-li-bil-i-ty
Fal-lo-pi-an
fal-set-tos
fal-si-fi-ca-tion
fal-si-ty
Fal-staff-i-an

fal-ter
fa-mil-iar
fa-mil-i-ar-i-ty
fa-mil-iar-ize
fam-i-ly
fam-ish
fa-mous
fam-u-lus
fa-nat-i-cal
fa-nat-i-cism
fan-ci-er
fan-ci-ful
Fan-euil
fan-gled
fan-ta-sia
fan-ta-size
fan-tas-tic
fan-ta-sy
far-ad
Far-a-day
fa-rad-ic
far-a-dism
far-ci-cal
fa-ri-na
far-i-na-ceous
far-i-nose
farm-er
far-ther
far-thing
far-thin-gale
fas-ces
fas-ci-cle
fas-cic-u-lar
fas-ci-na-tor
fas-ci-o-li-a-sis
fas-cism
Fas-cist
Fa-scis-ti
fash-ion-a-ble
fas-ten-er
fas-tid-i-ous
fas-tig-i-um
fa-tal-ism
fa-tal-i-ty
fa-ther
fath-om-a-ble
Fa-thom-e-ter
fat-i-ga-ble
fa-tigue
fa-tigu-ing-ly
Fat-i-ma
fa-tu-i-tous
fat-u-ous

fau-cal-ize
fau-cet
fau-nal
fau-vism
fa-ve-o-lus
fa-vism
fa-vor-ite
fa-vor-it-ism
fa-vrile
fa-yal-ite
fe-al-ty
fea-sance
fea-si-bil-i-ty
feath-er-ing
fea-tured
fe-bric-i-ty
fe-bric-u-la
fe-brif-ic
fe-brif-u-gal
feb-ri-fuge
fe-brif-u-gine
feb-rile
fe-bril-i-ty
Feb-ru-ar-y
fe-cal
fec-u-lent
fe-cund
fec-un-date
fe-cun-da-tive
fe-cun-di-ty
fed-er-a-cy
fed-er-al-ese
fed-er-a-tive
fee-ble
Feh-ling
feld-spath-ic
feld-spath-oi-dal
fe-li-cide
fe-lic-i-tate
fe-lic-i-tous
fe-line
fe-lin-i-ty
fel-on
fe-lo-ni-ous
fel-o-ny
felt-er
Felt-ham
fe-luc-ca
fem-i-ne-i-ty
fem-i-nin-i-ty
fem-i-nism
fem-o-ral
fe-mur

fen-chene
fen-chone
fen-chyl
fen-ci-ble
fend-er
fe-nes-tra
fen-es-tra-tion
Fe-ni-an
fe-ra-cious
Fer-di-nand
fer-ment-a-ble
fer-men-ta-tion
fer-ment-a-tive
fer-ment-er
fer-men-tive
fer-mi-um
fe-ro-cious
fe-roc-i-ty
fer-rif-er-ous
fer-ri-na-trite
fer-rit-ic
fer-ri-tin
fer-ro-cene
fer-ro-cy-a-nide
fer-rom-e-ter
fer-ru-gi-nous
fer-rule
fer-til-i-ty
fer-til-iz-a-ble
fer-til-iz-er
fe-ru-lic
fer-va-nite
fer-ven-cy
fer-vor
fes-ter
fes-ti-val
fes-tiv-i-ty
fes-toon
fe-tal
fet-e-ri-ta
fe-ti-cide
fet-id
fe-tid-i-ty
fet-ish-ism
fe-tus
feu-dal-ism
feud-ist
feuil-le-ton
fe-ver-ous
fi-an-ce
Fi-ber-glas
fi-ber-ize
fi-bril-la-tion

fi-brin-o-gen-ic
fi-bri-nog-e-nous
fi-broid
fi-bro-in
fi-bro-sis
fi-bro-si-tis
fi-brous
fib-u-la
fick-le
fic-tile
fic-ti-tious
fid-dler
fi-del-i-ty
fidg-et-y
fi-du-ci-ar-y
field-er
fiend-ish
fi-er-y
fi-es-ta
fight-er
fig-ur-al
fig-u-ra-tion
fig-u-ra-tive
fig-u-rine
fil-a-men-tous
fi-lar-i-al
fil-a-ri-a-sis
fil-bert
fil-i-al
fil-i-bus-ter
fil-i-gree
Fil-i-pi-no
fill-er (filled)
fil-ler (money unit)
fil-let
fil-o-selle
fil-ter-er
filth-i-ness
fil-tra-ble
fil-tra-tion
fin-a-ble
fi-na-gle
fi-nal-e
fi-nal-i-ty
fi-nan-cial
fin-an-cier
fi-nanc-ing
find-er
fin-er-y
fi-nesse
fin-ger
fin-i-cal
fin-ick-y

fi-nis
fin-ished
fi-nite
fin-i-tude
Finn-ish
fir-ing
fir-kin
fir-ma-ment
firm-er
fis-cal
fisch-er-ite
fish-er-y
fis-sion
fis-sip-a-rous
fis-sure
fist-i-cuff
fis-tu-la
fis-tu-lous
fix-a-tive
flac-cid-i-ty
flag-el-lant
flag-el-la-tor
flag-eo-let
fla-gi-tious
flag-on
fla-grant
flam-beau
flam-boy-ant
fla-min-go
flam-ma-ble
flang-er
flank-er
flap-er-on
flar-ing
flat-u-lence
flau-tist
flav-a-none
fla-van-throne
fla-ves-cence
fla-vi-an-ic
fla-vin
fla-vo-nol
fla-vo-pur-pu-rin
fla-vor
fledg-ling
fletch-er-ize
flex-i-bi-lize
flex-om-e-ter
flex-or
flex-ur-al
flick-er-y
flin-ders
flir-ta-tious

float-er
floc-cu-lant (n.)
floc-cu-la-tor
floc-cu-lent (adj.)
flood-om-e-ter
flo-ral
Flor-ence
flor-enc-ite
Flor-en-tine
flo-res-cence
flo-ret
flo-ri-cul-tur-al
Flor-i-da
Flo-rid-i-an
flor-id-ness
flo-rif-er-ous
flo-ri-gen
flor-in
flo-rist
flo-riv-o-rous
flor-u-lent
flo-tage
flo-ta-tion
flo-til-la
flot-sam
floun-der
flour-ish
fluc-tu-ate
flu-en-cy
fluff-i-ness
flu-id-i-ty
flu-mer-in
flu-o-bo-rate
flu-o-bo-rite
flu-o-ran-thene
flu-or-ap-a-tite
flu-o-rene
flu-o-re-nyl
flu-o-res-ce-in
flu-o-res-cence
flu-o-ri-date
flu-o-ride
flu-o-ri-dize
flu-o-ri-nate
flu-o-rine
flu-o-rite
flu-o-ro-a-ce-tic
flu-o-ro-graph-ic
flu-o-rog-ra-phy
flu-o-rom-e-ter
flu-o-ro-scope
flu-o-ros-co-py
flu-o-ro-sis

flu-o-sil-i-cate
flu-o-si-lic-ic
flus-ter
flut-ist
flu-vi-al
flu-vi-ol-o-gy
flux-i-ble
flux-ion-al
flux-me-ter
Foam-ite
fo-cal-ize
fo-com-e-ter
fo-cus-er
fo-cus-ing
foi-ble
fol-de-rol
fo-li-a-ceous
fo-li-age
fo-lic
fo-lin-ic
fo-li-o-late
fol-lic-u-lar
fol-lic-u-li-tis
fo-men-ta-tion
fon-dant
fond-ling
fool-er-y
fool-ish
foo-zle
for-age
fo-ra-men
fo-ram-i-na
Fo-ram-i-nif-er-a
fo-ram-i-nif-er-ous
fo-ram-i-nous
for-ay
for-bear-ance
for-ceps
forc-er
forc-i-ble
forc-ing
fore-clo-sure
for-eign-er
fo-ren-si-cal
fore-see-a-ble
for-est-a-tion
for-est-er
for-est-ry
for-feit-er
for-feit-ure
forg-er
for-ger-y
fo-rint

for-mal
form-al-de-hyde
For-ma-lin
for-mal-ist
for-mal-i-ty
for-mal-ize
form-am-ide
form-am-i-dine
form-ant
for-mate
for-ma-tion
form-a-tive
form-a-zan
form-er (one who forms)
for-mer (previous)
for-mic
For-mi-ca
for-mi-cide
for-mi-da-ble
for-mol-ize
For-mo-san
for-mu-la
for-mu-la-ri-za-ble
for-mu-lar-i-za-tion
for-mu-lar-y
for-mu-la-tor
for-myl-ate
for-ni-ca-tion
for-syth-i-a
for-ti-eth
for-ti-fi-ca-tion
for-ti-fy
for-tis-si-mo
for-ti-tude
for-tress
for-tu-i-tous
for-tu-i-ty
for-tu-nate
for-ty
fo-rum
fos-sil-if-er-ous
fos-sil-ize
fos-so-ri-al
fos-ter
fou-lard
foun-da-tion
found-er (n.)
foun-der (v.; also as n.,
    act of foundering)
found-ling
found-ry
foun-tain
Four-drin-i-er

Fou-ri-er
four-ra-gere
fo-ve-o-late
Fow-ler
fowl-er
fra-cas
frac-tion-ate
frac-tious
frac-tog-ra-phy
frac-tur-al
frag-ile
fra-gil-i-ty
frag-men-tal
frag-men-tar-y
frag-ment-ize
fra-grance
frail-ty
fram-er
fran-chise
fran-ci-um
fran-gi-ble
fran-gi-pan-i
frank-furt-er
fran-kin-cense
fran-ti-cal-ly
fra-ter-nal
fra-ter-ni-ty
frat-er-nize
frat-ri-ci-dal
fraud-u-lent
frau-lein
freck-led
free-dom
freez-er
freight-er
fre-net-ic
fren-zied
fre-quen-cy
fre-quen-ta-tion
fresh-et
Freud-i-an
fric-an-deau
fric-as-see
frig-ate
fright-ened
frig-id
Frig-i-daire
fri-gid-i-ty
frig-o-rim-e-ter
fris-ket
frisk-i-ly
fri-vol-i-ty
friv-o-lous

frizz-ing
frol-icked
fron-des-cence
front-age
fron-tal
fron-ta-lis
fron-tier
fron-tis-piece
fron-to-gen-e-sis
front-o-ly-sis
fron-to-pa-ri-e-tal
frost-i-ness
froth-i-ly
frow-zy
fro-zen
fruc-tif-er-ous
fruc-ti-fy
fruc-tose
fru-gal-i-ty
fruit-age
fru-i-tion
frump-ish
frus-trate
frus-tum
fru-tes-cence
fu-ca-ceous
fuch-sia
fuch-sin-o-phil
fu-coi-dal
fu-cos-ter-ol
fu-el-er
fu-ga-cious
fu-gac-i-ty
fu-gi-tive
ful-crum
ful-fill-ing
ful-gen-ic
ful-gide
ful-gu-rant
ful-gu-ra-tion
ful-gu-rite
fu-lig-i-nous
full-ness
ful-mi-nate
ful-min-ic
ful-min-u-ric
fu-ma-rase
fu-mar-ic
fu-mar-o-yl
fum-bler
fu-mig-a-cin
fu-mi-ga-tor
fu-mu-lus

fu-nam-bu-list
fun-da-men-tal
fun-dus-co-py
fu-ner-al
fu-ne-re-al
fun-gi-ble
fun-gi-ci-dal
fun-giv-o-rous
fun-goid
fun-gous (adj.)
fun-gus (n.)
fu-ni-cle
fu-nic-u-lar
fun-neled
fu-ra-nose
fu-ran-o-side
fur-be-low
fur-bish
fur-fu-ra-ceous
fur-fu-ral
fur-fu-ryl-i-dene
fu-ri-ous
fur-long
fur-lough
fur-nace
fur-nish-er

fur-ni-ture
fu-ro-ic
fu-ror
fur-ring
fur-ther
fur-thest
fur-tive
fu-run-cle
fu-run-cu-lo-sis
fu-ryl
fu-sar-i-um
fu-see
fu-sel
fu-se-lage
fu-si-ble
fu-si-lier
fu-sil-lade
fu-sion
fu-so-spi-ro-chete
fus-tian
fu-tile
fu-til-i-ty
fu-tu-ram-ic
fu-tur-ist
fu-tu-ri-ty
fuzz-i-ness

G

gab-ar-dine (fabric)
ga-ba-rit
gab-er-dine (gown)
ga-bi-on
ga-bling
Ga-bon
Gab-o-nese
Ga-bri-el
gadg-et-eer
gadg-et-ry
gad-o-le-ic
gad-o-lin-i-um
Gael-ic
gaf-fer
gag-er
gai-ner (diving)
gain-er (one who gains)
Gains-bor-ough
gait-er (harness)
gai-ter (overshoe)

ga-lac-ta-gogue
ga-lac-tic
ga-lac-to-lip-id
gal-ac-tom-e-ter
gal-ac-ton-ic
ga-lac-to-poi-e-sis
ga-lac-tos-a-mine
ga-lac-to-sid-ase
gal-ac-to-sis
ga-lac-tu-ron-ic
Ga-la-pa-gos
gal-a-te-a
ga-lax-i-al
gal-ax-y
ga-le-gine
ga-le-na
ga-le-nic (mineral)
ga-len-ic (medicinal)
ga-le-no-bis-mu-tite
Ga-li-cian

Gal-i-le-an
gal-lant-ry
gal-le-in
gal-ler-y
gal-li-na-ceous
gal-li-nule
Gal-lip-o-li
gal-li-vant
gal-lo-cy-a-nine
gal-lop
gal-op
ga-lore
ga-losh
gal-van-ic
gal-va-nism
gal-va-ni-za-tion
gal-va-nom-e-ter
gal-va-no-met-ric
gal-van-o-scope
Gam-bi-an
gam-bling
gam-boled
game-ster
ga-mete
ga-met-ic
ga-me-to-cide
gam-e-toid
gam-in
gam-ing
gam-ut
gan-der
Gan-dha-ra
Gan-dhi
gan-gling
gan-gli-on-at-ed
gan-gli-on-ic
gan-gli-o-side
gan-gre-nous
gang-ster
gan-is-ter
ga-nom-a-lite
gant-let (track)
Gan-tri-sin
gan-try
gap-er
ga-rage
gar-an-cine
Ga-rand
gar-bage
gar-bling
gar-den-er
gar-de-nia
Gar-di-nol

gar-gan-tu-an
gar-gling
gar-goyle
gar-ish
gar-land
gar-lick-y
gar-ner
gar-ni-er-ite
gar-nish-ee
gar-ni-ture
gar-ru-li-ty
gas-con-ade
gas-e-ous
gas-i-fy
gas-ket
gas-o-line
gas-om-e-ter
gas-o-met-ric
gas-sing
gas-ter-o-sto-ma-ta
gas-tral-gi-a
gas-tra-li-um
gas-trec-to-my
gas-tric
gas-tri-tis
gas-tro-cne-mi-us
gas-tro-en-ter-os-to-my
gas-tro-in-tes-ti-nal
gas-trol-o-ger
gas-tro-nom-ic
gas-tron-o-my
gas-tro-pod
Gas-trop-o-da
gas-tros-co-py
gas-tros-to-my
gath-er-ing
Ga-tun
gau-che-rie
gau-chos
gaud-i-ness
gau-lei-ter
Gaull-ist
gaunt-let
ga-vage
gav-el-er
ga-votte
gawk-i-ness
ga-zelle
gaz-er
ga-zette
gaz-et-teer
Gei-ger
gei-sha

gel-a-tin-ase
ge-lat-i-nate
ge-lat-i-ni-za-tion
ge-lat-i-niz-er
ge-lat-i-no-chlo-ride
ge-lat-i-nous
ge-la-tion
geld-ing
ge-lid-i-ty
gel-ig-nite
gel-ling
gel-ose
gel-se-mic
gem-i-na-tive
Gem-i-ni
gem-mif-er-ous
gen-dar-mer-y
gen-der
gen-e-al-o-gist
gen-e-al-o-gy
gen-er-a-lis-si-mo
gen-er-al-i-ty
gen-er-al-ize
gen-er-a-tor
ge-ner-i-cal
gen-er-os-i-ty
gen-e-sis
gen-et
ge-net-i-cal
Ge-ne-va
ge-nial
ge-ni-al-i-ty
gen-ic
ge-nic-u-late
ge-nie
gen-in
ge-ni-o-plas-ty
ge-nis-te-in
gen-i-tal
gen-i-tive
gen-i-to-u-ri-nar-y
ge-nius
Gen-o-a
gen-o-ci-dal
ge-nome
ge-no-mere
gen-o-type
genth-ite
gen-tian-in
gen-tian-ose
gen-til-i-ty
gen-ti-o-bi-ose
gen-tis-ic

gen-ti-sin
gent-ly
gen-try
gen-u-flec-to-ry
gen-u-ine
ge-nus
ge-o-ce-rite
ge-oc-ro-nite
ge-o-des-ic
ge-od-e-sy
ge-o-det-i-cal
ge-od-ic
ge-o-dim-e-ter
ge-og-e-nous
ge-og-nos-tic
ge-og-o-ny
ge-og-ra-pher
ge-o-graph-ic
ge-og-ra-phy
ge-oi-dal
ge-o-log-i-cal
ge-ol-o-gist
ge-ol-o-gy
ge-om-a-lism
ge-om-e-ter
ge-o-met-ri-cal
ge-om-e-triz-er
ge-om-e-try
ge-o-pon-ics
geor-gette
Geor-gian
ge-os-co-py
ge-ot-ri-cho-sis
ge-o-trop-ic
ge-ot-ro-pism
ge-ran-ic
ge-ra-ni-ol
ge-ra-ni-um
ge-ra-nyl
Ge-rard
ge-rat-ic
ger-a-tol-o-gy
ge-rent
ger-i-a-tri-cian
ger-i-at-rics
ger-mane
ger-ma-nite
ger-ma-ni-um
ger-mi-ci-dal
ger-mi-nal
ger-mi-na-tor
Ge-ron-i-mo
ger-on-toc-ra-cy

ge-ron-to-log-i-cal
ger-on-tol-o-gy
Ger-trude
ger-und
ger-un-di-val
ge-run-dive
ge-sell-schaft
Ge-stalt
Ge-sta-po
ges-ta-tion
ges-tic-u-late
ges-ture
Geth-sem-a-ne
gey-ser
Gha-na-ian
gher-kin
ghoul-ish
gibbs-ite
Gi-bral-tar
gi-gan-tic
gi-gan-tism
gild-er
gil-son-ite
gim-baled
gin-ger
ging-ham
gin-gi-val
gin-gi-vi-tis
gink-go
gin-seng
gi-raffe
Gi-rard
gird-er
gir-dling
girl-ish
gi-tal-in
gi-tox-i-gen-in
giv-en
gla-bres-cent
gla-brous
gla-cial
gla-ci-a-tion
gla-cier
gla-ci-ol-o-gy
gla-ci-om-e-ter
glad-i-a-tor
glad-i-o-lus
glam-or-ous
glam-our
glan-ders
glan-du-lar
glar-ing
glass-ine

glass-i-ness
glau-ber-ite
glau-co-cer-i-nite
glau-co-ma
glau-co-ma-tous
glau-co-nite
glau-cous
glaz-er
gla-zier
glis-ten
gloam-ing
glob-al-ism
glo-bal-i-ty
glo-boid
glob-u-lar
glob-ule
glob-u-lif-er-ous
glob-u-lin
glo-mer-u-lar
gloom-i-ly
glo-ri-fy
glo-ri-ous
glos-sa-ry
gloss-i-ness
gloss-me-ter
Glouces-ter
glov-er
glu-ca-mine
glu-car-ic
glu-cin-i-um
glu-ci-tol
glu-ci-tyl
glu-co-nate
glu-con-ic
glu-co-py-ran-o-side
glu-co-sa-mine
glu-cose
glu-co-si-dase
glu-co-side
glu-cu-ron-ic
glu-cu-ron-i-dase
glu-cu-ro-nide
glu-ey-ness
glu-ing
glut-a-con-ic
glu-ta-mate
glu-tam-ic
glu-ta-min-ase
glu-ta-mine
glu-ta-min-ic
glu-tam-o-yl
glu-ta-thi-one
glu-te-al

glu-ten
glu-te-nin
glu-ten-ous
glu-ti-nous
glyc-er-ate
gly-ce-mi-a
gly-ce-mic
glyc-er-al-de-hyde
gly-cer-ic
glyc-er-ide
glyc-er-in
glyc-er-ol
glyc-er-o-phos-phor-ic
glyc-er-yl
glyc-ide
gly-cid-ic
glyc-i-dol
gly-cine
gly-co-cy-a-mine
gly-co-gen
gly-co-gen-ol-y-sis
gly-co-gen-o-lyt-ic
gly-col-y-sis
gly-co-lyt-ic
gly-co-si-dase
glyc-u-re-sis
gly-cyl
gly-ox-yl-ic
glyp-tol-o-gy
gnath-ism
gneiss-oid
gnom-ish
gno-se-ol-o-gy
gno-sis
gnos-tic
goa-tee
gob-ble-dy-gook
gob-bler
Go-be-lin
gob-lin
Goe-thals
goi-ter
goi-tro-gen-ic
goi-tro-ge-nic-i-ty
goi-trous
gold-en
Go-li-ath
go-nad-ec-to-my
go-nad-o-tro-phin
gon-do-la
gon-fa-lon
go-nid-i-al
go-nid-i-um

go-ni-om-e-ter
go-ni-o-met-ric
gon-o-coc-ci
gon-or-rhe-al
goo-gol-plex
go-pher
gor-geous
go-ril-la
gor-lic
Go-shen
gos-pel-er
gos-sa-mer
gos-syp-i-trin
Goth-am-ite
Goth-ic
gour-man-diz-er
gov-ern-ess
gov-ern-men-tal
gov-er-nor
goy-a-zite
Graaf-i-an
grac-ile
gra-cious
gra-da-tion
grad-a-to-ry
grad-er
gra-di-ent
gra-di-om-e-ter
grad-u-al
grad-u-ate
graft-er
gra-ham
grai-ning (fish)
grain-ing (of grain)
gram-i-cid-in
gram-i-na-les
gram-ine
gra-min-e-ous
gram-mar-i-an
gram-mat-i-cal
gra-na-ry
gran-dam
gran-deur
gran-dil-o-quent
gran-di-ose
grang-er
gran-ite
gra-nit-ic
gran-o-blas-tic
gran-o-di-o-rite
grant-ee
grant-er
Grant-ham

grant-or
gran-u-lar-i-ty
gran-u-late
gran-ule
gran-u-lo-ma-to-sis
gran-u-lous
graph-eme
gra-phe-mic
graph-i-cal
graph-ite
gra-phit-ic
gra-phol-o-gy
graph-o-met-ric
grap-pling
grasp-er
grat-er
grat-i-cule
grat-i-fy
grat-in
gra-tis
grat-i-tude
gra-tu-i-tous
gra-va-men
grav-eled
grav-el-ly
grav-en
grav-id
gra-vid-i-ty
gra-vim-e-ter
grav-i-met-ri-cal-ly
gra-vim-e-try
grav-i-sphere
grav-i-tat-er
grav-i-tom-e-ter
grav-i-ty
gra-vure
graz-er
greas-er
greas-i-ness
Gre-cian
greed-i-ness
green-sward
gre-gar-i-ous
Gre-go-ri-an
grei-sen
gre-nade
gren-a-dier
gren-a-dine
Gresh-am
grid-i-ron
griev-ance
griev-ous
Gri-gnard

gril-lage
grim-ace
gri-mal-kin
grind-er
grin-gos
griph-ite
gris-e-o-ful-vin
gris-tly
griz-zly
gro-cer-y
gro-per (fish)
grop-er
gro-schen
gros-grain
gro-tesque
gro-tes-que-rie
ground-ling
grou-per (fish)
group-er
grou-ser (timber; cleats)
grous-er
grout-er
grov-el-er
growl-er
grum-bler
gru-mose
grun-ion
Gru-yere
guai-ac
guai-a-col
Gua-ma-ni-an
gua-na-mine
gua-ni-dine
gua-nif-er-ous
gua-nine
gua-nyl-ic
gua-ra-ni
guar-an-tee (n., v.)
guar-an-ty (n.) (legal)
guard-i-an
Gua-te-ma-la
gua-va
gua-yu-le
gu-ber-na-to-ri-al
gudg-eon
guer-don
Guern-sey
guer-ril-la
guid-ance
gui-don
guil-lo-tine
guilt-i-ly
Guin-ea

gui-pure
gui-tar
gul-den
gul-li-ble
gu-lose
Gun-ite
gur-gi-ta-tion
gur-gling
gur-nard
gush-er
gus-set
gus-ta-to-ry
Gu-ten-berg

gut-tur-al
Guy-a-nese
gym-na-si-um
gym-nas-tic
gym-no-sto-ma-ta
gym-no-stom-a-tous
gyn-e-coc-ra-cy
gyn-e-col-o-gy
gyp-se-ous
gyp-sif-er-ous
gy-ra-to-ry
gy-roi-dal
gy-ro-scop-ic

H

ha-be-as
ha-ben-dum
hab-er-dash-er-y
ha-bil-i-ment
hab-it-a-ble
hab-i-ta-tion
ha-bit-u-al
ha-bit-u-e
ha-chure
ha-ci-en-da
hack-ler
Ha-des
haf-ni-um
Ha-ga-nah
hag-i-ol-o-gy
Hai-fa
hai-kwan
Hai-tian
ha-la-tion
hal-a-zone
hal-berd-ier
hal-cy-on
hal-i-but
ha-lide
hal-i-dom
hal-i-eu-tics
hal-i-ste-re-sis
ha-lite
hal-i-to-sis
hal-le-lu-jah
Hal-low-een

hal-lu-ci-na-tion
ha-lo
hal-o-gen-a-tion
ha-log-e-nous
hal-o-hy-drin
ha-lom-e-ter
ha-lot-ri-chite
halt-er (one who halts)
hal-ter (other meanings)
ham-burg-er
Ham-mar-skjold
ham-per
ham-ster
hand-i-cap
hand-i-craft
hand-i-ly
hand-i-work
han-dle-a-ble
han-dler
han-dling
hand-som-est
hang-ar
hang-er
han-ker
Han-o-ver
Ha-nuk-kah
hap-pi-ness
har-a-kir-i
ha-rangued
ha-rangu-er
har-assed

har-bin-ger
har-bor
hard-en-er
har-di-ness
Har-ding
har-dy
ha-rem
har-i-cot
hark-en
har-le-quin
har-ma-line
har-mo-ni-al
har-mon-i-ca
har-mo-ni-ous
har-mo-nize
har-ness
harp-ist
har-poon
harp-si-chord
har-te-beest
Hart-ley
har-um-scar-um
har-vest-er
hash-ish
has-sled
has-tate
has-ten
hast-i-ly
Hast-ings
hatch-er-y
hatch-et
ha-tred
haugh-ti-ness
hau-teur
Ha-va-na
ha-ven
hav-er-sack
hav-oc
Ha-wai-ian
haw-ser
haz-ard-ous
ha-zel
haz-ing
head-quar-ters
health-i-est
heart-i-ly
heat-er
hea-then
heath-er
heav-en
heav-i-ly
Heav-i-side
heb-dom-a-dal

He-bra-ic
He-brew
Heb-ri-des
Hec-a-te
hec-a-tomb
heck-ler
hec-o-gen-in
hec-tare
hec-to-li-ter
hec-to-me-ter
hed-er-in
he-don-ics
he-do-nism
he-do-nis-tic
he-do-nom-e-ter
he-dral
heg-e-mon-ic
he-gem-o-ny
he-gi-ra
heif-er
hei-li-gen-schein
hei-nous
Hel-e-na
hel-e-nin
he-li-a-cal
he-li-an-the-mum
he-li-an-thus
hel-i-cal
hel-i-ces
hel-i-coi-dal
Hel-i-con
hel-i-cop-ter
he-li-o-graph
he-li-og-ra-phy
he-li-om-e-ter
he-li-o-met-ric
he-li-om-e-try
he-li-o-pho-bic
he-li-o-trope
he-li-ot-ro-pism
hel-i-port
he-li-um
he-lix
he-lix-om-e-ter
Hel-len-ic
Hel-le-nism
Hel-les-pont
hel-min-thic
hel-min-tho-spo-rin
hel-ot-ism
hel-ter–skel-ter
hel-vite
hel-vol-ic

he-ma-cy-tom-e-ter
he-ma-fi-brite
he-mag-glu-ti-nin
he-mal-bu-men
he-man-gi-o-ma-to-sis
he-ma-poi-e-sis
he-mar-thro-sis
he-ma-tal
he-ma-te-in
he-mat-ic
hem-a-tin-om-e-ter
hem-a-tite
hem-a-tit-ic
hem-a-to-cele
hem-a-to-crit
hem-a-tog-e-nous
hem-a-to-lite
he-ma-tol-o-gy
he-ma-to-ma
he-ma-tom-e-ter
hem-a-to-por-phy-rin
he-ma-to-sis
he-ma-tox-y-lin
hem-i-ac-e-tal
hem-i-cy-clic
hem-i-he-dral
hem-i-kar-y-on
he-min
he-mip-ter-oid
hem-i-spher-ic
hem-i-stich-al
he-mo-chro-mo-gen
he-mo-chro-mom-e-ter
he-mo-co-ni-o-sis
he-mo-cy-a-nin
he-mo-cyte
he-mo-cy-tol-y-sis
he-mo-glo-bin
he-mo-glo-bi-nom-e-ter
he-mol-y-sin
he-mol-y-sis
he-mo-lyt-ic
he-mom-e-ter
hem-or-rhag-ic
hem-or-rhoi-dal
he-mo-sid-er-in
he-mo-sid-er-o-sis
he-mo-stat-ic
hemp-en
hen-e-quen
hep-a-rin
he-pat-i-ca
hep-a-ti-tis

hep-a-to-cu-pre-in
hep-a-to-fla-vin
hep-a-tos-co-py
hep-ta-dec-yl
hep-tag-o-nal
hep-tam-e-ter
hep-tar-chy
hep-tu-lose
hep-tyl-ene
her-ald
he-ral-dic
her-ba-ceous
herb-age
her-bar-i-um
her-bi-ci-dal
her-biv-o-rous
Her-cu-les
her-e-dit-a-ment
he-red-i-tar-y
Her-e-ford
her-e-sy
her-e-tic
he-ret-i-cal
her-it-age
her-maph-ro-dite
her-me-neu-tics
her-met-i-cal
her-mit-age
her-ne-ar-in
her-ni-a
her-ni-ot-o-my
he-ro-ic
her-o-ine
her-o-ism
her-on
her-pes
her-pe-tol-o-gy
Hertz-i-an
hes-i-tan-cy
hes-i-tat-er
hes-i-ta-tion
hes-per-i-din
Hes-per-is
Hes-sian
hess-ite
het-er-o-aux-in
het-er-o-cy-clic
het-er-o-dox-y
het-er-o-ge-ne-ous
het-er-og-e-nous
het-er-o-ki-ne-sis
het-er-ol-o-gy
het-er-ol-y-sis

het-er-o-ou-si-a
het-er-o-pol-y
het-er-os-co-py
hex-a-chlo-ro-eth-ane
hex-a-gon
hex-ag-o-nal
hex-a-he-dral
hex-am-e-ter
hex-a-no-yl
hex-es-trol
hex-os-a-mine
hex-u-lose
hex-u-ron-ic
hex-yl-ene
hi-a-tus
hi-ber-na-tor
hick-o-ry
hid-e-ous
hi-dro-sis
hi-drot-ic
hi-er-ar-chy
hi-er-o-glyph-ic
high-fa-lu-tin
hi-lar-i-ous
hill-ocked
hi-lus
Hi-ma-la-yan
hin-der (v.)
hind-er (adj.)
hin-drance
Hin-du-stan-i
hint-er
hin-ter-land
Hip-po-crat-ic
hip-po-pot-a-mus
hip-pu-ric
Hir-o-shi-ma
hir-su-tal
His-pa-ni-a
His-pan-ic
his-pa-ni-dad
his-tam-i-nase
his-ta-mine
his-ti-dine
his-to-log-i-cal
his-tol-o-gy
his-tol-y-sis
his-to-ri-an
his-tor-i-cal
his-to-ric-i-ty
his-to-ry
his-tri-on-ic
hith-er-to

hock-ey
hod-o-graph
Hoh-en-zol-lern
hoist-er
hold-er
hol-i-day
ho-li-ness
hol-lan-daise
Hol-land-er
hol-mi-um
hol-o-caust
hol-o-graph
hol-o-he-dral
hol-o-pho-tal
ho-loph-ra-sis
hol-ster
Hol-yoke
hom-age
ho-me-ol-o-gy
ho-me-o-path-ic
ho-me-op-a-thy
ho-me-o-sta-sis
hom-i-ci-dal
hom-i-let-ics
hom-i-ly
hom-ish
hom-o-cys-teine
ho-mog-a-my
ho-mo-ge-ne-i-ty
ho-mo-ge-ne-ous
ho-mog-e-ni-za-tion
ho-mog-e-niz-er
ho-mog-e-nous
hom-o-log
ho-mol-o-gous
ho-mol-y-sis
hom-o-nym-ic
ho-mo-thet-ic
Hon-du-ran
hon-ey
Hon-i-ton
Hon-o-lu-lu
hon-or-a-ble
hon-o-rar-i-um
hon-or-ar-y
hon-or-if-ic
Hoo-ver
ho-ra-ry
ho-ri-zon
hor-i-zon-tal
hor-mo-nal
hor-mon-ic
ho-rol-o-gy

hor-o-scope
ho-ros-co-py
hor-ren-dous
hor-rif-ic
hor-ta-to-ry
hor-ti-cul-tur-al
ho-san-na
ho-sier-y
hos-pi-ta-ble
hos-pi-tal-i-za-tion
hos-tage
host-al
hos-tel-ry
host-ess
hos-til-i-ty
hos-tler
Hou-dry
hous-ing
hov-el
hov-er
how-it-zer
howl-er
how-lite
hua-ra-che
huck-ster
Hue-ne-me
Hu-gue-not
hul-la-ba-loo
hu-man-i-tar-i-an
hu-man-ize
hum-bling
hu-mec-tant
hu-mer-us
hu-mid-i-ty
hu-mil-i-a-tion
hu-min
hum-ite
hu-mi-ture
hu-mor-ous
hu-mous (adj.)
hu-mu-lene
hu-mus (n.)
hun-dred
Hun-gar-i-an
hun-ger
hun-gry
hunt-er
hur-dler
hurl-er
Hu-ron
hur-ried-ly
hur-ter (bumper)
hurt-er

hur-tling
hus-band-ry
husk-i-ness
hus-ting
hus-tler
hy-a-cin-thine
Hy-a-des
hy-a-les-cence
hy-a-lin-i-za-tion
hy-a-li-no-sis
hy-al-o-gen
hy-al-o-phane
hy-a-lu-ro-nate
hy-a-lu-ron-i-dase
hy-brid-ize
hy-dan-to-in-ate
hy-da-tid-o-sis
hy-da-to-gen-ic
hy-drac-ry-late
hy-dra-cryl-ic
hy-dral-a-zine
hy-dra-mat-ic
hy-dra-mine
hy-dran-ge-a
hy-drar-gil-lite
hy-dras-ti-nine
hy-dra-tor
hy-drau-lic
hy-dra-zide
hy-draz-i-dine
hy-dra-zine
hy-dra-zin-i-um
hy-dra-zo-ate
hy-dra-zone
hy-dre-mi-a
hy-dri-od-ic
hy-dri-o-dide
hy-dro-ab-i-et-yl
hy-dro-cal-u-mite
hy-dro-cele
hy-dro-ce-phal-ic
hy-dro-ceph-a-lous (adj.)
hy-dro-ceph-a-lus (n.)
hy-dro-chlo-ric
hy-dro-flu-or-ide
hy-dro-form-ate
hy-dro-gen-a-tion
hy-dro-gen-a-tor
hy-drog-e-nous
hy-drog-no-sy
hy-drog-ra-pher
hy-dro-graph-ic
hy-dro-lase

hy-drol-o-gy
hy-drol-y-sate
hy-drol-y-sis
hy-dro-lyze
hy-drom-e-ter
hy-dro-met-ric
hy-dro-ni-um
hy-drop-a-thy
hy-dro-pho-bi-a
hy-dro-pon-ics
hy-drox-ide
hy-drox-im-i-no
hy-drox-y-am-i-no
hy-drox-y-bu-tyr-ic
hy-drox-yl-a-mine
hy-drox-yl-ate
hy-drox-y-zine
hy-e-tom-e-ter
hy-gi-en-ic
hy-gien-ist
hy-grom-e-ter
hy-gro-met-ric
hy-gro-scop-ic
hy-me-ne-al
hy-me-no-cal-lis
hy-per-bo-la
hy-per-bo-le
hy-per-bol-i-cal
hy-per-bo-loi-dal
hy-per-crit-i-cal
hy-per-e-mi-a
hy-per-go-lic-i-ty
hy-per-i-cin
hy-per-in
hy-per-o-pi-a

hy-per-sthene
hy-per-ten-sive
hy-per-troph-ic
hy-per-tro-phy
hy-phen-ate
hyp-no-sis
hyp-not-ic
hyp-no-tism
hy-po-bro-mous
hy-po-chlo-rous
hy-po-chon-dri-a
hy-poc-ri-sy
hyp-o-crite
hy-po-der-mic
hy-poid
hy-po-i-o-dous
hy-po-mor-pho-sis
hy-pos-ta-sis
hy-pot-e-nuse
hy-poth-e-cate
hy-poth-e-sis
hy-po-thet-i-cal
hy-pox-e-mi-a
hy-pox-i-a
hyp-som-e-ter
hys-taz-a-rin
hys-ter-ec-to-my
hys-ter-e-sis
hys-te-ri-a
hys-ter-i-cal
hys-ter-or-rha-phy
hys-ter-os-co-py
hys-ter-ot-o-my
hy-ther-graph

I

i-at-ro-gen-ic
i-at-ro-ge-nic-i-ty
I-be-ri-an
Ice-land-er
Ice-lan-dic
ich-neu-mon
ich-nog-ra-phy
Ich-thy-ol
ich-thy-o-sis
i-ci-cle
ic-ing

i-con-o-clast
i-co-nog-ra-phy
i-co-nol-a-try
i-co-nom-e-ter
i-con-o-scope
ic-ter-ic
I-da-ho-an
i-de-al-ism
i-de-al-ist
i-de-al-i-za-tion
i-den-ti-cal

i-den-ti-fi-a-ble
i-de-oc-ra-cy
i-de-og-ra-phy
i-de-o-log-i-cal
i-de-ol-o-gy
id-i-o-cy
i-di-o-gram-mat-ic
id-i-om
id-i-o-mat-ic
id-i-om-e-ter
id-i-o-path-ic
id-i-op-a-thy
id-i-o-syn-cra-sy
id-i-ot-i-cal
id-i-tol
i-dol-a-ter
i-dol-a-trous
i-dol-ize
i-dyl-lic
i-dyll-ist
ig-loo
ig-ne-ous
ig-nit-a-ble
ig-nit-er
ig-ni-tron
ig-no-min-i-ous
ig-no-min-y
ig-no-ra-mus
ig-no-rance
Ig-o-rot
il-e-i-tis
il-e-os-to-my
il-e-um
il-leg-i-ble
il-lic-it
il-lim-it-a-ble
Il-li-nois-an
il-lu-mi-nant
il-lu-mi-na-tor
il-lu-min-er
il-lu-mi-nom-e-ter
il-lu-sive
il-lu-so-ry
il-lus-tra-tive
il-lu-vi-al
il-men-ite
I-lo-i-lo
im-age-ry
i-mag-i-na-ble
i-mag-i-nar-y
i-mag-i-na-tive
i-ma-go
im-be-cil-i-ty

im-bri-cate
im-bro-glio
im-id-az-ole
im-id-az-o-line
im-ide
im-i-do
im-in-az-ole
im-i-no
im-i-ta-tive
im-mac-u-late
im-ma-nence
im-mar-gin-ate
im-me-di-a-cy
im-mem-o-ra-ble
im-me-mo-ri-al
im-men-si-ty
im-men-su-ra-ble
im-mers-i-ble
im-mers-ing
im-mer-sion
im-mi-gra-tion
im-mi-nent
im-mis-ci-ble
im-mo-late
im-mu-ni-ty
im-mu-ni-za-tion
Im-mu-no-gen
im-mu-nol-o-gy
im-mu-ta-ble
im-pac-tive
im-pal-pa-ble
im-par-ta-tion
im-part-i-ble
im-pass-a-ble
im-pas-si-ble
im-pas-sive
im-pa-tience
im-pe-cu-ni-ous
im-ped-ance
im-ped-i-ble
im-ped-i-men-tal
im-pe-dom-e-ter
im-pe-dor
im-pel-ling
im-per-a-tive
im-pe-ra-tor
im-per-cep-ti-ble
im-per-fo-rate
im-pe-ri-al
im-per-iled
im-pe-ri-ous
im-per-scrip-ti-ble
im-per-son-a-tor

im-per-sua-si-ble
im-per-turb-a-ble
im-per-vi-ous
im-pe-ti-go
im-pet-u-os-i-ty
im-pe-tus
im-ping-er
im-ping-ing
im-pi-ous
imp-ish
im-plac-a-ble
im-plan-ta-tion
im-plau-si-ble
im-ple-men-tal
im-pli-cate
im-plic-it-ly
im-plo-sion
im-pol-i-tic
im-por-tance
im-por-tant
im-port-er
im-por-tu-nate
im-post-er
im-pos-tor (deceiver)
im-pos-ture
im-po-tence
im-pov-er-ish
im-prec-a-to-ry
im-preg-na-tor
im-pre-sar-i-o
im-pre-scrip-ti-ble
im-press-a-ble
im-press-i-ble
im-pres-sive
im-pri-ma-tur
im-promp-tu
im-prov-i-dent
im-prov-i-sa-tion
im-pro-vise
im-pu-dence
im-pul-sive
im-pu-ni-ty
im-pu-ri-ty
im-put-a-ble
im-pu-ta-tion
in-ad-vert-ent
in-am-o-ra-ta
in-an-i-mate
in-a-ni-tion
in-an-i-ty
in-au-gu-ra-tion
in-cal-cu-la-ble
in-ca-les-cent

in-can-des-cent
in-ca-pac-i-tate
in-car-cer-ate
in-car-nate
in-cen-di-ar-y
in-cen-tive
in-cep-tive
in-ces-tu-ous
in-cho-ate
in-ci-den-tal
in-cin-er-a-tor
in-cip-i-ent
in-ci-sive
in-ci-sor
in-cit-ant
in-ci-ta-tion
in-cit-er
in-clem-ent
in-clin-a-ble
in-cli-na-tion
in-cli-na-to-ry
in-cli-nom-e-ter
in-clud-a-ble
in-clu-sive
in-cog-ni-to
in-com-pa-ra-ble
in-com-pat-i-ble
in-con-cus-si-ble
in-con-gru-ous
in-cor-po-ra-tor
in-cor-ri-gi-ble
in-creas-er
in-cred-i-ble
in-cre-du-li-ty
in-cred-u-lous
in-cre-ment
in-crim-i-nate
in-crus-ta-tion
in-cu-ba-tor
in-cu-bous (adj.)
in-cu-bus (n.)
in-cum-bent
in-cu-nab-u-lum
in-cur-a-ble
in-cur-ra-ble
in-cur-sive
in-da-mine
in-da-zole
in-de-fat-i-ga-ble
in-dem-ni-fi-ca-tion
in-dene
in-den-ta-tion
in-dent-er

in-den-ture
in-de-pend-ent
in-de-struct-i-ble
In-di-an
In-di-an-a
In-di-an-ap-o-lis
In-di-an-i-an
in-di-can
in-di-ca-tion
in-dic-a-tive
in-di-ca-tor
in-di-ci-a
in-dic-o-lite
in-dict-a-ble
in-dict-er
In-dies
in-dig-e-nous
in-di-gent
in-di-gest-i-ble
in-di-go
in-dig-o-lite
In-di-go-sol
in-dig-o-tin
in-di-ru-bin
in-dis-pen-sa-ble
in-dis-pu-ta-ble
in-dis-sol-u-ble
in-di-um
in-di-vid-u-al-ize
in-di-vis-i-ble
in-doc-tri-nate
in-dole-a-ce-tic
in-do-lent
in-do-line
in-do-lyl
in-dom-i-ta-ble
In-do-ne-sian
in-do-phe-nin
in-dox-yl
in-du-bi-ta-ble
in-duc-er
in-duc-i-ble
in-duct-ance
in-duct-ee
in-duc-tive
in-duc-tom-e-ter
in-duc-tor
in-duc-to-ri-um
in-dul-gence
in-du-line
in-du-ra-tive
in-dus-tri-al-i-za-tion
in-e-bri-ate

in-ef-fa-ble
in-ef-face-a-ble
in-e-luc-ta-ble
in-ep-ti-tude
in-ert-ance
in-er-tial
in-ev-i-ta-ble
in-ex-o-ra-ble
in-ex-press-i-ble
in-ex-pres-sive
in-ex-pung-i-ble
in-ex-tir-pa-ble
in-ex-tri-ca-ble
in-fa-mous
in-fan-ti-cide
in-fan-tile
in-fan-try
in-fat-u-ate
in-fect-ant
in-fect-i-ble
in-fec-tious
in-fec-tive
in-fe-lic-i-tous
in-fer-a-ble
in-fer-ence
in-fe-ri-or-i-ty
in-fer-nal
in-fest-ant
in-fes-ta-tion
in-fil-tra-tor
in-fil-trom-e-ter
in-fi-nite
in-fin-i-tes-i-mal
in-fin-i-ti-val
in-fin-i-ty
in-fir-ma-ry
in-fir-mi-ty
in-flat-a-ble
in-flect-i-ble
in-flict-er
in-flo-res-cence
in-flu-en-tial
in-for-mal-i-ty
in-for-ma-lize
in-form-ant
in-for-ma-tion
in-form-a-tive
in-form-er
in-fract-i-ble
in-fran-gi-ble
in-fring-er
in-fun-dib-u-lum
in-fu-ri-ate

in-fu-si-ble
in-fu-so-ri-al
in-ge-nious
in-ge-nue
in-ge-nu-i-ty
in-gen-u-ous
in-ges-tant
in-got
in-gra-ti-ate
in-grat-i-tude
in-gra-ves-cence
in-grav-i-date
in-gre-di-ent
in-gui-nal
in-gur-gi-tate
in-hab-it-a-bil-i-ty
in-hab-it-ant
in-hab-it-er
in-hal-ant
in-ha-la-tion
in-ha-la-tor
in-her-ent
in-her-it-a-ble
in-her-it-ance
in-hib-it-er
in-hi-bi-tion
in-hib-i-tor (chem.)
in-hib-i-to-ry
in-hos-pit-a-ble
in-im-i-cal
in-im-i-ta-ble
in-iq-ui-tous
i-ni-tial
i-ni-ti-a-tive
in-jec-tor
in-junc-tive
in-ju-ri-ous
in-kling
in me-mo-ri-am
in-nas-ci-ble
in-noc-u-ous
in-no-va-to-ry
in-nu-en-do
in-nu-mer-a-ble
in-oc-u-late
in-or-di-nate
i-no-si-tol
in per-so-nam
in-quir-er
in-quir-y
in-qui-si-tion
in-quis-i-tive
in-sa-tia-ble

in-scrib-a-ble
in-scrib-er
in-scru-ta-ble
in-sec-ti-ci-dal
in-sec-tiv-o-ra
in-sec-tiv-o-rous
in-sec-tol-o-gy
in-sem-i-na-tion
in-sen-sate
in-ser-tive
in-sid-i-ous
in-sig-ne
in-sig-ni-a
in-sig-nif-i-cant
in-sip-id
in-si-pid-i-ty
in-sist-ence
in-sist-er
in-so-lence
in-sol-u-ble
in-sol-vent
in-sou-ci-ance
in-sou-ci-ant
in-spec-tor
In-spec-to-scope
in-spir-a-ble
in-spi-ra-tion
in-spir-a-tive
in-stal-la-tion
in-stalled
in-stan-ta-ne-ous
in-sti-ga-tor
in-stinc-tive
in-sti-tu-tor
in-struct-i-ble
in-struc-tive
in-struc-tor
in-stru-men-tal-i-ty
in-su-lar
in-su-la-tor
in-su-lin
in-su-per-a-ble
in-sur-ance
in-sur-er
in-sur-gen-cy
in-tagl-io
in-tan-gi-ble
in-te-ger
in-te-gral
in-te-gra-tor
in-teg-ri-ty
in-teg-u-men-tal
in-tel-lec-tu-al

in-tel-li-gen-tsi-a
in-tend-ant
in-ten-si-fy
in-ten-si-tom-e-ter
in-ten-si-ty
in-ten-sive
in-ter-ca-lar-y
in-ter-cede
in-ter-cep-tor
in-ter-cos-tal
in-ter-est
in-ter-fer-ence
in-ter-fer-om-e-ter
in-ter-im
in-te-ri-or
in-ter-jec-tor
in-ter-jec-tur-al
in-ter-lin-gua
in-ter-loc-u-to-ry
in-ter-lop-er
in-ter-me-di-ate
in-ter-mi-na-ble
in-tern
in-ter-nal
in-ter-ne-cine
in-ter-nist
in-ter-po-lat-er
in-ter-pret-a-ble
in-ter-pre-ta-tive
in-ter-pret-er
in-ter-pre-tive
in-ter-ro-gate
in-ter-rog-a-to-ry
in-ter-rupt-ed
in-ter-rupt-er
in-ter-rupt-i-ble
in-ter-rupt-ing
in-ter-stic-es
in-ter-sti-tial
in-ter-ven-er
in-ter-ve-nor (law)
in-tes-tate
in-tes-ti-nal
in-ti-ma-cy
in-ti-mat-er
in-tim-i-da-tor
in-to-nate
In-tox-im-e-ter
in-trac-ta-ble
in-tran-si-gent (n., adj.)
in-trav-a-sa-tion
in-tra-ve-nous
in-trep-id

in-tre-pid-i-ty
in-tri-ca-cy
in-trigu-er
in-trigu-ing
in-trin-si-cal
in-tro-duc-to-ry
in-tro-spec-tive
in-tro-ver-si-ble
in-trud-er
in-tru-sive
in-tu-i-tive
in-tu-mes-cence
in-u-lase
in-un-da-tor
in-vad-er
in-va-lid (n., v., adj., not well)
in-val-id (adj., not valid)
in-val-i-date
in-va-lid-i-ty
in-var-i-a-ble
in-vec-tive
in-vei-gle
in-vent-a-ble
in-ven-tor
in-ven-to-ry
in-vert-ase
in-ver-te-brate
in-vert-er
in-vert-i-ble
in-ver-tor (muscle)
in-ves-ti-ga-tor
in-ves-ti-ture
in-ves-tor
in-vet-er-ate
in-vid-i-ous
in-vig-o-rate
in-vin-ci-ble
in-vi-o-la-ble
in-vis-i-ble
in-vi-ta-tion
in-vit-er
in-vo-ca-tion
in-voc-a-tive
in-vo-lu-cre
i-o-di-nate
i-o-dine
i-o-din-oph-i-lous
i-o-do-a-ce-tic
i-o-do-form
i-o-do-hy-drin
i-o-dom-e-try
i-o-do-ni-um
i-o-do-phthal-ein

i-o-do-pyr-a-cet
i-o-dox-y-ben-zene
i-od-y-rite
I-o-ni-an
I-on-ic
i-o-ni-um
i-on-i-za-tion
i-o-nom-e-ter
i-o-none
i-on-o-spher-ic
I-o-wan
ip-e-cac
I-ra-ni-an
i-ras-ci-ble
ir-i-dec-to-my
ir-i-des-cence
i-rid-ic
i-rid-i-um
i-ron-i-cal
i-ron-y (of iron)
i-ro-ny (sarcasm)
Ir-o-quois
ir-ra-di-ate
ir-rad-i-ca-ble
ir-rec-on-cil-a-ble
ir-re-duc-i-ble
ir-ref-ra-ga-ble
ir-re-fu-ta-ble
ir-re-me-di-a-ble
ir-rep-a-ra-ble
ir-re-press-i-ble
ir-re-sist-i-ble
ir-re-spon-si-ble
ir-re-vers-i-ble
ir-rev-o-ca-ble
ir-ri-ga-ble
ir-ri-tant
i-sa-go-ge
i-sa-gog-ics
I-sa-iah
i-sa-tin-ic
is-che-mi-a
i-sin-glass
Is-lam-ic

is-land-er
is-let
i-so-am-yl-ene
i-so-bar-ic
i-so-bath-y-therm
i-soch-ro-nal
i-so-chrone
i-soch-ro-nism
i-so-cla-site
i-so-cli-nal
i-so-drin
i-sog-a-mous
i-so-gly-co-sa-mine
i-sog-o-nal
i-so-gon-ic
i-so-lat-a-ble
i-so-leu-cine
i-so-mer-ic
i-som-er-ize
i-so-met-ri-cal-ly
i-som-e-try
i-so-ni-a-zid
i-so-phthal-ic
i-so-pre-noid
i-so-pro-pe-nyl
i-so-pro-pyl
i-sos-ce-les
i-sos-ta-sy
i-so-ther-mal
i-so-top-ic
i-so-to-py
i-so-tron
Is-rae-li
Is-ra-el-ite
Is-tan-bul
isth-mus
it-a-con-ic
I-tal-ian
i-tal-i-cize
i-tem-ize
it-er-ate
i-tin-er-ar-y
i-vo-ry

J

ja-bot	jin-rik-i-sha
jack-al	jock-ey
jack-a-napes	jo-cos-i-ty
jack-et	joc-u-lar
Ja-cob	joc-und
Jac-o-be-an	jo-cun-di-ty
Ja-co-bi-an	jodh-pur
Jac-o-bin	joh-nin
jac-o-net	John-ston
jac-quard	join-der
Jacque-mi-not	joint-er
jag-uar	join-ture
jal-ap	jok-er
ja-lop-y	joke-ster
jal-ou-sie	Jo-nah
Ja-mai-can	jon-quil
jam-bo-ree	Jor-da-ni-an
jan-gling	jo-se-ite
jan-i-tor	Jo-seph
Jan-u-ar-y	Jo-se-phine
Ja-nus	Josh-u-a
Ja-pan	jos-tled
Jap-a-nese	jos-tling
ja-panned	jour-nal-ist
ja-pon-i-ca	jour-ney
jar-di-niere	jo-vi-al-i-ty
jar-gon-ize	ju-bi-lant
jar-ring	ju-bi-la-tion
jas-mine	Ju-da-ism
jas-per	judg-ment
jaun-dice	ju-di-ca-to-ry
jaunt-i-ly	ju-di-ca-ture
jav-a-nese	ju-di-cial
Jav-a-nese	ju-di-ci-ar-y
jeal-ous-y	ju-di-cious
Jef-fer-so-ni-an	ju-gal
Je-ho-vah	jug-gler
je-ju-nos-to-my	jug-gling
je-ju-num	jug-u-lar
Je-kyll	ju-jit-su
jeop-ard-ize	ju-jube
jeop-ard-y	Ju-lian
Je-ru-sa-lem	ju-li-enne
jes-sa-mine	Ju-li-et
Jes-u-it	Ju-lius
Je-sus	jum-bled
jew-eled	jump-er
Jez-e-bel	junc-tur-al
jin-gling	Ju-neau

jun-ior
ju-nior-i-ty
ju-ni-per
Jun-ius
Jun-ker
junk-er
jun-ket-eer
Ju-pi-ter
Ju-ras-sic
ju-rat
ju-rid-i-cal
ju-ris-dic-tion

ju-ris-pru-dence
ju-ris-tic
ju-ror
jus-tice
jus-ti-ci-a-ble
jus-ti-fi-ca-tion
jus-tif-i-ca-to-ry
ju-ve-nes-cence
ju-ve-nile
ju-ve-nil-i-ty
jux-ta-po-si-tion

K

Kad-iak
Kaf-fir
kai-nite
kai-nos-ite
kai-ser
ka-lei-do-scop-ic
kal-i-bo-rite
ka-lic-i-nite
ka-lig-e-nous
Kal-i-spell
ka-mi-ka-ze
kan-ga-roo
Kan-san
ka-o-lin-ic
ka-o-lin-ite
ka-pok
Ka-ra-chi
kar-y-o-gam-ic
kar-y-og-a-my
kar-y-o-ki-ne-sis
kar-y-ol-o-gy
kar-y-ol-y-sis
kar-y-o-mi-to-sis
kar-y-o-some
ka-tab-a-sis
kat-a-bat-ic
Ka-tan-gan
Kath-a-rine
ka-ty-did
kay-ak
keep-er
ken-o-tron
Ken-tuck-i-an
Ken-yan

ker-a-tin
ke-rat-i-nous
ker-a-ti-tis
Ker-a-tol
ker-a-tol-y-sis
ker-a-to-sis
ker-chiefed
ker-mes-ite
ker-neled
ker-o-gen
ker-o-sene
ker-sey
ke-ta-zine
Ketch-i-can
ke-tene
ke-ti-mine
ke-to-gen-e-sis
ke-to-glu-tar-ic
ke-tol-y-sis
ke-to-lyt-ic
ke-tone
ke-to-side
ke-to-sis
Keynes-i-an
kha-ki
Khar-toum
khe-dive
Khru-shchev
kib-itz
ki-bosh
kid-nap-er
kie-sel-guhr
kill-er
kil-o-cy-cle

kil-o-me-ter
kil-o-ton
kil-o-watt
ki-mo-no
ki-nase
kin-der-gar-ten
kin-der-gart-ner
kind-li-ness
kin-dling
kin-dred
kin-e-mat-ics
kin-e-scope
ki-ne-si-at-rics
ki-ne-sics
kin-e-sim-e-ter
ki-ne-si-o-log-ic
ki-ne-si-ol-o-gy
kin-es-the-si-a
ki-net-ic
ki-ne-to-phone
ki-ne-to-scope
kin-e-to-sis
Kings-ton
Kirch-hoff
Kirsch-ner
kitch-en-ette
Kjel-dahl
Klam-ath (river, etc.)
Klee-nex
klep-to-ma-ni-a
klys-tron
knav-ish
knick-er-bock-er

knock-er
knowl-edge-a-ble
knuck-led
ko-gas-in
Koh-i-noor
kohl-ra-bi
ko-jic
kok-sa-ghyz
ko-lin-sky
kol-khoz
Kom-man-da-tu-ra
ko-nim-e-ter
ko-ni-ol-o-gy
Koo-te-nay
ko-peck
Ko-ran
Ko-re-an
ko-ru-na
ko-sher
kreu-zer
kro-nen
kro-ner
kryp-ton
ku-lak
Kuo-min-tang
kur-to-sis
Ku-wait
Ku-wai-ti
Kwaj-a-lein
kwa-shi-or-kor
ky-mo-graph
ky-mog-ra-phy
kyn-u-ren-ine

L

lab-a-rum
lab-e-fac-tion
la-beled
la-bel-er
la-bi-al
la-bile
la-bi-lize
la-bi-um
lab-o-ra-to-ry
la-bor-er
la-bo-ri-ous
lab-ra-dor-ite
la-bur-num
lab-y-rin-thine

lac-er-ate
lach-es
lach-ry-mose
lack-a-dai-si-cal
la-con-ic
lac-o-nism
lac-quer
lac-ri-mal
la-crosse
lac-tal-bu-min
lac-tase
lac-te-al
lac-tes-cent
lac-tif-er-ous

lac-to-fla-vin
lac-tom-e-ter
lac-tose
la-cu-na
la-cus-trine
lad-en-ing
lad-ing
la-di-no
la-dler
la-drone
La-fay-ette
la-ger
la-gniappe
la-goon-al
la-gu-na
lai-tance
la-lop-a-thy
la-ma-ser-y
lam-bent
lam-bre-quin
la-mel-lar
lam-el-late
la-mel-lose
la-ment
lam-en-ta-ble
lam-en-ta-tion
lam-i-na-graph
lam-i-nag-ra-phy
lam-i-nal
lam-i-nar-in
lam-i-nate
lam-i-na-tor
lam-i-ni-tis
lam-poon
lam-prey
la-nat-o-side
Lan-ce-lot
lan-ce-o-lar
lanc-er
lan-cet
lan-ci-nate
lan-dau-let
Lang-shan
lan-guage
lan-guish
lan-guor-ous
lan-o-ce-ric
lan-o-lin
la-nos-ter-ol
Lan-ston
lan-tern
lan-tha-nide
lan-tha-num

lan-thi-o-nine
lap-a-rot-o-my
la-pel-er
lap-i-dar-y
la-pis
lap-is la-zu-li
La-o-tian
Lar-a-mie
lar-ce-nous
lar-da-ceous
lar-der
larg-er
lar-gess
larg-est
lar-i-at
lar-va
lar-vi-cid-al
lar-vic-o-lous
lar-viv-o-rous
la-ryn-ge-al
lar-yn-gec-to-my
lar-yn-git-ic
lar-yn-gi-tis
la-ryn-go-log-i-cal
lar-yn-gol-o-gy
la-ryn-go-scope
lar-yn-gos-co-py
lar-yn-got-o-my
lar-ynx
las-civ-i-ous
las-si-tude
Lat-a-ki-a
la-teen
la-ten-cy
lat-er
lat-er-al
lat-er-ite
la-tes-cent
lat-est
la-tex
lath-er-ing
lat-i-cif-er-ous
Lat-in-ize
la-tite
lat-i-tu-di-nous
la-trine
laud-a-ble
lau-dan-i-dine
lau-da-nine
lau-dan-o-sine
lau-da-num
laud-a-to-ry
launch-er

laun-der
Laun-der-om-e-ter
laun-dress
Laun-dro-mat
lau-rate
lau-re-ate
lau-reled
Lau-rence
Lau-ren-tian
lau-ric
lau-ro-len-ic
lau-ryl
la-vage
lav-a-liere
lav-a-to-ry
lav-en-der
lav-ish
Law-rence
law-renc-ite
lay-ette
Laz-a-rus
la-zi-ly
laz-u-rite
lead-er
lea-guer
leak-age
learn-ed (adj.)
leath-er-ine
leav-en
Leb-a-nese
le-bens-raum
lech-er-ous
lec-i-thin-ase
lec-tern
lec-tur-er
ledg-er
le-dol
leg-a-cy
le-gal-i-ty
le-gal-ize
leg-ate (n.)
le-gate (v.)
leg-a-tee
le-ga-tion
leg-end-ar-y
leg-er-de-main
le-ger-i-ty
leg-i-ble
le-gion-naire
leg-is-la-tive
leg-is-la-tor
leg-is-la-to-ri-al
le-git-i-ma-cy

leg-ume
le-gu-mi-nous
Leices-ter
leish-ma-ni-a-sis
lei-sure
lem-on-ade
lender
length-en
le-ni-en-cy
len-i-ty
Lent-en
len-ti-cel
len-tic-u-lar
len-ti-go
len-til
Leom-in-ster
Leon-ard
Le-o-nar-desque
le-o-nine
leop-ard
lep-er
lep-i-do-cro-cite
le-pid-o-lite
Lep-i-dop-ter-a
lep-i-do-sis
lep-rol-o-gy
lep-ro-sar-i-um
le-pro-sis
lep-ro-sy
lep-rous
lep-to-ceph-a-lus
lep-to-mat-ic
lep-to-spi-ro-sis
le-sion
Le-so-tho
les-pe-de-za
les-see
less-en
less-er
les-son
les-sor
le-thal
leth-ane
le-thar-gic
leth-ar-gy
leu-cite
leu-con-ic
leu-cop-te-rin
leu-co-sin
leu-co-sphe-nite
leu-cot-o-my
leu-cov-o-rin
leu-ke-mi-a

leu-ke-mic
leu-ker-gy
leu-ko-cyte
leu-ko-cyt-ic
leu-ko-cy-to-sis
leu-ko-poi-e-sis
leu-ko-poi-et-ic
leu-kor-rhe-a
leu-ko-sis
lev-an
Le-vant
Le-vant-er
Le-van-tine
le-va-tor
le-vee (reception)
lev-ee (dam)
lev-el-er
le-ver
le-ver-age
le-vi-a-than
lev-i-ga-tor
lev-i-tat-ing
lev-i-ty
le-vo-glu-co-san
lev-u-li-nate
lev-u-lin-ic
lev-u-lose
lev-y-ing
lew-is-ite
lex-i-cog-ra-pher
lex-i-co-graph-ic
lex-i-cog-ra-phy
lex-ig-ra-phy
li-ai-son
li-bel-ant
li-beled
li-bel-ous
lib-er-al-i-ty
lib-er-a-tor
lib-er-tar-i-an
lib-er-tine
lib-er-ty
li-bid-i-nous
li-bi-do
Li-bra
li-brar-i-an
li-bra-to-ry
li-bret-to
Lib-y-an
li-can-ic
li-cens-a-ble
li-censed
li-cens-ee

li-cens-er
li-cen-sor
li-cen-tious
li-chen-in
lic-o-rice
lid-o-caine
Lie-der-kranz
lien-ee
lien-or
lieu-ten-an-cy
lift-er
lig-a-men-tous
li-ga-tion
lig-a-ture
light-ened
light-en-ing (brightening)
light-er-age
light-ning (a flash)
lig-ne-ous
lig-nes-cent
lig-nite
lig-num vi-tae
lig-ro-in
lig-u-lar
lik-a-ble
lik-en
li-la-ceous
lil-li-pu-tian
lim-ber
Lim-burg-er
lime-ade
li-mic-o-lous
lim-i-ta-tion
lim-it-ed
li-miv-o-rous
lim-ner
lim-nim-e-ter
lim-nol-o-gy
Li-moges
lim-o-nene
li-mo-nite
lim-ou-sine
lim-pid-i-ty
lin-a-ble
lin-age
lin-al-o-ol
lin-a-mar-in
Lin-coln
lin-dane
lin-e-age
lin-e-al
lin-e-a-ment
lin-e-ar-i-ty

lin-en
lin-e-o-late
lin-er
lin-ger
lin-ge-rie
lin-gual
lin-guis-tics
lin-guist-ry
link-age

Lin-nae-us
li-no-le-ate
lin-o-le-ic
li-no-le-in
lin-o-le-nic
li-no-le-um
Li-no-type
li-nox-yn
lin-tel
lint-er
li-on-ess
li-on-ize
lip-a-rid
li-pe-mi-a
lip-ide
lip-i-do-sis
lip-o-chon-dri-on
lip-o-fus-cin
li-pog-e-nous
li-po-ic
lip-oi-do-sis
li-pol-y-sis
lip-o-lyt-ic
li-po-ma-to-sis
li-po-si-tol
lip-o-trop-ic
li-qua-tion
liq-ue-fa-cient
liq-ue-fy
li-ques-cent
li-queur
liq-uid
liq-ui-da-tor
li-quid-i-ty
liq-ui-dus
liq-uor
liroc-o-nite
lis-e-ran
lisp-er
lis-ten-er
lis-ter-el-lo-sis
lis-te-ri-a
lis-ter-ize
lit-a-ny

li-tchi
li-ter
lit-er-al-ly
lit-e-ra-ti
lit-e-ra-tim
lit-er-a-ture
lith-arge
li-the-mi-a
lith-i-a

li-thi-a-sis
li-thid-i-o-nite
lith-i-um
lith-o-cho-lic
lith-o-graph
li-thog-ra-pher
lith-o-graph-ic
li-thog-ra-phy
lith-ol-a-pax-y
lith-o-log-ic
li-thol-o-gy
lith-o-pone
lith-o-sol
li-thot-o-my
li-thot-ri-ty
Lith-u-a-ni-an
li-thu-ri-a
lit-i-ga-ble
lit-i-ga-tor
li-ti-gious
lit-ter-a-teur
lit-to-ral
li-tur-gi-cal
lit-ur-gy
liv-a-ble
live-li-hood
liv-er-y
liv-id
Liv-ing-stone
Li-vo-ni-an
lix-iv-i-ate
liz-ard
lla-ma
load-er
load-om-e-ter
loaf-er
loath-er
lo-bar
lo-bate
lob-bied
lo-bec-to-my
lo-be-li-a
lo-be-line
lo-bot-o-my

lob-u-lar
lob-u-lose
lo-cale
lo-cal-i-ty
lo-cal-iz-er
lo-cant
lo-cat-er
loc-a-tive
lo-ca-tor
lock-age
lock-er
lo-co-mo-tive
loc-u-late
lo-cust
lodg-er
lo-ga-nin
log-a-rith-mic
log-i-cal
lo-gi-cian
lo-gis-ti-cian
lo-gis-tics
log-o-gram-mat-ic
lo-gom-a-chy
log-o-pe-dic
log-o-type
loi-ter
lol-li-pop
Lom-bar-dy
lone-li-ness
long-er
lon-ger (cask)
lon-ge-ron
long-est
lon-gev-i-ty
lon-gi-fo-lene
lon-gi-tu-di-nal
loos-en
loot-er
lo-phine
lop-sid-ed
lo-qua-cious
lo-quac-i-ty
lo-ran
lor-gnette
Los An-ge-les
los-er
los-ing
loss-er
Lo-thar-i-o
Lou-i-si-an-i-an
lous-i-ness
lou-ver
lov-a-ble

lox-o-drom-ic
loy-al-ist
loz-enge
lu-bri-ca-tor
lu-bric-i-ty
lu-cid-i-ty
Lu-ci-fer
lu-cif-er-ase
lu-cite
lu-cra-tive
lu-cu-brate
lu-di-crous
lu-gu-bri-ous
lum-bar
lu-men
lu-miere
lu-mi-fla-vin
lu-mi-naire
lu-mi-nar-y
lu-mi-nes-cence
lu-mi-nif-er-ous
lu-mi-nom-e-ter
lu-mi-nos-i-ty
lu-mi-nous
lu-mis-ter-ol
lu-na-cy
lu-nar-i-an
lu-na-tic
lunch-eon
lu-nette
lu-nik
lu-nu-late
lu-pet-i-dine
lu-pin-ine
lu-pu-lone
lu-rid
lus-cious
Lu-si-ta-ni-a
lus-ter (shine)
lust-er (n.) (one who lusts)
lus-trous
lu-te-in-ize
lu-te-o-lin
lu-te-o-vi-res-cent
lu-te-ti-um
Lu-ther-an
lu-ti-din-ic
Lux-em-bourg-er
lux-u-ri-ant
lux-u-ri-ous
ly-ce-um
ly-co-pene
lydd-ite

lymph-ad-e-ni-tis
lymph-ad-e-nop-a-thy
lym-phan-gi-al
lym-phat-ic
lym-pho-cyte
lymph-oid
lym-pho-ma-to-sis

ly-o-phil-ic
ly-oph-i-lize
lyr-i-cal
ly-ser-gic
ly-sim-e-ter
ly-sine
ly-so-gen-ic

M

ma-ca-bre
mac-ad-am-ize
mac-a-ro-ni
mac-a-ron-ic
mac-a-roon
Ma-cas-sar
ma-caw
Mac-ca-be-an
Mac-e-do-ni-an
mac-er-a-tor
ma-che-te
Mach-i-a-vel-li-an
ma-chi-nal
mach-i-na-tion
ma-chin-er-y
ma-chin-ist
mack-er-el
mack-in-tosh
mac-ro-bi-o-sis
mac-ro-cosm
mac-ro-cy-clic
mac-ro-cy-to-sis
mac-ro-mol-e-cule
ma-cron
ma-crop-si-a
mac-ro-scop-ic
mac-u-la-ture
mad-am
ma-dame
Ma-dei-ra
ma-de-moi-selle
ma-don-na
Ma-dras
Ma-drid
mad-ri-gal
mael-strom
mae-stro
Ma-fi-a
maf-ic

mag-a-zine
Mag-da-len
Mag-de-burg
ma-gen-ta
mag-i-cal
ma-gi-cian
Ma-gi-not
ma-gis-ter
mag-is-te-ri-al
mag-is-tra-cy
mag-na-nim-i-ty
mag-nan-i-mous
mag-ne-sia
mag-ne-si-o-chro-mite
mag-ne-site
mag-ne-si-um
mag-ne-syn
mag-net-i-cal-ly
mag-net-ism
mag-net-ite
mag-net-ize
mag-ne-to-graph
mag-ne-tom-e-ter
mag-ne-to-met-ric
mag-ne-tom-e-try
mag-ne-tos
mag-ne-tron
mag-ni-fi-ca-tion
mag-nif-i-cence
mag-ni-fy
mag-nil-o-quent
mag-ni-tude
mag-no-lia
ma-guey
mah-jong
ma-hog-a-ny
Ma-hom-et
maid-en
mail-er

Main-er
main-te-nance
mai-so-nette
mai-tre d'ho-tel
ma-jes-tic
maj-es-ty
ma-jol-i-ca
ma-jor-i-ty
maj-us-cule
ma-jus-cu-lar
mak-er
mal-a-chite
mal-a-dy
Mal-a-ga
Mal-a-gas-y
mal-a-gue-na
mal-aise
ma-lar
ma-lar-i-al
ma-lar-i-om-e-try
mal-a-thi-on
Ma-la-wi
Ma-lay-an
Ma-lay-sian
ma-le-ate
mal-e-dic-tion
mal-e-fac-tor
ma-lef-i-cent
ma-le-ic
ma-lev-o-lent
mal-fea-sance
Ma-li-an
mal-ic
mal-ice
ma-li-cious
ma-lif-er-ous
ma-lign
ma-lig-nant
ma-lin-ger
mal-le-a-ble
mal-o-nate
ma-lo-nic
malt-ase
Mal-tese
mal-tha
Mal-thu-sian
malt-ose
mam-ma-li-an
mam-ma-lif-er-ous
mam-mal-o-gy
mam-ma-ry
mam-mif-er-ous
man-a-cle

man-age-a-ble
man-ag-er
man-e-ge-ri-al
Ma-na-gua
ma-ña-na
man-a-tee
Man-chu-ri-an
man-da-mus
man-da-rin-ate
man-da-to-ry
man-del-ate
man-di-ble
man-dib-u-lar
man-do-lin-ist
man-drake
man-drel
ma-nege
ma-neu-ver
man-ga-nate
man-ga-nese
man-gan-ic
man-ga-nif-er-ous
man-ga-nin
man-ga-nite
man-ga-no-site
man-ga-nous
man-ger
man-gler
man-gy
ma-ni-ac
ma-ni-a-cal
ma-ni-co-ba
man-i-cur-ist
man-i-fes-tant
man-i-fes-ta-tion
man-i-fold-er
man-i-kin
Ma-nil-a
ma-nil-la
man-i-oc
ma-nip-u-la-tor
man-nu-ron-ic
ma-nom-e-ter
man-o-met-ric
ma-nom-e-try
man-or
ma-no-ri-al
man-o-stat
man-sard
man-tel (arch)
man-tle (garment)
man-tling
man-u-al

man-u-duc-to-ry
man-u-fac-tur-er
ma-nure
ma-quette
ma-quis
mar-a-bou
ma-rac-a
mar-a-schi-no
ma-ras-mus
ma-raud-er
mar-bled
mar-ble-ize
mar-ca-site
mar-che-se
mar-chion-ess
mar-ga-rate
Mar-ga-ret
mar-gar-ic
mar-ga-rin
mar-ga-rite
mar-ga-ro-san-ite
mar-gin-al
mar-gi-na-li-a
mar-gin-ate
mar-gue-rite
Mar-i-an
Mar-i-co-pa
mar-i-gold
mar-i-hua-na
ma-rim-ba
ma-ri-na
ma-rine
mar-i-ner
Ma-ri-nist (of Marin)
ma-rin-ist (sea)
ma-ri-no-ra-ma
mar-i-o-nette
mar-i-tal
ma-rit-i-cide
mar-i-time
mar-jo-ram
Mar-jo-ry
mark-er
mar-ket-er
mar-la-ceous
marl-ite
mar-ma-lade
mar-mo-ra-ceous
mar-mo-re-al
mar-mo-set
ma-roon
mar-que-try
mar-quis

mar-qui-sette
mar-riage-a-ble
Mar-seil-laise
Mar-seilles
mar-shaled
mar-shal-er
mar-su-pi-al-ize
mar-tens-ite
mar-tial
mar-ti-net
mar-tin-gale
Mar-ti-ni
mar-tite
mar-tyr-ize
mar-vel-ous
Mar-y-land-er
Ma-sa-ryk
mas-cu-lin-i-ty
mask-er
mas-och-ism
mas-och-is-tic
Ma-son-ite
ma-son-ry
masqu-er
mas-quer-ade
Mas-sa-chu-setts-an
mas-sa-cred
mas-sag-er
mas-sive
mast-er (with masts)
mas-ter (owner, etc.)
mas-tic
mas-ti-cate
mas-tiff
mas-tit-ic
mas-ti-tis
mas-to-don
mas-toi-dal
mas-toid-i-tis
mas-toid-ot-o-my
ma-su-ri-um
mat-a-dor
mat-er
ma-te-ri-al-ize
ma-te-ri-a med-i-ca
ma-te-ri-el
ma-ter-ni-ty
math-e-mat-i-cal
math-e-ma-ti-cian
math-e-mat-ics
ma-thet-ic
mat-in-al
mat-i-nee

ma-tri-ar-chal
mat-ri-ces
ma-tri-ci-dal
ma-tric-u-late
mat-ri-mo-ni-al
ma-trix
ma-tron
mat-ro-nym-ic
mat-u-ra-tion
mat-u-ra-tive
ma-tu-ri-ty
ma-tu-ti-nal
mat-zoth
maud-lin
maul-er
maun-der
Mau-re-ta-ni-an
Mau-rice
Mau-ri-ti-us (island)
Mau-ser
mau-so-le-um
mau-vine
mav-er-ick
mawk-ish
max-i-miz-er
max-i-mum
may-on-naise
may-or-al-ty
maz-a-rine
ma-zur-ka
mea-con-ing
mead-ow
mea-ger
meal-y-mouthed
me-an-der
mea-sles
mea-sly
meas-ur-a-ble
meas-ured
me-a-tus
me-cap-rine
me-chan-i-cal
mech-a-ni-cian
mech-a-nism
mech-a-ni-za-tion
mech-a-no-mor-phic
me-com-e-ter
me-con-ic
mec-o-nin
me-co-ni-um
med-aled
med-al-ist
me-dal-lion

med-dler
me-di-an
me-di-as-ti-ni-tis
me-di-as-ti-num
me-di-a-tor
me-di-ca-ble
med-ic-aid
med-i-cal
me-dic-a-ment
med-i-care
Med-i-ci
me-dic-i-nal
med-i-cine
me-di-e-val
Me-di-na
me-di-o-cre
me-di-oc-ri-ty
med-i-ta-tive
Med-i-ter-ra-ne-an
me-di-um
me-dul-la
med-ul-lar-y
meer-schaum
meg-a-lo-ma-ni-a
meg-a-lop-o-lis
meg-a-lo-pol-i-tan
meg-a-phone
meg-a-ton
meg-ohm-me-ter
me-grim
mei-o-nite
mei-ot-ic
mei-ster
me-lac-o-nite
mel-a-mine
mel-an-cho-li-a
mel-an-chol-y
me-lange
me-lan-ger
me-lan-ic
mel-a-nin
mel-a-no-ma-to-sis
mel-a-no-sis
mel-a-no-stib-i-an
me-lan-ter-ite
me-lee
me-lez-i-tose
mel-i-bi-ose
mel-i-lite
me-lio-ra-tive
Me-lis-sa
mel-i-tose
mel-lif-lu-ous

mel-li-tate
mel-lit-ic
me-lod-ic
me-lo-di-on
me-lo-di-ous
mel-o-dra-ma
mel-o-dy
mel-o-ma-ni-a
mel-o-nite
mel-o-plas-ty
melt-er
mem-bra-nate
mem-bra-nous
me-men-tos
mem-oir
mem-o-ra-ble
mem-o-ran-dums
me-mo-ri-al-iz-ing
mem-o-riz-er
men-ace
men-a-di-one
me-nag-er-ie
me-naph-thone
men-da-cious
men-dac-i-ty
men-de-le-vi-um
Men-de-li-an
men-de-lye-ev-ite
mend-er
men-di-cant
men-dic-i-ty
men-ha-den
me-ni-al
Me-ni-ere
men-i-lite
me-nin-ge-al
me-nin-gi-o-ma
men-in-git-ic
men-in-gi-tis
me-nin-go-cele
me-nin-go-coc-cus
me-nin-go-my-e-li-tis
me-nis-cus
Men-non-ite
Me-nom-i-nee
men-o-pau-sal
me-no-rah
men-ses
men-stru-al
men-su-ra-ble
men-su-ral
men-su-ra-tion
men-tal-i-ty

men-tha-di-ene
men-thane
men-tha-nol
men-the-none
men-tho-lat-ed
men-thyl
men-ti-cide
me-per-i-dine
me-phen-e-sin
Meph-is-to-phe-li-an
me-phit-ic
me-phi-tis
me-pro-ba-mate
mer-al-lu-ride
mer-can-tile
mer-cap-to
mer-cap-tom-er-in
mer-cap-tu-ric
Mer-ca-tor
mer-ce-nar-y
mer-cer-ize
mer-chan-dise
mer-chant-a-ble
mer-cu-rate
mer-cu-ri-al
mer-cu-ric
mer-cu-rous
me-ren-gue
me-re-ol-o-gy
mer-e-tri-cious
mer-gan-ser
mer-gence
Mer-gen-tha-ler
merg-er
me-rid-i-an
me-rid-i-o-nal
me-ringue
me-ri-nos
mer-it-ed
mer-i-to-ri-ous
mer-o-crine
mer-o-gon-ic
me-rog-o-ny
mer-o-he-dral
Mer-o-pe
me-ro-pi-a
me-rot-o-mize
me-rox-ene
mer-sal-yl
Mer-thi-o-late
mes-al-liance
mes-ar-te-ri-tis
mes-en-ce-phal-ic

mes-en-ceph-a-lon
mes-en-chy-ma
mes-en-chym-a-tous
mes-en-chyme
mes-en-ter-ic
mes-en-ter-i-tis
me-sic
mes-i-dine
mes-i-tyl
me-sit-y-lene
mes-mer-ism
mes-o-blast
mes-o-car-di-a
mes-o-ce-phal-ic
mes-o-derm
mes-o-lite
mes-o-mer-ic
me-som-er-ism
mes-on
mes-o-phyll
mes-o-sphere
mes-ox-al-ic
mes-ox-a-lyl
Mes-o-zo-ic
mes-quite
mes-sage
mes-sen-ger
mes-si-an-ic
mes-ti-zos
mes-yl
me-tab-a-sis
met-a-bi-o-sis
met-a-bi-ot-ic
met-a-bol-ic
me-tab-o-lism
me-tab-o-liz-a-ble
met-a-bo-rate
met-a-car-pus
me-tag-ra-phy
met-al-de-hyde
me-tal-lic
met-al-lif-er-ous
met-al-lize
met-al-log-ra-phy
met-al-lur-gi-cal
met-al-os-co-py
met-a-mer-ic
me-tam-er-ism
met-a-mor-phism
met-a-mor-pho-sis
met-a-phor-i-cal
met-a-phys-ics
met-ar-te-ri-ole

met-a-so-ma-to-sis
met-a-sta-ble
me-tas-ta-sis
me-tath-e-sis
me-tem-psy-cho-sis
me-te-or-ic
me-te-or-ite
me-te-or-it-ics
me-te-or-o-graph
me-te-or-og-ra-phy
me-te-or-oid
me-te-or-o-log-i-cal
me-te-or-ol-o-gist
me-te-or-ol-o-gy
me-te-or-om-e-ter
me-te-or-o-scope
me-te-or-os-co-py
me-ter
meth-ac-ry-late
meth-a-cryl-ic
meth-a-done
meth-al-lyl
meth-ane
meth-a-nol
meth-a-no-lic
meth-a-nol-y-sis
meth-a-nom-e-ter
meth-an-the-line
me-the-na-mine
meth-ene
meth-ide
meth-i-on-ic
me-thi-o-nine
me-thi-um
meth-od
me-thod-i-cal
Meth-od-ist
meth-od-ize
meth-od-ol-o-gy
me-tho-ni-um
meth-ox-ide
me-thox-y-car-bon-yl
meth-ox-yl
Me-thu-se-lah
meth-yl-a-mine
meth-yl-ate
meth-yl-ene
meth-yl-en-i-mine
meth-yl-eth-yl-pyr-i-dine
me-thyl-i-dyne
meth-yl-naph-tha-lene
meth-yl-ol-u-re-a
me-tic-u-lous

me-tier
me-ton-y-my
me-top-ic
met-o-pon
met-o-pos-co-py
Met-ra-zol
met-ric
met-ri-cal
me-tri-tis
me-trol-o-gy
met-ro-nome
me-tro-nym-ic
met-ro-pole
me-trop-o-lis
met-ro-pol-i-tan
mev-a-lon-ic
mez-za-nine
mho-me-ter
mi-ar-gy-rite
mi-ca-ceous
mi-cel-lar
mi-celle
Mi-chael
Mich-ael-mas
Mich-i-gan-ite
mi-cri-nite
mi-cro-bi-al
mi-cro-cosm
mi-crog-ra-phy
mi-cro-lite
mi-cro-me-rit-ics
mi-crom-e-ter
mi-cro-met-ri-cal
mi-crom-e-try
mi-cro-mho
mi-cron-ize
mi-cro-phon-ic
mi-crop-si-a
mi-cro-scop-ic
mi-cros-co-py
mi-crot-o-my
mid-dling
midg-et
mi-gnon-ette
mi-graine
mi-grain-oid
mi-grant
mi-gra-tet-ics
mi-gra-to-ry
mi-ka-do
Mi-lan
Mil-a-nese
mil-i-a-ri-a

mil-i-ar-y
mi-lieu
mil-i-tant
mil-i-ta-rism
mil-i-tate
mi-li-tia
milk-er
mil-le-nar-y
mil-len-ni-um
mill-er
mil-les-i-mal
mil-let
mil-li-am-me-ter
mil-li-ner-y
mil-lion-aire
Mim-e-o-graph
mi-met-ic
mim-e-tite
mim-ick-er
mim-ic-ry
mi-mo-sa
mi-mo-sine
min-a-ble
min-a-ret
minc-ing
mi-nen-wer-fer
min-er
min-er-ag-ra-phy
min-er-al-iz-er
min-er-al-og-i-cal
min-er-al-o-gy
Mi-ner-va
min-e-stro-ne
mi-nette
min-gling
min-i-a-ceous
min-i-a-ture
Min-ie
min-i-mize
min-i-mum
min-ion
min-is-te-ri-al
min-is-try
min-i-track
Min-ne-so-tan
mi-nom-e-ter
mi-nor-i-ty
min-strel
mint-age
mint-er
min-u-et
mi-nus-cu-lar
min-us-cule

min-ute (time)
mi-nute (small)
min-ute-ly (every minute)
mi-nute-ly (precisely)
mi-nu-ti-a
mi-o-sis
mi-ot-ic
mi-rab-i-lite
mir-a-cle
mi-rac-u-lous
mi-rage
mis-an-throp-ic
mis-an-thro-py
mis-ceg-e-na-tion
mis-cel-la-ne-ous
mis-cel-la-ny
mis-chie-vous
mis-ci-bil-i-ty
mis-cre-ant
mis-de-mean-or
mis-er-a-ble
Mis-e-re-re
mi-ser-ly
mis-er-y
mis-fea-sance
mis-no-mer
mi-sog-y-nist
mis-pri-sion
mis-sil-eer
mis-sile-ry
Mis-sis-sip-pi-an
mis-sive
Mis-sou-ri-an
mis-spelled
mis-tak-a-ble
mis-tak-en
mis-ter
mis-tle-toe
mis-tral
mis-tress
mi-ter
mit-i-ga-tor
mi-to-chon-dri-a
mi-to-sis
mi-tot-ic
mi-trail-leuse
mi-tral
mix-ture
mne-mon-ic
mo-bile
mo-bil-i-ty
mo-bi-li-za-tion
mo-bil-om-e-ter

mob-oc-ra-cy
moc-ca-sin
mo-cha
mock-er-y
mod-al-ism
mo-dal-i-ty
mod-eled
mod-er-a-tor
mod-ern-is-tic
mod-ern-ize
mod-es-ty
mod-i-cum
mod-i-fy
mod-ish
mo-diste
mod-u-la-bil-i-ty
mod-u-lar
mod-u-la-tor
mod-u-lus
mo-dus op-e-ran-di
Mo-ham-med-an
Mo-ha-ve
moi-e-ty
moi-re
moist-en-er
mois-ture
mo-lar-i-ty
mo-la-ry
mo-las-ses
mold-er
mo-lec-u-lar
mol-e-cule
mo-les-ta-tion
mol-ten
molt-er
mo-lyb-date
mo-lyb-de-num
mo-lyb-do-me-nite
mol-y-site
mo-men-tar-i-ly
mo-men-tar-y
mo-men-tous
mo-men-tum
mom-ism
Mon-a-can
mo-nad
mo-nad-ic
mo-nan-dry
mo-nar-chal
mo-nar-chi-cal
mon-ar-chist
mon-as-te-ri-al
mon-as-ter-y

mo-nas-tic
mon-a-tom-ic
mon-a-zite
mo-nel
mo-ne-sia
mon-e-tar-y
mon-e-tite
mon-e-tize
mon-eys
mon-ger
Mon-go-li-an
Mon-gol-oid
mon-grel
mon-i-ker
mo-nim-o-lite
mon-ism
mo-nis-tic
mon-i-to-ry
mon-keys
monk-ish
mon-o-ac-e-tin
mon-o-ac-id
mon-o-a-cid-ic
mon-o-am-ide
mon-o-a-mine
mon-o-chro-mous
mo-noch-ro-nous
mon-o-cle
mon-o-coque
mo-noc-ra-cy
mon-o-crot-ic
mo-noc-u-lar
mo-nog-a-my
mo-nog-o-ny
mon-o-gramed
mon-o-gram-mat-ic
mo-nog-ra-pher
mon-o-graph-ic
mo-nog-y-ny
mon-o-lith-ic
mon-o-log
mo-nol-o-gist
mo-nom-a-chy
mon-o-ma-ni-a
mon-o-mer
mo-nom-e-ter
mo-no-mi-al
mon-o-nu-cle-o-sis
mon-o-plane
mo-nop-o-lize
mo-nop-so-ny
mon-o-rail
mon-o-the-ism

mon-o-tone
mo-not-o-nous
mo-not-ro-py
mon-ox-ide
mon-sei-gneur
mon-sieur
mon-si-gnor
mon-ster
mon-stros-i-ty
mon-strous
mon-tage
Mon-tan-an
Mon-te-ne-grin
Mon-tes-so-ri
mon-tic-u-lous
mont-mo-ril-lon-ite
Mon-tre-al
mon-troy-dite
mon-u-men-tal
mon-zo-nite
Moor-ish
mo-quette
mo-raine
mor-al
mo-rale
mor-al-ist
mo-ral-i-ty
mor-al-ize
mo-rass-ic
mor-a-to-ri-um
Mo-ra-vi-an
mo-ra-vite
mor-bid-i-ty
mor-bose
mor-da-cious
mor-dac-i-ty
mor-dant
mo-reen
mo-rel-lo
mo-ren-cite
mo-res
mor-ga-nat-ic
mor-i-bund
mo-rin-done
mo-rin-ite
Mor-mon-ite
morn-ing
Mo-roc-co
mo-ron-ic
mo-ros-i-ty
mor-pheme
mor-phe-mics
Mor-pheus

mor-phine
mor-phog-ra-phy
mor-pho-line
mor-pho-log-i-cal
mor-phol-o-gy
mor-phom-e-try
mor-pho-sis
mor-phot-o-my
mor-tal-i-ty
mort-ga-gee
mort-ga-gor
mor-ti-cian
mor-ti-fi-ca-tion
mor-tis-er
mor-tu-ar-y
mo-sa-i-cism
mo-ses-ite
mos-qui-toes
mo-tel
moth-er
mo-til-i-ty
mo-ti-vate
mo-tor
mo-to-ri-al
mou-lage
mou-lin
moun-tain-eer
moun-te-bank
mount-er
mourn-er
mous-er
mous-que-taire
mousse-line
mov-a-ble
mov-ant
mov-er
mov-ie
mu-ce-dine
mu-ced-i-nous
mu-cic
mu-cif-er-ous
mu-ci-lage
mu-ci-lag-i-nous
mu-cin-o-gen
mu-cin-oid
mu-ci-no-lyt-ic
mu-coi-dal
mu-co-i-tin
mu-co-lyt-ic
mu-con-ic
mu-co-sa
mu-cos-i-ty
mu-cous (adj.)

mu-cus (n.)
mud-dled
muf-fler
Muh-len-berg
mu-lat-toes
mulch-er
mu-le-teer
mul-ish
mul-li-ga-taw-ny
mull-ite
mul-ti-far-i-ous
mul-tif-er-ous
Mul-ti-graph
Mul-ti-lith
mul-til-o-quent
mul-tim-e-ter
mul-tim-e-try
mul-tip-a-rous
mul-ti-par-tite
mul-ti-ple
mul-ti-plic-a-ble
mul-ti-pli-ca-tion
mul-ti-plic-i-ty
mul-ti-tu-di-nous
mul-ti-va-lent
mum-bling
Mun-chau-sen
mun-dane
Mu-nich
mu-nic-i-pal
mu-nif-i-cent
mu-ni-tion
mu-ral
mu-rar-i-um
mur-der-ous
mu-ri-at-ic
mu-rine
mu-ri-um
mur-mur-ous
mus-ca-dine
mus-ca-rine
mus-ca-tel
mus-cle
Mus-co-vite
mus-cu-lar
mus-cu-la-ture
mus-cu-lo-trop-ic
mu-se-ol-o-gy
mu-se-um
mu-si-cal
mu-si-col-o-gy
mus-ing
mus-ket-eer

mus-tache
mus-tard
mu-ta-bil-i-ty
mu-ta-gen-ic
mu-tant
mu-tase
mu-ta-tive
mu-ti-late
mu-ti-nous
mut-ism
mu-tu-al-ism
mu-zhik
muz-zling
my-al-gi-a
My-an-e-sin
my-as-the-ni-a
my-as-then-ic
my-ce-li-um
my-ce-to-ma
my-co-my-cin
my-co-sis
myc-ter-ic
my-dri-a-sine
my-dri-a-sis
myd-ri-at-ic
my-e-li-tis
my-e-lo-cyte
my-e-loid
my-e-lo-ma-to-sis
my-e-lom-a-tous
my-e-lop-a-thy

my-e-lo-sis
my-o-car-di-tis
my-op-a-thy
my-o-pi-a
my-op-ic
my-o-sin
my-o-si-tis
my-os-mine
my-ot-o-my
myr-i-ad
myr-i-am-e-ter
my-ric-e-tin
my-ric-i-trin
myr-i-cyl
myr-in-gi-tis
myr-in-got-o-my
my-ris-tate
myr-mi-don
myrrh-ic
myr-tle
mys-te-ri-ous
mys-ter-y
mys-ti-cal
mys-ti-fi-ca-tion
mys-tique
myth-i-cal
myth-o-log-i-cal
my-thol-o-gy
myx-o-bac-te-ri-al
myx-o-ma-to-sis

N

na-bob
na-celle
na-cre-ous
na-crite
na-dir
nad-or-ite
Na-ga-sa-ki
nah-co-lite
nail-er
nain-sook
na-ive
na-ive-te
na-ked
nam-a-ble
na-no-gram
na-palm

na-per-y
na-phaz-o-line
naph-tha
naph-tha-lene
naph-tha-len-ic
naph-thal-ic
naph-thene
naph-the-nic
naph-thi-o-nate
naph-thi-on-ic
naph-thol-ate
naph-tho-res-or-cin-ol
naphth-ox-y-a-ce-tic
naph-tho-yl
naph-thyl-a-mine
naph-thy-lene

Na-ples
Na-po-le-on
na-prap-a-thy
nar-cis-sism
nar-co-lep-sy
nar-co-sis
nar-cot-ic
nar-co-tol-ine
na-res
nar-in-gen-in
na-rin-gin
Nar-ra-gan-sett
nar-rat-a-ble
nar-ra-tor
na-sa-lis
na-sal-i-ty
nas-cent
na-so-scope
nas-ti-ly
nas-tur-tium
na-tal
na-tant
na-ta-to-ri-al
na-ta-to-ri-um
Natch-ez
Na-than-iel
na-tion-al-ist
na-tiv-is-tic
na-tiv-i-ty
na-tri-um
na-tro-lite
na-troph-i-lite
nat-u-ral-ist
nat-u-ral-ize
na-ture
na-tur-o-path
na-tur-op-a-thy
naugh-ti-ness
nau-pli-us
nau-se-ate
nau-seous
nau-ti-cal
nau-ti-lus
nau-to-phone
Nav-a-ho
na-val
nav-ar
na-vel
na-vic-u-lar
nav-i-ga-ble
nav-i-ga-tor
na-vite
Naz-a-rene

na-zism
Ne-an-der-thal
Ne-a-pol-i-tan
near-est
ne-ar-thro-sis
Ne-bras-kan
neb-u-lar
ne-bu-li-um
neb-u-los-i-ty
neb-u-lous
nec-es-sar-i-ly
ne-ces-si-tate
ne-ces-si-tous
nec-ro-bi-o-sis
nec-ro-log-i-cal
ne-crol-o-gy
nec-ro-man-cy
ne-crop-o-lis
ne-crop-sy
ne-cros-co-py
nec-ro-sin
ne-cro-sis
ne-crot-ic
ne-crot-o-my
nec-tar-ine
nec-ta-ry
nee-dler
ne-far-i-ous
ne-ga-tion
neg-a-tive
neg-a-to-ry
neg-a-tron
ne-glect-er
neg-li-gee
neg-li-gence
neg-li-gi-ble
ne-go-ti-a-ble
ne-go-ti-a-tor
Ne-gress
Ne-grit-ic
Ne-gro
Ne-groid
Ne-gus
neigh-bor
nei-ther
ne-mat-ic
nem-a-to-ci-dal
nem-a-tode
nem-a-to-di-a-sis
nem-a-tol-o-gy
Nem-bu-tal
ne-mes-ic
nem-e-sis

ne-moph-i-ly
nem-o-ral
Ne-o-ant-er-gan
ne-o-ars-phen-a-mine
ne-o-dym-i-um
ne-og-a-my
ne-o-lith-ic
ne-o-log-i-cal
ne-ol-o-gy
ne-o-my-cin
ne-on-tol-o-gy
ne-o-phyte
ne-o-pla-si-a
ne-o-prene
ne-o-stig-mine
Ne-o-sy-neph-rine
ne-o-ter-ic
ne-ot-o-cite
Ne-pal
Nep-a-lese
ne-pen-the
neph-e-lin-ite
neph-e-lite
neph-e-lom-e-ter
neph-e-lo-scope
neph-ew
ne-phol-o-gy
neph-o-scope
ne-phrec-to-my
neph-ric
ne-phrid-i-al
neph-rite
ne-phrit-ic
ne-phri-tis
ne-phrol-o-gy
neph-rop-to-sis
ne-phro-sis
ne-phrot-ic
ne-phrot-o-my
nep-i-on-ic
ne-pot-ic
nep-o-tism
nep-tu-ni-um
ne-rit-ic
ne-rol-i-dol
nerv-ate
nerv-ine
ner-von-ic
nerv-ous
ner-vule
ne-science
nest-ling (n.)
nes-tling (v.)

Nes-tor
neth-er
Ne-trop-sin
net-tled
Neuf-châ-tel
neu-ral-gia
neur-as-the-ni-a
neur-as-then-ic
neu-rec-to-my
neu-rine
neu-rit-ic
neu-ri-tis
neu-ro-blas-to-ma
neu-ro-crine
neu-ro-gen-ic
neu-rog-ra-phy
neu-roid
neu-ro-log-i-cal
neu-rol-o-gy
neu-rol-y-sis
neu-ro-path-ic
neu-rop-a-thy
neu-ro-sis
neu-rot-ic
neu-rot-i-cism
neu-rot-o-my
neu-ro-trop-ic
neu-rot-ro-pism
neu-ter
neu-tral-i-ty
neu-tral-iz-er
neu-tri-no
neu-tro-dyne
neu-tron
Ne-vad-an
ne-vus
new-com-er
New-to-ni-an
New Zea-land-er
nex-us
ni-a-cin-a-mide
Ni-ag-a-ra
nib-bling
Nic-a-ra-guan
ni-ce-ty
nick-el-if-er-ous
nick-el-ine
nick-el-o-de-on
nic-o-tin-a-mide
nic-o-tin-ate
nic-o-tin-ic
nic-o-ti-no-yl
nic-o-tin-u-ric

ni-dic-o-lous
nid-i-fi-cate
ni-dol-o-gy
Nietz-sche-ism
Ni-ger
Ni-ge-ri-a
ni-ger-ite
night-in-gale
ni-gres-cence
ni-grine
ni-grom-e-ter
ni-gro-sine
ni-grous
ni-hi-list
ni-lom-e-ter
nim-bly
nim-bo-stra-tus
ni-mi-e-ty
Nin-hy-drin
Ni-o-be
ni-o-bic
ni-o-bi-um
nip-e-cot-ic
Nip-pon-ese
Nir-va-na
Ni-sei
ni-sin
ni-ter
ni-tra-mine
ni-trate
ni-tra-tor
ni-tric
ni-trid-ize
ni-tri-fi-ca-tion
ni-trite
ni-tro-an-i-line
ni-tro-fu-ra-zone
ni-tro-gen-ate
ni-tro-gen-ize
ni-trog-e-nous
ni-tro-lic
ni-trom-e-ter
ni-tro-ni-um
ni-tros-a-mine
ni-tro-sate
ni-tro-so
ni-tro-tol-u-ene
ni-tro-tol-u-ol
ni-trous
ni-trox-yl-ene
ni-tryl
No-bel
no-bel-i-um

no-bil-i-ty
no-blesse
no-bly
no-car-di-o-sis
no-cer-ite
no-ci-cep-tor
noc-tam-bu-list
noc-ti-lu-cine
noc-tiv-a-gant
noc-tur-nal
noc-turne
noc-u-ous
nod-al
no-dal-i-ty
nod-u-lar
nod-ule
no-e-ma-ta-chom-e-ter
nois-i-ly
noi-some
no-lo con-ten-de-re
no-mad-ic
no-men-cla-ture
no-mi-al
nom-i-nal-ize
nom-i-nat-ed
nom-i-na-tion
nom-i-na-tive
no-moc-ra-cy
nom-o-gram
nom-o-graph-ic
no-mog-ra-phy
non-a-co-sane
non-a-dec-ane
non-a-ge-nar-i-an
no-nane
non-a-no-ic
no-na-nol
non-cha-lance
non-de-script
no-nene
non-en-ti-ty
no-no-ic
non-pa-reil
non-plused
non pro-se-qui-tur
non se-qui-tur
non-yl-ene
no-nyl-ic
noo-dle
no-ol-o-gy
no-pi-nene
Nor-dic
nor-di-hy-dro-guai-a-ret-ic

nor-mal-i-ty
nor-mal-iz-er
nor-ma-tive
North-amp-ton
north-ern
North-um-ber-land
Nor-we-gian
no-se-lite
no-sog-ra-phy
no-sol-o-gist
nos-tal-gi-a
nos-tril
nos-trum
nos-y
no-ta-ble
no-tam
no-tar-i-al
no-ta-ry
notch-er
noth-ing
no-tice-a-ble
no-ti-fi-ca-tion
no-to-ri-e-ty
no-to-ri-ous
nou-gat
nour-ish
nou-veau
nov-el-ette
nov-el-ist
no-vel-la
nov-el-ty
No-vem-ber
no-ve-na
nov-ice
no-vi-ti-ate
no-vo-cain
nox-ious
Nu-bi-an
nu-cle-ar
nu-cle-ate
nu-cle-in-a-tion
nu-cle-og-o-ny
nu-cle-o-his-tone

nu-cle-o-lar
nu-cle-ol-y-sis
nu-cle-om-e-ter
nu-cle-on-ics
nu-cle-o-tid-ase
nu-cle-us
nu-clide
nu-clid-ic
nudg-er
nud-ism
nu-di-ty
nu-ga-to-ry
nui-sance
nul-li-ty
num-bered
nu-mer-al
nu-mer-a-tive
nu-mer-a-tor
nu-mer-i-cal
nu-mer-ol-o-gy
nu-mis-mat-ics
nu-mis-ma-tist
num-skull
nun-ci-a-ture
nup-tial
nup-ti-al-i-ty
Nur-em-berg
nurs-er
nurs-er-y
nur-tur-al
nu-tri-a
nu-tri-ent
nu-tri-lite
nu-tri-tious
nu-tri-tive
nyc-ta-lo-pi-a
ny-lon
nym-pha
nymph-al
nys-tag-mus
nys-ta-tin
ny-tril

O

oak-en
oa-kum
o-a-sis
ob-bli-ga-to
ob-du-ra-cy

ob-du-rate
o-be-di-ence
o-bei-sance
o-be-li-al
ob-e-lisk

o-be-si-ty
ob-fus-ca-to-ry
o-bit-u-ar-y
ob-jec-tee
ob-jec-tiv-ism
ob-jec-tiv-i-ty
ob-jec-tor
ob-ju-ra-tion
ob-jur-gate
ob-last
ob-la-to-ry
ob-li-ga-tor
o-blig-a-to-ry
ob-li-gee
o-blig-ing
ob-li-gor
o-blique
ob-liq-ui-ty
ob-lit-er-ate
ob-li-ves-cence
ob-liv-i-on
ob-liv-i-ous
ob-long-at-ed
ob-lo-quy
ob-mu-tes-cence
ob-nox-ious
ob-nu-bi-la-tion
ob-o-lus
ob-scen-i-ty
ob-scu-ran-tism
ob-scu-ri-ty
ob-se-qui-ous
ob-seq-ui-ty
ob-se-quy
ob-serv-ance
ob-serv-ant
ob-ser-va-tion
ob-serv-a-to-ry
ob-serv-er
ob-ses-sion
ob-sid-i-an
ob-so-les-cence
ob-so-lete
ob-sta-cle
ob-ste-tri-cian
ob-stet-rics
ob-sti-na-cy
ob-strep-er-ous
ob-struc-tive
ob-struc-tor
ob-tru-sive
ob-tund-ent
ob-tu-ra-tor

ob-tu-si-ty
ob-ver-tend
oc-a-ri-na
oc-ca-sion
oc-ci-den-tal
oc-cip-i-ta-lis
oc-cip-i-to-pa-ri-e-tal
oc-ci-put
oc-clu-sal
oc-clu-sion
oc-cul-ta-tion
oc-cult-ism
oc-cu-pan-cy
oc-cu-pa-tive
oc-curred
oc-cur-rence
o-cea-nar-i-um
o-ce-an-ic
o-cean-o-graph-ic
o-cean-og-ra-phy
oc-el-late
o-ce-lot
o-cher-ous
och-loc-ra-cy
o-chro-no-sis
oc-ta-co-sane
oc-ta-dec-a-di-e-no-ic
oc-ta-dec-ane
oc-ta-dec-a-no-ic
oc-ta-dec-yl
oc-ta-gon
oc-tag-o-nal
oc-ta-he-dron
oc-ta-mer
oc-tam-er-ous
oc-tam-e-ter
oc-tane
oc-tan-gu-lar
oc-ta-no-ate
oc-ta-nol
oc-ta-no-yl
oc-ta-vos
Oc-to-ber
oc-to-ge-nar-i-an
oc-tog-e-nar-y
oc-to-ic
Oc-top-o-da
oc-to-pus
oc-to-roon
oc-tose
oc-tu-ple
oc-tup-let
oc-tyl-ene

oc-u-lar
oc-u-list
oc-u-lo-gy-ric
o-da-lisque
odd-i-ty
o-dif-er-ous
o-di-om-e-ter
o-di-ous
od-ist
o-di-um
o-dom-e-ter
o-don-ti-tis
o-don-to-gen-ic
o-don-tol-o-gy
o-don-tom-e-ter
o-don-tot-o-my
o-dor-ant
o-dor-if-er-ous
o-dor-om-e-ter
o-dor-ous
Od-ys-sey
oed-i-pal
oe-nan-thic
oer-sted
of-fal
of-fend-er
of-fen-sive
of-fer-to-ry
of-fi-cer
of-fi-cial
of-fi-ci-ate
of-fic-i-nal
of-fi-cious
off-ing
of-ten
o-gi-val
o-gre-ish
O-hi-o-an
ohm-ic
ohm-me-ter
oil-er
oi-ti-ci-ca
o-ken-ite
O-ki-na-wan
O-kla-ho-man
ok-o-nite
o-kra
old-en
old-ster
o-le-ag-i-nous
o-le-an-der
o-le-an-drin
o-lec-ra-non

o-le-fin-ic
o-le-ic
o-le-in-ic
o-le-og-ra-phy
o-le-o-mar-ga-rine
o-le-om-e-ter
o-le-o-res-in
o-le-o-yl
ol-fac-tom-e-ter
ol-fac-to-ry
ol-i-gar-chi-cal
ol-i-gar-chy
ol-i-ge-mi-a
ol-i-go-chro-ne-mi-a
ol-i-go-clase
ol-i-go-dy-nam-ic
ol-i-go-nite
ol-i-gop-o-ly
ol-i-gop-so-ny
ol-i-va-ceous
ol-i-var-y
o-liv-en-ite
ol-i-ves-cence
ol-i-vine
O-lym-pi-an
O-ma-ha
om-bro-graph
om-brom-e-ter
om-buds-man
o-me-ga
om-e-let
o-men-ol-o-gy
om-i-cron
om-i-nous
o-mis-si-ble
o-mis-sion
o-mit-ted
om-ni-bus
om-nif-i-cence
om-nim-e-ter
om-nip-o-tence
om-ni-science
om-niv-o-rous
om-pha-li-tis
on-a-ger
on-co-gen-ic
on-cog-e-ny
on-col-o-gy
on-col-y-sis
on-com-e-ter
on-cot-o-my
on-dom-e-ter
on-du-le

O-nei-da
on-er-ous
on-ion
on-o-ma-si-ol-o-gy
on-o-mat-o-poe-ia
On-on-da-ga
On-tar-i-an
on-tog-e-ny
on-to-log-i-cal
on-tol-o-gy
on-y-chol-y-sis
on-y-cho-my-co-sis
on-y-choph-a-gy
on-y-cho-sis
o-ol-o-gy
o-pa-cim-e-ter
o-pac-i-ty
o-pal-es-cent
o-pal-ine
o-paqu-er
o-paqu-ing
o-pei-do-scope
op-er-a
op-er-a-ble
op-er-and
op-er-ate
op-er-at-ic
op-er-a-tive
op-er-a-tor
o-per-cu-lar
oph-i-cleide
o-phid-i-an
o-phi-ol-o-gy
o-phit-ic
oph-thal-mi-a
oph-thal-mic
oph-thal-mo-log-ic
oph-thal-mol-o-gy
oph-thal-mom-e-ter
oph-thal-mo-met-ric
oph-thal-mo-scope
oph-thal-mos-co-py
o-pi-an-ic
o-pi-ate
o-pin-ion-at-ed
o-pin-ion-a-tor
op-i-som-e-ter
o-pis-tho-gas-tric
o-pi-um
o-pos-sum
op-po-nent
op-por-tun-ism
op-por-tun-ist

op-por-tu-ni-ty
op-pos-al
op-po-site
op-press-i-ble
op-pres-sive
op-pres-sor
op-pro-bri-um
op-ti-cal
op-ti-cian
op-ti-mal-ize
op-ti-me
op-tim-e-ter
op-ti-mism
op-ti-mis-tic
op-ti-mum
op-tom-e-ter
op-to-met-ric
op-tom-e-try
op-u-lent
or-a-cle
o-rac-u-lar
o-ral-ly
or-ange
o-ran-ge-lo
or-ange-ry
o-rang-u-tan
o-ra-tion
or-a-tor
or-a-tor-i-cal
or-a-to-ri-o
or-bic-u-lar
or-bit-al
or-bit-ed
or-bit-er
or-bit-ing
or-chard
or-ches-tra
or-chi-da-ceous
or-chid-ol-o-gy
or-cin-ol
or-deal
or-dered
or-di-nal
or-di-nance
or-di-nar-i-ly
or-di-nar-y
ord-nance
Or-do-vi-cian
Or-e-go-ni-an
or-gan-dy
or-gan-ic
or-ga-nism
or-gan-ist

or-ga-niz-a-ble
or-ga-ni-za-tion
or-ga-niz-er
or-gan-o-gel
or-ga-no-gen-ic
or-ga-nog-e-ny
or-ga-nog-ra-phy
or-ga-nos-co-py
or-gan-o-sol
or-gi-as-tic
o-ri-el
O-ri-ent
o-ri-en-tal
o-ri-en-ta-lia
o-ri-en-ta-tor
o-ri-en-tite
or-i-fi-cial
or-i-flamme
or-i-gin
o-rig-i-nal-i-ty
o-rig-i-nat-ing
o-rig-i-na-tive
o-ri-ole
O-ri-on
or-is-mol-o-gy
or-i-son
Or-lan-do
Or-le-ans
Or-lon
or-mo-lu
or-na-men-tal
or-ner-y
or-ni-thine
or-ni-tho-log-i-cal
or-ni-thol-o-gy
or-ni-thop-ter
or-ni-tho-rhyn-chus
or-ni-tho-sis
or-ni-thot-o-my
or-nith-u-ric
o-rog-e-ny
o-rog-ra-phy
o-ro-ide
o-rol-o-gy
o-rom-e-ter
or-o-met-ric
o-ro-tun-di-ty
or-phan-age
or-pi-ment
or-ris
or-sel-lin-ic
or-tha-nil-ic
or-thi-con

or-tho-ar-se-nate
or-tho-ben-zo-qui-none
or-tho-clase
or-tho-don-ti-a
or-tho-don-tist
or-tho-dox-y
or-tho-e-py
or-tho-for-mic
or-thog-o-nal
or-thog-ra-phy
or-thom-e-try
or-tho-pe-dic
or-tho-pe-dist
or-thop-ne-a
Or-thop-ter-a
or-thop-tics
or-tho-sis
or-tho-typ-ic
or-to-lan
o-ryc-tol-o-gy
o-ryc-tog-no-sy
o-sa-zone
Os-car
os-cil-la-tor
os-cil-la-to-ry
os-cil-lom-e-ter
os-cil-lo-scope
os-ci-tant
os-cu-la-to-ry
os-cu-lom-e-ter
O-si-ris
os-mi-dro-sis
os-mi-rid-i-um
os-mi-um
os-mom-e-ter
os-mo-met-ric
os-mom-e-try
os-mo-sis
os-mot-ic
os-phre-sis
os-prey
os-se-ous
os-si-cle
os-sic-u-lar
os-si-cu-lec-to-my
os-sif-i-ca-to-ry
os-si-fy
os-te-al
os-te-it-ic
os-te-i-tis
os-ten-si-ble
os-ten-ta-tious
os-te-o-chon-dro-sis

os-te-ol-o-gy
os-te-ol-y-sis
os-te-o-ma
os-te-o-ma-tous
os-te-om-e-try
os-te-o-my-e-li-tis
os-te-o-path
os-te-op-a-thy
os-te-ot-o-my
os-tra-cism
os-tra-cize
os-trich
o-tal-gi-a
o-the-o-scope
oth-er
o-ti-ose
o-ti-os-i-ty
o-ti-tis me-di-a
o-tog-e-nous
o-to-lar-yn-go-log-i-cal
o-to-lar-yn-gol-o-gy
o-tos-co-py
o-to-sis
oua-ba-in
ou-bli-ette
ou-ri-cu-ry
oust-er
out-er
out-land-ish
out-law-ry
out-ra-geous
out-rag-er
ou-trance
out-rid-er
out-sid-er
o-val-i-form
o-val-i-ty
o-var-i-an
o-var-i-ec-to-my
o-var-i-ole
o-var-i-ot-o-my
o-va-ri-tis
o-va-ry
ov-en
o-ver-head
o-ver-land-er
o-ver-se-er
o-ver-ture
o-vi-ci-dal
o-vic-u-lar

O-vid-i-an
o-vi-na-tion
o-vip-a-ra
o-vi-par-i-ty
o-vip-a-rous
o-vi-pos-i-tor
o-vu-lar
o-vu-la-to-ry
ow-ing
own-er
ox-a-late
ox-al-ic
ox-al-u-ric
ox-a-lyl
ox-am-ide
ox-am-i-dine
ox-an-i-late
ox-a-nil-ic
ox-a-zine
ox-a-zol-i-dine
ox-i-dant
ox-i-dase
ox-i-da-tion
ox-ide
ox-i-dim-e-try
ox-i-diz-a-ble
ox-i-diz-er
ox-id-u-lat-ed
ox-im-e-ter
ox-i-met-ric
ox-in-dole
ox-o-ni-um
ox-o-phen-ar-sine
ox-y-a-can-thine
ox-y-a-cet-y-lene
ox-y-gen
ox-y-gen-ate
ox-y-gen-ize
ox-y-lu-cif-er-in
ox-y-tet-ra-cy-cline
ox-y-to-cin
oys-ter
Oz-al-id
O-zark-i-an
o-zo-ke-rite
o-zon-ate
o-zon-ide
o-zon-iz-er
o-zon-ol-y-sis
o-zo-no-sphere

P

pab-u-lum
pac-er
pa-chi-si
pach-no-lite
pach-y-der-ma-tous
pa-chym-e-ter
pac-i-fi-a-ble
pa-cif-ic
pac-i-fi-ca-tion
pa-cif-i-ca-to-ry
pac-i-fist
pac-i-fy
pack-ag-er
pack-et
pad-dling
pa-dre
pa-dro-ne
Pad-u-an
pae-an
pa-gan-ism
pag-eant-ry
pag-er
pag-i-nal
pag-i-nate
pag-ing
pa-go-da
pains-tak-ing
paint-er
pais-ley
Pak-i-stan-i
pal-ace
pa-la-ceous
pal-a-din
pal-an-quin
pal-at-a-bil-i-ty
pal-at-a-ble
pal-a-tal-ize
pal-ate (roof of mouth)
pa-la-tial
pa-lat-i-nate
pal-a-tine
pal-a-ti-tis
pal-a-to-gram
pa-lav-er
pa-le-a-ceous
pa-le-og-ra-pher
pa-le-ol-o-gy

pa-le-on-tol-o-gy
Pa-le-o-zo-ic
Pal-es-tin-i-an
pal-ette (artist's board)
pal-frey
pa-lil-o-gy
pal-imp-sest
pal-in-drome
pal-i-sade
pal-la-di-um
pal-let (a bed)
pal-let-ize
pal-lette (armor)
pal-li-a-tive
pal-mate
palm-er
pal-met-to
palm-is-try
pal-mit-ic
pal-mit-o-le-ic
pal-o-mi-no
pal-pa-ble
pal-pi-tate
pal-sy
pal-try
pal-u-drine
pa-lus-trine
pal-y-nol-o-gy
pam-a-quine
Pam-e-la
pam-pas
pam-pe-an
pam-per
pam-phlet
pam-phlet-eer
pam-phlet-ize
pan-a-ce-a
pa-nache (headdress)
pa-na-che (food)
Pan-a-ma-ni-an
pan-a-ry
pan-a-tel-a
pan-car-di-tis
pan-chro-mat-ic
pan-cre-as
pan-cre-a-tec-to-my
pan-cre-a-tin

pan-cre-a-ti-tis
pan-cre-o-zy-min
pan-dem-ic
pan-de-mo-ni-um
pan-der
pan-e-gyr-ic
pan-e-gy-rize
pan-el-ist
pan-go-lin
pan-icked
pan-i-cle
pa-nic-u-late
pan-mne-si-a
pan-nic-u-li-tis
pan-nier
pa-no-cha
pan-o-ply
pan-o-ram-a
pan-o-ram-ic
pan-soph-ic
pan-tag-a-my
Pan-ta-gru-el
pan-ta-loon
pan-tarch-y
pan-te-the-ine
pan-the-ism
pan-the-on
pan-ther
pant-i-soc-ra-cy
pan-to-chro-mism
pan-to-graph
pan-tog-ra-pher
pan-to-ic
pan-tol-o-gy
pan-tom-e-ter
pan-to-mime
pan-to-then-ic
pan-to-yl
pan-try
pa-pa-cy
pa-pa-in-ase
Pa-pa-ni-co-laou
pa-par-chy
pa-pav-er-ine
pa-paw
pa-pay-a
pa-per
pa-pier ma-che
pa-pil-la
pap-il-lar-y
pap-il-lo-ma-to-sis
pap-il-lom-a-tous
pa-pism

pa-poose
pa-pri-ka
Pap-u-an
pap-u-lar
pap-y-ra-ceous
pap-y-rin
pa-py-rus
par-a-ban-ic
par-a-ba-sic
pa-rab-a-sis
par-a-bi-o-sis
par-a-ble
pa-rab-o-la
par-a-bol-i-cal
pa-rab-o-loi-dal
par-a-chor
par-a-chord-al
pa-rach-ro-nism
par-a-chut-ist
par-a-clete
pa-rad-er
par-a-digm
par-a-dise
par-a-di-si-a-cal
par-a-dox
par-af-fin-ic
par-a-gly-co-gen
par-a-go-ge
par-a-gog-ic
par-a-gon
pa-rag-o-nite
par-a-graph-er
Par-a-guay-an
par-a-keet
par-al-de-hyde
par-al-lac-tic
par-al-leled
par-al-lel-e-pi-ped
par-al-lel-e-pip-e-don
par-al-lel-ing
par-al-lel-om-e-ter
pa-ral-o-gize
pa-ral-y-sis
par-a-lyt-ic
par-a-lyzed
pa-ram-e-ter
par-a-mide
par-a-mi-no-ben-zo-ic
par-a-mor-phism
par-a-mour
par-a-noi-a
par-a-noi-ac
par-a-noi-dal

par-ant-he-lion	par-o-dis-tic
par-a-pet-ed	par-o-dy
par-a-pha-si-a	pa-rol
par-a-pher-na-lia	pa-role
par-a-phrase	pa-rol-ee
pa-raph-ra-sis	par-o-nych-i-a
pa-raph-y-sis	par-o-nym
par-a-ple-gi-a	pa-ron-y-mous
par-a-ple-gic	pa-rot-id
pa-rap-sis	pa-rot-i-dec-to-my
par-a-se-le-ne	par-o-tit-ic
par-a-sit-e-mi-a	par-o-ti-tis
par-a-sit-i-cal	par-ox-ysm
par-a-sit-i-ci-dal	par-ox-ys-mal
par-a-sit-ism	par-quet-ry
par-a-si-tize	par-ri-ci-dal
par-a-si-to-sis	par-si-mo-ni-ous
par-a-sol	pars-ley
pa-rat-ro-phy	pars-nip
par-celed	par-son-age
par-don-a-ble	par-tage
par-e-gor-ic	par-tak-er
pa-ren-chy-ma	part-er
par-en-chym-a-tous	par-terre
par-ent-age	Par-the-non
pa-ren-tal	par-ti-al-i-ty
par-en-ter-al	par-tial-ly
pa-ren-the-sis	par-ti-bil-i-ty
par-en-thet-i-cal	par-tic-i-pant
par-er-gon	par-tic-i-pa-tor
pa-re-sis	par-ti-cip-i-al
pa-ret-ic	par-ti-ci-ple
par-he-lion	par-ti-cle
pa-ri-ah	par-tic-u-lar-i-ty
pa-ri-e-tal	par-tic-u-late
pa-ri-e-to-fron-tal	par-ti-san
par-i-mu-tu-el	par-ti-tion-er
par-i-nar-ic	par-ti-tive
par-ing	par-tridge
Par-is	par-tu-ri-tion
par-ish	pa-ru-lis
pa-rish-ion-er	par-ve-nu
Pa-ri-sian	pas-chal
Pa-ri-si-enne	pa-sha
par-i-son	pas-i-graph-ic
par-i-ty	pa-sig-ra-phy
Par-ker	pas-quin-ade
park-er	pass-a-ble
par-lance	pas-sa-ca-glia
par-lia-men-tar-i-an	pas-sage
par-lia-men-ta-ry	pas-sé
par-lous	pas-sen-ger
pa-ro-chi-al	pas-ser (bird)

pass-er
pas-si-ble
pas-sim-e-ter
pass-ing
pas-sion-ate
pas-si-va-tor
pas-siv-ist
pas-siv-i-ty
pas-som-e-ter
pass-o-ver
pas-tel
past-er
pas-tern
pas-teur-i-za-tion
pas-tiche
pas-tille
pas-time
pas-tor
pas-to-ral
pas-to-rale
pas-tor-ate
pas-tra-mi
pas-try
pas-tur-age
Pat-a-go-ni-an
Pa-taps-co
patch-er-y
patch-ou-li
pa-tel-la
pat-ent-ee
pat-en-tor
pa-ter-fa-mil-i-as
pa-ter-nal
pa-ter-ni-ty
pa-ter-nos-ter
pa-thet-ic
path-o-don-ti-a
path-o-gen-ic
path-o-ge-nic-i-ty
pa-thog-e-ny
pa-thog-no-my
path-o-log-i-cal
pa-thol-o-gist
pa-thol-o-gy
pa-thom-e-ter
pa-thos
pa-tho-sis
pa-tien-cy
pat-i-na
pat-i-o
pa-tois
pa-tri-ar-chal
pa-tri-arch-ate

pa-tri-arch-y
pa-tri-cian
pat-ri-cid-al
pat-ri-mo-ni-al
pat-ri-mo-ny
pa-tri-ot-ic
pa-tri-ot-ism
pa-tris-tic
pa-trolled
pa-trol-ling
pa-tron-age
pa-tron-ess
pat-ro-nite
pa-tron-ize
pat-ro-nym-ic
pa-tron-y-my
pa-troon
pat-terned
pau-ci-ty
Pau-li-na
Pau-line
Paul-ine (of Paul)
Paul-ist
pau-lo-post
pau-per-ize
paus-al
pav-er
pa-vil-ion
Pav-lov-i-an
pav-o-nite
pawn-ee (pledgee)
Paw-nee (Indian)
pay-ee
pay-o-la
peace-a-ble
peaked (topped)
peak-ed (pale)
pearl-es-cent
pearl-ite
peas-ant-ry
pe-can
pec-ca-ble
pec-ca-dil-lo
pec-cant
pec-ca-ry
pec-tin-ase
pec-ti-nate
pec-tin-ic
pec-to-lyt-ic
pec-to-ral
pec-to-ril-o-quy
pec-tous (chemistry)
pec-tus (zoology)

pe-cu-liar
pe-cu-li-ar-i-ty
pe-cu-ni-ar-y
ped-a-gog
ped-a-gog-i-cal
ped-a-gog-y
ped-aled
ped-al-ine
ped-ant
pe-dan-tic
ped-ant-ry
ped-dler
Pe-der-sen
ped-es-tal
pe-des-tri-an
pe-di-at-ric
pe-di-a-tri-cian
ped-i-cel
ped-i-cle
pe-dic-u-lar
Pe-dic-u-lar-is
pe-dic-u-lo-sis
pe-dic-u-lous (adj.)
Pe-dic-u-lus (n.)
ped-i-cure
ped-i-gree
ped-o-cal
pe-dol-o-gy
pe-dom-e-ter
ped-o-met-ri-cal
pe-dun-cu-lar
peel-er
peep-er
peer-age
pee-vish
Peg-a-sus
peg-ma-tite
peg-ma-tit-ic
peign-oir
pei-ram-e-ter
pej-o-ra-tive
Pe-king-ese
pe-koe
pe-lag-ic
pel-ar-go-nate
pel-ar-gon-ic
pel-ar-gon-i-din
pel-ar-go-nin
pel-er-ine
pel-i-can
pe-lisse
pel-la-gra
pel-let-er

pel-lu-cid-i-ty
pel-mat-o-gran
pe-lo-rus
pelt-er (n.)
pel-ter (v.)
pelt-ry
pel-vic
pel-vim-e-ter
pem-mi-can
pe-nal-ize
pen-al-ty
pen-ance
pe-na-tes
pench-ant
pen-ciled
pend-ant (n.)
pend-en-cy
pend-ent (adj.)
pen-du-los-i-ty
pen-du-lum
Pe-nel-o-pe
pen-e-tra-ble
pen-e-tram-e-ter
pen-e-tra-tive
pen-e-tra-tor
pen-e-trom-e-ter
pen-guin
pen-i-cil-lin
pen-i-cil-lin-ase
pen-i-cil-li-o-sis
pe-nin-su-lar
pen-i-tent
pen-i-ten-tia-ry
pen-ni-nite
Penn-syl-va-nian
Pe-nob-scot
pe-no-log-i-cal
pe-nol-o-gy
Pen-sa-co-la
pen-sive
pent-ac-id
pen-ta-cle
pen-tad
pen-ta-dec-ane
pen-ta-dec-yl
pen-ta-e-ryth-ri-tol
pen-ta-gon
pen-tag-o-nal
pen-ta-he-dral
pen-ta-hy-drite
pen-ta-mer
pen-tam-er-al
pen-tam-er-ous (adj.)

pen-tam-er-us (n.)
pen-tam-e-ter
pent-am-i-dine
pen-tane
pen-ta-no-ic
pen-ta-ploi-dic
pen-tarch-y
pen-ta-rone
Pen-ta-teuch
pen-tath-lon
pen-ta-tom-ic
pen-ta-va-lent
Pen-te-cos-tal
pen-te-nyl
pen-ti-tol
pen-to-bar-bi-tal
pen-tode
pen-tom-ic
pen-to-san
Pen-to-thal
pent-ox-ide
pen-tryl
pen-tu-lose
pen-tyl-ene
pen-tyl-i-dene
pe-nul-i-mate
pe-num-bra
pe-nu-ri-ous
pen-u-ry
pe-on-age
pe-o-ny
peo-ple
Pe-o-ri-a
pe-pi-no
pep-lum
pep-si-gogue
pep-sin-if-er-ous
pep-sin-o-gen
pep-ti-dase
pep-to-nate
pep-to-nize
per-a-ce-tic
per-am-bu-la-tor
per-bo-rate
Per-bu-nan
per-ca-line
per-ceiv-a-ble
per-ceiv-er
per-cent-age
per-cent-ile
per-cep-ti-ble
per-cep-tive
per-cep-tu-al

perch-er
Per-che-ron
per-chlo-rate
per-chlo-ryl
per-cip-i-ent
per-co-la-tor
per cu-ri-am
per-cus-sive
per-e-gri-nate
pe-rei-ra
pe-remp-tive
pe-remp-to-ry
pe-ren-ni-al
per-fect-er
per-fect-i-ble
per-fec-tor
per-fer-vid
per-fid-i-ous
per-fi-dy
per-fo-ra-tor
per-form-ance
per-form-er
per-fum-er-y
per-func-to-ry
per-i-anth
per-i-ar-thri-tis
per-i-as-tron
per-i-car-di-tis
per-i-car-di-um
per-i-cla-site
Per-i-cle-an
pe-ric-o-pe
per-i-cop-ic
pe-rid-i-um
pe-rid-o-tite
per-i-gee
pe-rig-y-nous
per-i-he-lion
per-iled
per-il-ous
pe-rim-e-ter
per-i-met-ri-cal
pe-rim-e-try
per-i-ne-al
per-i-ne-or-rha-phy
per-i-neph-ri-um
per-i-ne-um
pe-ri-od-ic (at intervals)
per-i-od-ic (chemistry)
pe-ri-od-i-cal
pe-ri-o-dic-i-ty
per-i-os-te-um
per-i-pa-tet-ic

pe-riph-er-al-ly
pe-riph-er-y
per-i-phrase
pe-riph-ra-sis
pe-rip-ter-al
pe-rip-ter-y
pe-rique
pe-ris-cil
per-i-scop-ic
per-ish
per-i-som-al
pe-ris-sad
per-i-stal-tic
per-i-sta-sis
per-i-sty-lar
pe-rit-o-my
per-i-to-ne-os-co-py
per-i-to-ne-um
per-i-to-nit-ic
per-i-to-ni-tis
per-i-win-kle
per-jur-er
per-ju-ri-ous
per-ju-ry
per-lite
per-ma-frost
Perm-al-loy
per-ma-nent
per-man-ga-nate
per-me-a-ble
per-me-am-e-ter
Per-mi-an
per-mis-si-ble
per-mit-tee
per-mut-a-ble
per-mu-ta-tor
per-ni-cious
per-ni-o-sis
per-o-ne-al
Pe-ro-nist
per-o-ra-tion
pe-ro-sis
per-ox-i-dase
per-ox-ide
per-ox-y-a-ce-tic
per-ox-y-di-sul-fate
per-pen-dic-u-lar
per-pe-tra-tor
per-pet-u-al
per-pe-tu-i-ty
per-qui-site
per-se-cu-tion
per-se-cu-to-ry

Per-se-id
per-se-i-tol
per-se-ver-ance
per-sev-er-a-tive
Per-shing
Per-sian
per-si-flage
per-sist-ence
per-sist-er
per-snick-e-ty
per-son-a-ble
per-son-al-i-ty
per-son-al-ty
per-son-nel
per-spec-tive
per-spec-tom-e-ter
per-spi-ca-cious
per-spi-cac-i-ty
per-spi-cu-i-ty
per-spic-u-ous
per-spir-a-ble
per-spi-ra-tion
per-spir-a-tive
per-spir-a-to-ry
per-suad-er
per-sua-si-ble
per-sua-sive
perth-ite
per-ti-na-cious
per-ti-nac-i-ty
per-ti-nent
per-turb-a-ble
per-tur-ba-tion
per-turb-er
pe-rus-al
Pe-ru-vi-an
per-va-sive
per-ver-sion
per-ver-si-ty
per-vert-i-ble
per-vi-ca-cious
per-vi-cac-i-ty
per-vi-ous
per-y-lene
pe-se-ta
Pe-sha-war
pes-sa-ry
pes-si-mis-tic
pes-tered
pes-ti-ci-dal
pes-tif-er-ous
pes-ti-lence
pes-tle

pes-tol-o-gy
pet-al-if-er-ous
pet-al-ite
pet-al-ous
pet-al-y
pe-tard
pe-te-chi-al
Pe-ter
pet-i-o-lar
pet-i-ole
pet-it
pe-tite
pe-ti-tion-er
Pe-trar-chan
Pe-trarch-ist
pe-trel
pe-tres-cence
pe-tri
pet-ri-fac-tion
pe-tro-chem-i-cal
pe-trog-e-ny
pe-trog-ra-pher
pet-ro-graph-i-cal
pe-trog-ra-phy
pet-rol
pet-ro-lage
pet-ro-la-tum
pet-ro-lene
pe-tro-le-um
pe-trol-ic
pet-ro-lif-er-ous
pet-ro-lize
pet-ro-log-ic
pe-trol-o-gy
pe-tro-sal
pet-rous
pe-trox-o-lin
pet-u-lant
pe-tu-nia
pe-yo-te
pha-com-e-ter
pha-e-ton
phag-o-cyte
phag-o-cyt-ic
phag-o-cy-to-sis
pha-lange
pha-lan-ge-al
pha-lanx
phal-loi-dine
phan-er-ite
phan-er-o-gram
phan-er-os-co-py
phan-er-o-sis

phan-o-tron
phan-tas-ma-go-ri-al
phan-tas-mal
phan-tom
phan-to-scope
Phar-aoh
phar-i-sa-i-cal
Phar-i-see
phar-ma-ceu-ti-cal
phar-ma-cist
phar-ma-cog-no-sy
phar-mac-o-lite
phar-ma-col-o-gy
phar-ma-co-peia
pha-ryn-ge-al
phar-yn-gi-tis
pha-ryn-go-log-i-cal
phar-yn-gol-o-gy
pha-ryn-go-scope
phar-ynx
phase-me-ter
pha-se-o-lin
phas-er (one who phases)
pha-sic
pha-si-tron
pha-sor (electrical)
pheas-ant
phel-lan-drene
phen-ac-e-tin
phen-a-cite
phen-a-cyl
phen-an-threne
phen-an-thri-dine
phe-nan-thri-din-i-um
phe-nan-thro-line
phe-nan-thryl
phen-ar-sa-zine
phen-a-zine
phe-net-i-dine
phen-e-tole
phe-nic
phen-mi-az-ine
phe-no-bar-bi-tal
phe-no-cop-ic
phe-no-crys-tic
phe-nol
phe-no-lase
phe-no-late
phe-no-lic
phe-no-log-i-cal
phe-nol-o-gy
phe-nol-phthal-ein
phe-nom-e-nal

phe-nom-e-no-log-i-cal
phe-nom-e-nol-o-gy
phe-no-plast
phe-no-type
phen-ox-ide
phe-nox-y-a-ce-tic
phen-tol-a-mine
phen-yl-ac-et-al-de-hyde
phen-yl-ate
phen-yl-ene
phen-yl-eph-rine
phen-yl-eth-yl-ene
phe-nyl-ic
phen-yl-ke-to-nu-ric
phe-nyt-o-in
phe-o-chro-mo-cy-to-ma
phe-o-phor-bide
phe-o-phy-tin
Phil-a-del-phi-an
phi-lan-der
phil-an-throp-ic
phi-lan-thro-pist
phi-lan-thro-py
phil-a-tel-ic
phi-lat-e-list
phi-lat-e-ly
phil-har-mon-ic
phil-i-a-ter
phi-lip-pic
Phil-ip-pine
Phil-is-tine
phil-o-den-dron
phil-o-graph
phi-log-y-ny
phil-o-log-i-cal
phi-lol-o-gy
phil-o-pe-na
phi-los-o-pher
phil-o-soph-i-cal
phi-los-o-phiz-er
phi-los-o-phy
phil-ter
phle-bit-ic
phle-bi-tis
phleb-o-graph-ic
phle-bog-ra-phy
phle-bot-o-my
phleg-mat-ic
phlob-a-phene
phlo-em
phlo-gis-ton
phlog-o-pi-ti-za-tion
phlo-i-on-ic

phlor-e-tin
phlor-i-zin-ize
phlor-o-glu-cin-ol
phlo-rol
phlox-ine
pho-bi-a
pho-bo-tax-is
phoe-be
Phoe-ni-cian
Phoe-nix
phon-as-the-ni-a
phon-au-to-graph
pho-ne-mat-ic
pho-ne-mic
pho-ne-mic-i-ty
pho-nen-do-scope
pho-net-ic
pho-ne-ti-cian
Phone-vi-sion
pho-ni-at-ric
phon-ic
pho-no-gen-ic
pho-no-graph-i-cal
pho-nog-ra-phy
pho-no-lite
pho-nol-o-gy
pho-nom-e-ter
pho-nom-e-try
pho-no-phore
pho-noph-o-rous
pho-ny
phor-bin
pho-re-sis
pho-ret-ic
pho-rom-e-ter
pho-rom-e-try
pho-rone
pho-rop-tor
phos-gen-ite
phos-pham-ic
phos-pha-tase
phos-pha-te-mi-a
phos-phat-ic
phos-phi-nate
phos-phin-ic
phos-pho-a-mi-no-lip-ide
phos-pho-di-es-ter-ase
phos-pho-nate
phos-phon-ic
phos-pho-rate
phos-pho-re-al
phos-pho-res-cence
phos-phor-ic

phos-phor-o-gen
phos-pho-ro-gen-ic
phos-pho-rol-y-sis
phos-pho-rous (adj.)
phos-pho-rus (n.)
phos-pho-ryl-ase
phos-vi-tin
pho-tics
pho-to-chro-my
pho-to-gen-ic
pho-to-gram-me-try
pho-tog-ra-pher
pho-to-graph-ic
pho-tog-ra-phy
pho-to-gra-vure
pho-tol-y-sis
pho-to-lyt-ic
pho-tom-e-ter
pho-to-met-ric
pho-tom-e-try
pho-ton
pho-to-nas-tic
pho-top-a-thy
pho-to-pho-re-sis
phot-op-tom-e-ter
pho-to-stat-ed
pho-to-trop-ic
pho-tot-ro-pism
pho-tron-ic
phras-a-ble
phra-se-o-gram
phra-se-og-ra-phy
phra-se-ol-o-gy
phras-er
phras-ing
phren-ic
phren-i-cot-o-my
phre-ni-tis
phren-o-log-i-cal
phre-nol-o-gy
phren-o-sin
Phryg-i-an
phtha-lam-ic
phthal-ate
phthal-ein
phthal-ic
phthal-im-ide
phthal-in
phthal-o-ni-trile
phthal-o-yl
phthi-o-col
phthi-ri-a-sis
phthis-ick-y

phthis-i-ol-o-gy
phthi-sis
phy-col-o-gy
phy-lac-tery
phyl-lo-por-phy-rin
phy-lo-ge-net-ic
phy-log-e-ny
phy-lum
phy-ma-to-sis
phys-i-at-rics
phys-ic
phys-i-cal
phy-si-cian
phys-i-cist
phys-i-og-no-my
phys-i-og-ra-phy
phys-i-ol-a-ter
phys-i-o-log-i-cal
phys-i-ol-o-gy
phys-i-om-e-try
phys-i-os-o-phy
phy-sique
phy-so-car-pous
phy-so-stig-mine
phy-tase
Phy-tin
phy-to-flu-ene
phy-tog-a-my
phy-to-gen-ic
phy-tol-o-gy
phy-tom-e-ter
phy-to-met-ric
phy-toph-a-gous
phy-to-sis
phy-tos-te-rol
phy-tyl
pi-a-nis-si-mo
pi-an-ist
pi-a-niste
pi-a-nis-tic
pi-an-o-for-te
pi-as-sa-va
pi-as-ter
pic-a-resque
pic-a-yune
Pic-ca-dil-ly
pic-ca-lil-li
pic-e-in
pi-cene
pick-et-er
pick-led
pick-ling
pic-nick-er

pic-o-line
pic-o-lin-ic
pic-ram-ic
pic-ram-ide
pic-rate
pic-ric
pic-ro-cro-cin
pic-ro-lon-ic
pic-rom-er-ite
pic-ryl
pic-to-graph-ic
pic-tog-ra-phy
pic-to-ri-al
pic-tur-a-ble
pic-tur-esque
pic-ul
pid-dler
pi-ece de re-sis-tance
piec-er
pierc-er
pi-e-ty
pi-e-zom-e-ter
pi-e-zom-e-try
pi-geon-eer
pig-men-tar-y
pi-gnon
pik-er
pi-las-ter
pil-chard
pil-er
pil-fer-age
pil-grim-age
pi-lif-er-ous
pil-lag-er
pil-lo-ry
pi-lo-car-pi-dine
pi-lose
pi-lo-sine
pi-los-i-ty
pi-lot-age
Pil-sner
pil-u-lar
pim-an-threne
pi-mar-ic
pim-e-late
pi-men-ta
pi-men-to
pi-mien-to
pim-ply
pin-a-coi-dal
pin-a-col
pi-nac-o-late
pi-nac-o-lone

pin-a-cy-a-nol
pi-nane
pin-cers
pinch-er
pin-e-al
pi-nene
pin-er-y
pi-nic
pin-ion
pi-nite
pi-ni-tol
pink-er
pin-na-cle
pi-no-cam-phe-ol
pi-noch-le
pi-no-lin
pi-ñon
pi-non-ic
pi-no-syl-vin
pin-tle
pi-nyl
pi-o-neered
pi-os-i-ty
pi-ous
pip-age
pi-pec-o-line
pip-er
pi-per-a-zine
pi-per-ic
pi-per-i-dine
pip-er-ine
pi-per-o-nyl-ic
pip-er-ox-an
pi-per-y-lene
pi-pet
pi-quan-cy
pi-quant
pi-qué (fabric)
pi-quet
pi-ra-cy
pi-ra-nha
pi-rat-i-cal
pi-rogue
pir-ou-ette
pis-ca-to-ri-al
Pis-ces
pis-cine
pi-si-form
pis-tach-i-o
pis-til-late
pitch-er
pit-e-ous
pith-e-can-thro-poid

pith-e-col-o-gy
pith-i-ness
pit-i-a-ble
pi-tom-e-ter
pi-ton
pi-tu-i-tar-y
Pi-tu-i-trin
pi-val-ic
piv-ot-al
piv-ot-er
pix-i-lat-ed
piz-ze-ri-a
plac-a-ble
plac-ard (n.)
pla-card (v.)
pla-cat-er
pla-ca-to-ry
place-a-ble
pla-ce-bo
pla-cen-ta
plac-en-tar-y
plac-en-ti-tis
plac-er
plac-id
pla-cid-i-ty
plack-et
pla-coi-dal
pla-gia-rism
pla-gia-rize
pla-gi-o-clase
pla-gi-o-nite
plagued
plagu-er
pla-gui-ly
pla-guy
plain-tiff
plain-tive
plait-er
pla-nar-i-ty
pla-na-tion
plan-chet
plan-chette
pla-ner (tree)
plan-er
plan-et
plan-e-tar-i-um
plan-e-tar-y
plan-e-tes-i-mal
plan-et-oi-dal
plan-et-o-log-ic
plan-e-tol-o-gy
plan-gen-cy
pla-nig-ra-phy

pla-nim-e-ter
pla-ni-met-ric
plan-i-sphere
plank-tiv-o-rous
pla-no-con-cave
plan-o-graph
pla-nog-ra-phy
pla-nom-e-ter
plan-o-sol
plan-tain
plan-tar
plan-ta-tion
plant-er
pla-num
pla-quette
plas-ma-pher-e-sis
plas-min-o-gen
plas-mo-di-a-sis
plas-mo-di-um
plas-mol-y-sis
plas-mo-lyt-ic
plas-ter
plas-ti-ca-tor
plas-ti-cim-e-ter
plas-tic-i-ty
plas-ti-ciz-er
plas-ti-line
plas-ti-noid
plas-ti-sol
plas-to-mer
plas-tom-e-ter
plas-tron
pla-teau
plat-ed
plat-en
plat-er
pla-ti-na
pla-tin-ic
plat-i-no-type
plat-i-num
plat-i-tu-di-nar-i-an
pla-ton-ic
Pla-to-nist
pla-toon
plat-y-nite
plat-y-pus
plau-dit
plau-si-ble
plead-er
pleas-ant-ry
pleas-ur-a-ble
pleat-er
ple-be-ian

pleb-i-scite
pledg-ee
pledge-or (law)
pledg-er
pledg-et
Ple-ia-des
plei-o-bar
plei-ot-ro-py
Pleis-to-cene
ple-na-ry
plen-i-po-ten-tia-ry
plen-i-tude
plen-te-ous
plen-ti-ful
ple-num
ple-o-nasm
ple-rot-ic
pleth-o-ra
ple-thor-ic
pleu-ral
pleu-ri-sy
pleu-rit-ic
pleu-ro-dont
plex-im-e-ter
plex-us
Pli-o-cene
plom-bage
plov-er
plu-ma-ceous
plum-age
plu-mate
plum-ba-gin
plum-ba-go
plum-bate
plumb-er
plum-bif-er-ous
plum-bite
plum-bous
plu-mose
plump-er
plun-der
plung-er
plu-ral-i-ty
plu-ri-va-lent
plu-tar-chy
plu-toc-ra-cy
plu-to-crat
plu-to-nism
plu-to-ni-um
plu-vi-og-ra-phy
plu-vi-om-e-ter
plu-vi-o-met-ric
plu-vi-ous

Plym-outh
pneu-drau-lic
pneu-mat-ic
pneu-ma-tic-i-ty
pneu-ma-tol-y-sis
pneu-ma-tom-e-ter
pneu-ma-to-sis
pneu-mec-to-my
pneu-mo-coc-cus
pneu-mol-y-sis
pneu-mo-nia
pneu-mon-ic
penu-mo-ni-tis
poach-er
po-choir
pock-et
po-dal-ic
po-di-a-trist
po-di-a-try
po-di-um
po-do-lite
pod-zol-ize
po-et-as-ter
po-et-i-cal
po-et-ry
po-go-not-ro-phy
po-grom
poign-an-cy
poign-ant
poi-ki-lit-ic
poi-kil-o-cy-to-sis
poin-ci-an-a
poin-set-ti-a
point-er
Poi-ret
pois-er
poi-son-ous
pok-er
po-lar
po-lar-im-e-ter
po-lar-i-met-ric
Po-la-ris
po-lar-i-scope
po-lar-i-stro-bom-e-ter
po-lar-i-ty
po-lar-iz-er
po-lar-o-graph-ic
po-lar-og-ra-phy
Po-lar-oid
po-lar-on
po-lem-ic
pol-e-mize
pol-er

po-li-a-nite
po-lic-ing
pol-i-cy
po-li-o-my-e-li-tis
po-li-o-sis
Pol-ish
pol-ish-er
Po-lit-bu-ro
po-lit-i-cal
pol-i-ti-cian
pol-i-tics
po-litz-er
pol-len-iz-er
poll-er
pol-li-na-tion
pol-li-nif-er-ous
pol-lin-i-um
pol-li-no-sis
pol-lu-cite
pol-lut-ant
pol-lut-er
pol-lu-tion
pol-o-naise
po-lo-ni-um
pol-troon
pol-y-a-cryl-ic
pol-y-am-ide
pol-y-an-dry
pol-y-ar-gy-rite
pol-y-ba-site
pol-y-chro-mat-ic
pol-y-chro-my
pol-y-clin-ic
pol-y-crase
pol-y-cy-the-mi-a
po-lyd-y-mite
pol-y-ene
pol-y-es-ter
pol-y-eth-yl-ene
pol-y-gam-ic
po-lyg-a-my
po-lyg-e-ny
pol-y-glot
pol-y-gon
po-lyg-o-nal
pol-y-graph-ic
po-lyg-ra-phy
pol-y-he-dral
pol-y-hi-dro-sis
pol-y-i-so-bu-tyl-ene
pol-y-i-so-top-ic
pol-y-kar-y-on
pol-y-mer-ic

po-lym-er-i-za-tion
po-lym-er-iz-er
po-lym-er-ous
pol-y-me-ter
pol-ym-nite
pol-y-mor-phous
Pol-y-ne-sian
pol-y-no-mi-al
pol-y-nu-cle-o-sis
pol-yp-ec-to-my
po-lyph-a-gous
po-lyph-o-ny
pol-y-ploid-dic
pol-yp-ous
pol-yp-tych
pol-y-pus
pol-y-so-ma-ty
pol-y-sty-rene
pol-y-tech-ni-cal
pol-y-trop-ic
pol-y-u-ro-nide
pol-y-va-lent
pol-y-vi-nyl
pom-ace
po-made
po-ma-tum
pome-gran-ate
Pom-er-a-ni-an
pom-meled
po-mo-log-i-cal
po-mol-o-gy
pom-pa-dour
pom-pa-no
Pom-pe-ian
pom-pos-i-ty
pomp-ous
Pon-a-pe-an
pon-cho
pond-age
pon-der-o-sa
pon-der-os-i-ty
pon-der-ous
pon-iard
pon-tage
pon-tif-i-cal
pon-tif-i-ca-tor
poo-dle
pop-e-line
pop-lit-e-al
pop-ping
pop-u-lace
pop-u-lar-i-ty
pop-u-lar-ize

pop-u-lous
por-ce-lain
por-ce-la-ne-ous
por-cine
por-cu-pine
po-ri-ci-dal
po-rif-er-ous
po-ri-tes
por-nog-ra-pher
por-no-graph-ic
po-rom-e-ter
po-ro-scope
po-ros-co-py
po-rose
po-ro-sim-e-ter
po-ros-i-ty
po-rot-ic
po-rous
por-phin
por-phy-rin
por-phy-rit-ic
por-phyr-ox-ine
por-phy-ry
por-poise
port-a-ble
por-tage
por-tal
por-ten-tous
por-ter
port-fo-li-o
por-ti-co
por-tiere
port-man-teau
por-trai-ture
Por-tu-guese
por-tu-lac-a
pos-er
po-seur
po-si-tion-er
pos-i-ti-val
pos-i-tiv-ism
pos-i-tri-no
pos-i-tro-ni-um
po-sol-o-gy
pos-sessed
pos-sess-es
pos-ses-sive
pos-ses-sor
pos-si-bil-i-ty
post-age
post-al
post-er
pos-te-ri-or

pos-ter-i-ty
pos-ter-o-dor-sal
post-hu-mous
pos-tu-lant
pos-tur-al
po-ta-ble
po-tage
po-tam-ic
pot-a-mog-ra-phy
pot-a-mom-e-ter
pot-ash
pot-as-sam-ide
po-tas-sic
po-tas-si-um
po-ta-to-ry
Pot-a-wat-o-mi
po-ten-cy
po-ten-tate
po-ten-ti-al-i-ty
po-ten-ti-om-e-ter
po-tom-e-ter
pot-pour-ri
pot-sherd
poul-tice
poul-try
pounc-er
pound-age
pound-er
pour-par-ler
pousse ca-fe
pout-er
pov-er-ty
pow-dered
pow-ered
poz-zo-la-nic
prac-ti-ca-ble
prac-ti-cal-i-ty
prac-tic-er
prac-ti-tion-er
prae-ci-pe
prag-mat-ic
prag-ma-tism
prai-rie
prais-er
pra-line
pranc-er
pran-di-al
prank-ster
pra-se-o-dym-i-um
pras-oid
pra-tique
prat-tler
prax-e-ol-o-gy

pray-er
preach-er
pre-am-ble
pre-car-i-ous
prec-a-to-ry
pre-ced-a-ble
prec-e-dence
pre-ce-dent (adj.)
prec-e-dent (n., v.)
pre-ced-ing
pre-cep-tor
pre-ci-os-i-ty
pre-cious
prec-i-pice
pre-cip-i-tant
pre-cip-i-ta-tor
pre-cip-i-tin-o-gen
pre-cip-i-tous
Pre-cip-i-tron
pre-ci-sion
pre-ci-sive
pre-clu-sive
pre-co-cious
pre-coc-i-ty
pre-cor-di-um
pre-cur-sor
pre-da-ceous
pre-dac-i-ty
pred-a-to-ry
pred-e-ces-sor
pre-den-ta-ry
pre-des-ti-nate
pred-i-ca-ble
pre-dic-a-ment
pred-i-cate
pred-i-ca-to-ry
pre-dict-able
pre-dic-tion
pre-dic-tor
pred-i-lec-tion
pred-nis-o-lone
pred-ni-sone
pre-dom-i-nance
pre-emp-to-ry
pre-fab-ri-ca-tor
pref-ace
pref-a-to-ry
pre-fec-ture
pre-fer
pref-er-a-ble
pref-er-ence
pref-er-en-tial
pre-fer-ment

pre-for-ma-tion
preg-nan-cy
preg-nen-in-o-lone
preg-nen-o-lone
pre-hen-si-ble
pre-hen-sile
prehn-ite
prehn-i-tene
prehn-it-ic
prej-u-di-cial
prel-ate
pre-lim-i-nar-y
prel-ude
pre-lu-di-al
pre-ma-ture
pre-med-i-ta-tive
pre-mier
pre-miere
prem-ise (n.)
pre-mise (v.)
pre-mi-um
pre-mo-ni-tion
pre-mon-i-to-ry
prep-a-ra-tion
pre-par-a-to-ry
pre-par-er
pre-pon-der-ant
pre-po-si-tion (before)
prep-o-si-tion
pre-pos-ter-ous
pre-puce
pre-req-ui-site
pre-rog-a-tive
pres-age (n.)
pre-sage (v.)
pres-by-o-phre-ni-a
pres-by-o-pi-a
Pres-by-te-ri-an
pres-by-ter-y
pre-science
pre-scient
pre-scis-sion
pre-scrib-er
pre-scrip-ti-ble
pre-scrip-tive
pres-ent (adj. and n.)
pre-sent (v.; also as n.,
  military term)
pre-sent-a-ble
pres-en-ta-tion
pre-sen-ta-tive
pre-sent-er
pre-sen-ti-ment

pre-sen-tive
pres-er-va-tion
pre-serv-a-tive
pre-serv-er
pres-i-den-cy
pres-i-den-tial
pre-sid-i-o
pre-sid-i-um
press-er
pres-sor
pres-sur-ize
pres-ti-dig-i-ta-tor
pres-tig-i-ous
Pres-tone
pre-sum-a-ble
pre-sump-tion
pre-sump-tive
pre-sump-tu-ous
pre-tend-er
pre-tense
pre-ten-tious
pret-er-it
pre-ter-i-tal
pre-ter-mit
pre-to-ri-al
pret-ti-ness
pret-zel
pre-vail
prev-a-lence
pre-var-i-ca-tor
pre-vent-a-tive
pre-vent-er
pre-ven-tive
pre-vi-ous
pric-er
prick-ling
pri-ma-cy
pri-ma fa-ci-e
pri-ma-quine
pri-mar-i-ly
pri-mar-y
pri-mate
Pri-ma-tes
pri-ma-tol-o-gy
pri-ma-ve-ral
prim-er
prim-e-val
prim-i-tiv-ism
pri-mo-gen-i-ture
pri-mor-di-al
prim-u-lav-er-in
prim-u-line
pri-mus

prin-cess
prin-ci-pal
prin-ci-ple
print-er-y
pri-or-i-ty
pri-o-ry
pris-mat-ic
pris-ma-toi-dal
pris-moi-dal
pri-som-e-ter
pris-on-er
pris-tine
pri-va-cy
pri-va-teer
pri-va-tion
priv-a-tive
pri-vat-ize
priv-et
priv-i-leged
priv-i-ty
priz-a-ble
prob-a-bil-i-ty
prob-a-ble
pro-ba-tion-er
pro-ba-tive
pro-bi-ty
prob-lem-at-i-cal
prob-o-la
pro-bos-cis
pro-caine
pro-ce-dur-al
pro-ce-dure
proc-ess (n., v.)
proc-ess-ing
pro-ces-sion
proc-es-sor
pro-claim
proc-la-ma-tion
pro-clam-a-to-ry
pro-clit-ic
pro-cliv-i-ty
pro-cli-vous
proc-ne-mi-al
pro-cras-ti-na-tor
pro-cre-a-tor
pro-crus-te-an
proc-ti-tis
proc-to-log-i-cal
proc-tol-o-gy
proc-to-ri-al
proc-to-scop-ic
proc-tos-co-py
pro-cur-a-ble

proc-u-ra-cy
proc-u-ra-to-ry
pro-cur-er
pro-cur-ess
prod-i-gal-i-ty
pro-dig-i-o-sin
pro-di-gious
prod-i-gy
pro-drome
pro-duce (v.)
prod-uce (n.)
pro-duc-er
pro-duc-i-ble
prod-uct (n.)
pro-duct-i-ble
pro-duc-tion
pro-duc-tiv-i-ty
prof-a-na-tion
pro-fan-i-ty
pro-fess-ant
pro-fessed
pro-fes-sion
pro-fes-sor
pro-fes-so-ri-al
prof-fered
pro-fi-cient
pro-fil-er
pro-fil-o-graph
pro-fi-lom-e-ter
prof-it-a-ble
prof-it-eer
prof-it-er
prof-li-ga-cy
prof-li-gate
prof-lu-ence
pro-fun-di-ty
pro-fu-sion
pro-gen-i-tor
prog-e-ny
pro-ges-ter-one
prog-na-thous
prog-no-sis
prog-nos-ti-ca-tor
pro-grammed
pro-gram-er
pro-gram-ing
pro-gram-ist
pro-gram-mat-ic
prog-ress (n.)
pro-gress (v.)
pro-gres-sion
pro-gres-sive
pro-hib-it-er

pro-hi-bi-tion
pro-hib-i-tive
pro-hib-i-to-ry
proj-ect (n.)
pro-ject (v.)
pro-jec-tile
pro-jec-tive
pro-jec-tor
pro-ji-cient
pro-lam-in
pro-la-tive
pro-le-gom-e-non
pro-lep-sis
pro-le-tar-i-an
pro-lif-er-a-tive
pro-lif-ic
pro-li-fic-i-ty
pro-line
pro-lix
pro-log
pro-lon-ga-tion
pro-lu-so-ry
prom-e-nad-er
Pro-me-the-us
pro-me-thi-um
prom-i-nence
prom-is-cu-i-ty
pro-mis-cu-ous
prom-is-ee
prom-i-sor
prom-is-so-ry
Prom-i-zole
prom-on-to-ry
pro-mot-er
prompt-er
promp-ti-tude
pro-mul-ga-tion
pro-mul-ga-tor
pro-na-tor
pro-nom-i-nal
pro-no-tum
pro-nounce-a-ble
pro-nun-ci-a-tion
proof-er
pro-pa-di-ene
prop-a-ga-ble
prop-a-gan-dist
prop-a-ga-tor
pro-pam-i-dine
pro-pa-no-ic
pro-pa-nol
pro-par-gyl
pro-par-ox-y-tone

pro-pel-lant (n.)
pro-pel-lent (adj.)
pro-pel-ler
pro-pe-no-ic
pro-pen-si-ty
pro-pe-nyl
pro-per-din
prop-er-ly
prop-er-ty
proph-e-cy (n.)
proph-e-sy (v.)
proph-et
pro-phet-ic
pro-phy-lac-tic
pro-phy-lax-is
pro-pin-qui-ty
pro-pi-o-late
pro-pi-o-lic
pro-pi-o-nate
pro-pi-on-ic
pro-pi-o-ni-trile
pro-pi-o-nyl
pro-pi-on-y-late
pro-pi-ti-ate
pro-pi-tious
pro-po-de-um
pro-po-nent
pro-por-tion-ate
pro-pos-al
pro-pos-er
prop-o-si-tion
pro-pri-e-tar-y
pro-pri-e-tor
pro-pri-e-ty
pro-pox-y-ac-et-an-i-lide
pro-pul-sive
pro-pul-so-ry
pro-pyl-a-mine
pro-pyl-ene
pro-pyl-ic
prop-y-lite
pro ra-ta
pro-rat-a-ble
pro-rat-er
pro-ro-ga-tion
pro-rogue
pro-sa-i-cal-ly
pro-sce-ni-um
pro-scribe
pro-scrip-tive
pros-e-cu-to-ry
pros-e-cu-trix
pros-e-lyte

pros-e-lyt-iz-er
pro-sod-i-cal
pros-o-dy
pros-o-pite
pros-o-pla-si-a
pros-pect
pro-spec-tive
pros-pec-tor
pro-spec-tus
pros-per-i-ty
pros-per-ous
pro-spi-cience
pros-ta-tec-to-my
pros-tat-ic
pros-ta-ti-tis
pro-sthen-ic
pros-the-sis
pros-thet-ic
pros-the-tist
Pro-stig-min
pros-ti-tute
pros-tra-tor
prot-ac-tin-i-um
pro-ta-gon
pro-tag-o-nist
prot-a-mine
pro-ta-no-pi-a
pro-te-an
pro-te-ase
pro-tect-ant
pro-tec-tive
pro-tec-tor-ate
pro-te-ge
pro-te-ide
pro-tein
pro-tein-a-ceous
pro-tein-ase
pro tem-po-re
pro-te-ol-y-sin
Prot-er-o-zo-ic
pro-test
pro-tes-tant (law)
Prot-es-tant (religion)
prot-es-ta-tion
pro-test-er
pro-thon-o-tar-y
pro-throm-bin
pro-tide
pro-ti-um
pro-to-blast
pro-to-cat-e-chu-al-de-hyde
pro-to-clas-tic
pro-toc-neme

pro-to-col
pro-to-gen
pro-tog-y-ny
pro-ton-ate
pro-to-pine
pro-to-plas-mal
pro-to-trop-ic
pro-tot-ro-py
pro-to-type
pro-to-ver-a-trine
prot-ox-ide
pro-to-zo-a
pro-to-zo-i-a-sis
pro-tract-i-ble
pro-trac-tile
pro-trac-tor
pro-tru-si-ble
pro-tru-sive
pro-tu-ber-ance
proust-ite
prov-a-ble
prov-e-nance
prov-en-der
pro-ve-nience
prov-er
prov-erb
pro-ver-bi-al
pro-vide
prov-i-dence
prov-i-den-tial
pro-vid-er
prov-ince
pro-vin-cial
pro-vi-sion
pro-vi-so-ry
prov-o-ca-tion
pro-voc-a-tive
pro-voc-a-to-ry
pro-vost (military)
prov-ost-al
prow-ess
prowl-er
prox-i-mate
prox-im-i-ty
pru-dence
pru-den-tial
prud-er-y
prud-ish
pru-i-nes-cence
pru-na-sin
pru-nel-la
prun-er
pru-ne-tin

pru-ni-trin
pru-ri-ent
pru-rit-ic
pru-ri-tus
prus-si-ate
psalm-ist
psal-mod-ic
psal-ter-y
pseud-an-dry
pseud-ar-thro-sis
pseu-do-cu-mi-dine
pseu-do-i-o-none
pseu-do-ni-trole
pseu-do-nym
pseu-don-y-mous
pseu-dos-co-py
pseu-dos-to-ma
psil-an-thro-py
psi-lo-mel-ane
psi-lo-sis
psi-lot-ic
psit-ta-co-sis
psit-ta-cot-ic
pso-phom-e-ter
pso-ri-a-sis
pso-ro-sis
Psy-che
psy-che-om-e-try
psy-chi-at-ric
psy-chi-a-trist
psy-chi-a-try
psy-chi-cal
psy-cho-an-a-lyst
psy-cho-an-a-lyt-ic
psy-cho-an-a-lyze
psy-cho-gen-ic
psy-cho-ge-nic-i-ty
psy-cho-graph-ic
psy-chog-ra-phy
psy-cho-log-i-cal
psy-chol-o-gist
psy-chom-e-ter
psy-cho-met-ric
psy-chom-e-tri-cian
psy-chom-e-try
psy-cho-nom-ics
psy-cho-path-ic
psy-chop-a-thy
psy-cho-sis
psy-cho-so-mat-ic
psy-chot-ic
psy-cho-trine
psy-chrom-e-ter

psy-chrom-e-try
psyl-li-um
psyl-lyl
ptar-mi-gan
pter-i-dine
pter-o-dac-tyl
pte-ro-ic
pter-o-pod
Pte-rop-o-da
pter-o-yl
pte-ryg-i-um
pter-y-goid
Ptol-e-ma-ic
pto-maine
pto-sis
pu-ber-ty
pu-ber-u-lent
pu-ber-u-lon-ic
pu-bes-cent
pu-bic
pu-bi-ot-o-my
pub-li-ca-tion
pub-li-cist
pub-lic-i-ty
puck-ered
pu-den-dal
pueb-lo
pu-er-ile
pu-er-per-al
pu-er-pe-ri-um
puff-er
pu-gi-lism
pu-gi-list
pu-gi-lis-tic
pug-na-cious
pug-nac-i-ty
pu-is-sant
pul-chri-tu-di-nous
pu-le-gone
pu-li-cide
pul-ing
pull-er
pul-let
pul-lo-rum
pul-mom-e-ter
pul-mo-nar-y
pul-mon-ic
Pul-mo-tor
pulp-er
pul-pit-eer
pulp-ot-o-my
pulp-ous
pul-que

pul-sa-tance
pul-sa-to-ry
puls-er
pul-sim-e-ter
pul-som-e-ter
pul-ver-iz-er
pul-ver-u-lent
pul-vin-ic
pu-mi-cate
pum-ice
pu-mi-ceous
pump-age
pump-er
pum-per-nick-el
pun-cheon
punch-er
pun-chi-nel-lo
punc-tate
punc-ti-form
punc-til-i-o
punc-til-i-ous
punc-tu-al-i-ty
punc-tu-ate
punc-tur-a-ble
punc-tured
pun-dit
pun-gen-cy
Pu-nic
pu-nic-ic
pun-ish-er
pu-ni-tive
pun-ster
punt-er
Punx-su-taw-ney
pu-pa-tion
pu-pif-er-ous
pu-pil
pu-pil-late
pu-pil-lom-e-ter
pup-pet-eer
pup-pet-ry
pur-chas-er
pu-ree
pur-ga-tive
pur-ga-to-ry
purg-er
pu-ri-fi-ca-tion
pu-rine
pur-ist
pu-ris-tic
pu-ri-tan
pu-ri-ty
Pur-kin-je

pur-lieu
pur-lin
pur-loin
pu-ro-my-cin
pur-ples-cent
pur-plish
pur-pos-ive
pur-pu-ra
pur-pu-rin
pur-pu-rite
pur-pu-ro-gal-lin
pur-pu-rog-e-nous
purs-er
pur-su-ant
pur-suit-me-ter
pur-sui-vant
pur-te-nance
pu-ru-lence
pur-vey-or
pu-sil-la-nim-i-ty
pu-sil-lan-i-mous
pus-tu-lous
pu-ta-tive
pu-tre-fa-cient
pu-tre-fac-tion
pu-tres-cent
pu-tres-ci-ble
pu-tres-cine
pu-trid
put-ter (n., v.)
putt-er (golf club)
Puy-al-lup
puz-zler
pyc-nom-e-ter
pyc-no-sis
pyc-not-ic
py-e-lit-ic
py-e-li-tis
py-e-lo-graph-ic
Pyg-ma-li-on
pyg-my
pyk-rete
py-lor-ic
py-lo-ro-plas-ty
py-lo-rus
py-o-cy-a-nase
py-o-cy-a-nin
py-o-gen-ic
py-or-rhe-a
pyr-a-cene
Pyr-a-lin
pyr-a-mid
py-ram-i-dal

pyr-a-mid-er
pyr-a-mid-i-cal
py-ran
pyr-a-nom-e-ter
py-ran-o-side
pyr-ar-gy-rite
pyr-a-zin-a-mide
pyr-az-ine
pyr-az-ole
py-raz-o-lone
py-raz-o-lyl
py-rene
Pyr-e-ne-an
py-ren-em-a-tous
py-re-thrin
py-re-thrum
Py-rex
py-rex-in
pyr-ge-om-e-ter
pyr-he-li-om-e-ter
pyr-i-bole
py-rid-a-zine
py-rid-ic
pyr-i-dine
pyr-i-din-i-um
pyr-i-done
pyr-i-dyl
py-rim-i-dine
py-rite
py-ri-tes
py-rit-ic
py-rit-if-er-ous
py-ri-to-he-dral
py-ro-cat-e-chu-ic
py-ro-gal-lol
py-ro-ge-na-tion
py-rog-ra-phy
py-ro-lu-site
py-rol-y-sis
py-ro-lyze
py-ro-ma-ni-a
py-rom-e-ter
py-rone
py-ro-sis
py-ro-sphere
py-ro-tech-nic
py-rox-ene
pyr-ox-i-dine
py-rox-y-lin
pyr-rhic
pyr-rol-i-dine
pyr-ro-line
pyr-ro-lo-pyr-i-dine

pyr-ro-lyl
pry-uv-al-de-hyde
pyr-u-vic
py-ryl-i-um

Py-thag-o-re-an
Pyth-i-an
py-thon-ic

Q

quack-er-y
quad-ded
quad-ra-ges-i-mal
quad-ran-gle
quad-ran-gu-lar
quad-rant
quad-rat-ic
quad-ra-ture
quad-ra-tus
quad-ren-ni-al
quad-ric
quad-rille
quad-ril-lion
quad-ri-ple-gic
quad-ri-va-lent
quad-roon
quad-ru-ped
quad-ru-ple
quad-ru-plet
quad-ru-plex
quad-ru-pli-cate
quak-er
qual-i-fi-ca-tion
qua-lim-e-ter
qual-i-ta-tive
qualm-ish
quan-da-ry
quan-tile
quan-tim-e-ter
quan-ti-ta-tive
quan-ti-ty
quan-ti-za-tion
quan-tize
quan-tum
quar-an-tin-er
quar-reled
quar-tan
quar-tered
quar-tern
quar-tet
quar-tile
quartz-ite
quartz-it-ic

quartz-ose
qua-si
quas-si-a
qua-ter-nar-y
qua-ter-ni-on
qua-ter-ni-ty
qua-ter-ni-za-tion
qua-ter-phen-yl
qua-torze
quat-rain
qua-vered
que-brach-i-tol
que-bra-cho
quell-er
quench-er
quen-stedt-ite
quer-ce-tin
quer-ci-mer-i-trin
que-rist
quer-u-lous
que-ry
ques-tion-naire
quet-zal
queu-er
queu-ing
quib-bler
quick-en-ing
qui-es-cent
qui-e-tude
qui-e-tus
quin-a-chrine
quin-al-din-i-um
quin-a-mine
qui-naph-thol
qui-na-ry
quin-az-o-line
quin-i-dine
qui-nine
qui-nin-ic
qui-niz-a-rin
qui-noi-dine
quin-o-line
quin-o-lin-yl

qui-nol-o-gy
quin-o-lyl
qui-none
qui-non-ize
qui-no-nyl
qui-no-va-tan-nic
qui-no-vose
quin-sy
quin-tal
quin-tant
quin-ter-ni-on
quint-es-sence
quin-tet
quin-tile

quin-tu-ple
quin-tu-plet
qui-nu-cli-dine
quip-ster
quiv-ered
quix-ot-ic
quix-o-tism
quiz-zi-cal
quon-dam
quo-rum
quot-a-ble
quo-ta-tion
quot-er
quo-tient

R

rab-bet-ed
rab-bin-ate
rab-id
ra-bid-i-ty
ra-bies
rac-coon
rac-e-mate
ra-ceme
ra-ce-mic
rac-e-mi-za-tion
rac-e-mose
ra-chi-om-e-ter
ra-chis
ra-chit-ic
ra-chi-tis
ra-cial-ism
rac-ing
rac-ist
rack-et-eer
rack-et-y
ra-con
rac-on-teur
ra-dar
ra-di-ac
ra-di-al
ra-di-ant
ra-di-a-tor
rad-i-cal
rad-i-cand
rad-i-cle
ra-di-o
ra-di-o-graph-ic

ra-di-og-ra-phy
ra-di-o-i-so-tope
ra-di-o-log-i-cal
ra-di-ol-o-gy
ra-di-ol-y-sis
ra-di-om-e-ter
ra-di-o-met-ric
ra-di-on-ic
ra-di-o-nu-clide
ra-di-os-co-py
ra-di-o-sonde
rad-ish
ra-di-um
ra-di-us
ra-dome
ra-don
raf-fi-a
raf-fi-nase
raf-fi-nate
raf-fi-nose
raf-fled
raf-ter (roof)
raft-er (worker on rafts)
ra-gout
raid-er
rail-ler-y
rai-ment
rais-er
rai-sin
rais-ing
ra-jah
rak-er

rak-ish
Ra-leigh
ral-ston-ite
ram-bler
ram-bunc-tious
ram-e-kin
ram-ie
ram-i-fi-ca-tion
ra-mose
ram-pa-geous
ram-pag-er
ramp-ant
ram-part
ra-na-les
ranch-er
ran-che-ro
ran-cho
ran-cid-i-ty
ran-cor-ous
ran-dom-ize
rang-er
rang-ette
ra-nine
rank-er
ran-kled
ran-som-er
rant-er
ra-pa-cious
ra-pac-i-ty
ra-pa-ki-vi
rap-er
Raph-a-el
rap-id
ra-pid-i-ty
ra-pi-er
rap-ine
rap-proche-ment
rap-tur-ous
rar-e-fy
rar-i-ty
ras-cal-i-ty
rash-er
rasp-er
ras-ter
rat-a-ble
rat-a-fi-a
ratch-et
rat-er
rath-er
rat-i-fy
ra-tio
ra-ti-oc-i-na-tion
ra-ti-om-e-ter

ra-tion-ale
ra-tion-al-ize
rat-tler
rau-cous
rau-vite
Rau-wol-fi-a
rav-ag-er
rav-eled
rave-lin
rav-el-ing
ra-ven (bird)
rav-en (other meanings)
rav-en-ing
rav-en-ous
ra-vine
rav-ing
rav-ish-er
ra-win-sonde
ra-zon
ra-zor
re-act-ance
re-ac-tion-ar-y
re-ac-tive
re-ac-tor
read-er
read-i-ness
re-a-gent
re-a-gin
re-al-gar
re-al-ism
re-al-is-tic
re-al-ize
re-al-tor
ream-er
reap-er
rea-son-a-ble
Re-au-mur
re-bat-er
re-bel (v.)
reb-el (adj., n.)
re-bel-lious
re-but-ta-ble
re-cal-ci-trant
re-ca-les-cence
re-can-ta-tion
re-ca-pit-u-late
re-ced-ence
re-ced-er
re-ceipt-or
re-ceiv-a-ble
re-ceiv-er
re-cen-sion
re-cep-ta-cle

re-cep-ti-ble
re-cep-tiv-i-ty
re-cep-tor
re-cess-er
re-ces-sion-al
re-ces-sive
re-cher-che
re-cid-i-vist
Re-ci-fe
rec-i-pe
re-cip-i-ent
re-cip-ro-ca-ble
re-cip-ro-cal
rec-i-proc-i-ty
re-ci-sion
re-cit-al
rec-i-ta-tive
reck-on-ing
re-claim
rec-la-ma-tion
re-clin-a-ble
rec-li-na-tion
re-clin-er
rec-luse
re-clu-sive
rec-og-ni-tion
re-cog-ni-zance
rec-og-nize
re-cog-ni-zee
rec-og-niz-er
re-cog-ni-zor
re-col-lect (collect again)
rec-ol-lect (remember)
rec-om-men-da-tion
rec-om-mend-a-to-ry
rec-om-pens-er
re-con-cen-tra-do
rec-on-cil-a-ble
rec-on-cil-er
rec-on-cil-i-a-tion
rec-on-dite
re-con-nais-sance
rec-on-noi-ter
rec-ord (adj., n.)
re-cord (v.)
re-cord-a-ble
rec-or-da-tion
re-cord-er
re-coup
re-cov-er-y
rec-re-ant
rec-re-ate (refresh)
re-cre-ate (create again)

rec-re-a-tion
re-cre-a-tion
re-crim-i-na-to-ry
re-cru-des-cence
re-cruit-er
rec-tan-gle
rec-tan-gu-lar
rec-tan-gu-lom-e-ter
rec-ti-fi-er
rec-ti-lin-e-ar
rec-ti-tude
rec-tor-ate
rec-to-ry
rec-tum
re-cum-bent
re-cu-per-a-tive
re-cur-rence
re-cur-sive
rec-u-sant
re-dac-tor
re-demp-ti-ble
re-demp-tive
re-demp-tor
red-in-gote
red-o-lent
re-doubt-a-ble
re-dox
re-dress-a-ble
re-dress-er
re-duc-er
re-duc-i-ble
re-duc-tase
re-duc-tone
re-duc-tor
re-dun-dan-cy
reef-er
reel-er
re-fec-to-ry
ref-er-a-ble
ref-er-ee
ref-er-ence
ref-er-en-dum
ref-er-en-tial
re-fer-ring
re-fin-er-y
re-flec-tance
re-flect-i-ble
re-flec-tive
re-flec-tom-e-ter
re-flec-tom-e-try
re-flec-tor-ize
re-flex-iv-i-ty
ref-lu-ent

re-for-est-a-tion
re-form-a-ble
ref-or-ma-tion
re-form-a-to-ry
re-form-er
re-frac-tive
re-frac-tom-e-ter
re-frac-to-met-ric
re-frac-tom-e-try
re-frac-to-ry
re-fran-gi-ble
ref-re-na-tion
re-frig-er-ant
re-frig-er-at-ing
re-frig-er-a-tion
re-frig-er-a-tor
ref-uge
ref-u-gee
re-ful-gent
re-fus-al
ref-use (adj., n.)
re-fuse (v.)
re-fut-a-ble
ref-u-ta-tion
re-fut-er
re-ga-lia
re-gal-i-ty
re-ge-late
re-gen-cy
re-gen-er-a-tive
re-gen-er-a-tor
reg-i-cide
re-gime
reg-i-men
reg-i-men-tal
reg-i-men-ta-ry
Re-gi-na
re-gion-al
reg-is-tered
reg-is-tra-ble
reg-is-trar
reg-is-trate
reg-let
Re-gnault
reg-o-sol
re-gres-sive
re-gret-ta-ble
reg-u-lar-i-ty
reg-u-la-tive
reg-u-la-to-ry
reg-u-lus
re-gur-gi-tate
re-ha-bil-i-ta-tive

re-hears-al
re-hears-er
Re-ho-both
Reichs-tag
re-im-burs-a-ble
Rei-nec-ke
re-in-forced
re-it-er-ate
re-ject-a-ble
re-ject-er (one that rejects)
re-jec-tor (circuit)
re-joic-ing
re-join-der
re-ju-ve-na-tor
re-ju-ve-nes-cence
re-laps-er
re-lat-er
rel-a-tiv-ism
rel-a-tiv-i-ty
re-la-tor (law)
re-lax-om-e-ter
re-leas-er
rel-e-ga-ble
rel-e-vant
rel-ict (n.)
re-lict (adj.)
re-lief-er
re-liev-er
re-li-gion
re-li-gi-os-i-ty
re-li-gious
re-lin-quish
rel-i-quar-y
rel-ish
re-lu-cence
re-luc-tance
rel-uc-tiv-i-ty
re-lu-mine
re-main-der
rem-a-nence
re-mark-a-ble
re-me-di-a-ble
re-me-di-al
rem-e-di-less
rem-e-dy
re-mem-brance
re-mind-er
rem-i-nis-cence
rem-i-nis-cer
re-miss-i-ble
re-mis-sive
re-mit-tee
re-mod-eled

re-mon-strance
re-mon-stra-tive
re-mon-stra-tor
re-mov-al
re-mu-ner-a-ble
re-mu-ner-a-tive
ren-ais-sance
Re-nais-sant
re-nal
re-nas-cence
ren-der (v.)
rend-er (n.)
ren-dez-vous
rend-i-ble
ren-di-tion
ren-dzi-na
ren-e-gade
re-nege
ren-gue
re-nin
ren-o-va-tor
re-nowned
rent-al
rent-er (n.)
ren-ter (v.)
re-nun-ci-a-to-ry
re-pair-a-ble
rep-a-ra-ble
rep-a-ra-tion
rep-ar-tee
re-pa-tri-ate
re-peal-er
re-peat-er
re-pel-lant (n.)
re-pel-lent (adj.)
re-pent-ance
re-per-cus-sion
rep-er-to-ry
rep-e-tend
rep-e-ti-tion
re-pet-i-tive
re-place-a-ble
re-plen-ish-er
re-ple-tive
re-plev-in
re-plev-i-sor
rep-li-ca
rep-li-cate
re-port-er
rep-or-to-ri-al
rep-o-si-tion (n.)
re-po-si-tion (v.)
re-pos-i-to-ry

rep-re-hen-si-ble
rep-re-hen-so-ry
rep-re-sen-ta-tion
rep-re-sent-a-tive
rep-re-sent-er
re-press-er
re-press-i-ble
re-pres-sive
re-priev-al
rep-ri-mand
re-pris-al
rep-ro-ba-cy
rep-ro-bate
re-pro-duc-er
re-pro-duc-i-ble
rep-til-i-an
re-pub-li-can
re-pu-di-a-tor
re-pug-nant
re-pul-sive
rep-u-ta-ble
rep-u-ta-tion
re-pute
re-quest-er
req-ui-em
re-qui-es-cat
re-quir-er
req-ui-site
req-ui-si-tion
re-quit-al
res-az-ur-in
re-scind
re-scis-sion
re-scrip-tive
res-cu-a-ble
re-sect-a-ble
re-sem-blance
re-sem-bler
res-ene
re-ser-pic
Re-ser-pine
res-er-va-tion
re-served
re-serv-ist
res-er-voir
re-side
res-i-dence
res-i-den-tial
re-sid-u-al
re-sid-u-ar-y
res-i-due
re-sid-u-um
re-sign

res-ig-na-tion
re-sil-ience
re-sil-ien-cy
re-sil-i-om-e-ter
res-in-a-ceous
res-in-ate
res-in-ic
res-in-if-er-ous
re-sin-i-fi-ca-tion
res-in-og-ra-phy
res-in-oid
res-in-ol
res-in-ous
res-i-pis-cence
re-sist-ance
re-sist-er (one who resists)
re-sist-i-ble
re-sis-tiv-i-ty
re-sis-tor (device)
res-ite (resin)
res-i-tol
res ju-di-ca-ta
res-ol
re-sol-u-ble
res-o-lute
re-sol-u-tive
re-solv-ent
re-solv-er
res-o-nance
res-o-na-tor
res-or-cin-ol
res-or-cyl-ic
re-sorp-tive
res-o-ru-fin
re-spect-a-ble
re-spect-er
re-spec-tive
res-pi-ra-ble
res-pi-ra-tion
res-pi-ra-tor
res-pi-ra-to-ry
res-pi-rom-e-ter
res-pite
re-splend-ent
re-spond-ent
re-spond-er
re-spons-er
re-spon-si-ble
re-spon-sive
re-spon-sor
re-spon-so-ry
res-tau-rant
res-tau-ra-teur

res-ti-tu-tion
res-tive
res-to-ra-tion
re-stor-a-tive
re-stric-tive
re-sult-ant
re-sume (v.)
ré-su-mé (n.)
re-sump-tive
re-sur-gent
res-ur-rec-tor
re-sus-ci-ta-ble
re-sus-ci-ta-tor
re-tal-i-a-to-ry
re-tard-ant
re-tar-da-tion
re-tard-ed
re-tene
re-ten-tive
re-ten-tor
ret-ger-site
re-ti-ar-y
ret-i-cence
ret-i-cle
re-tic-u-late
ret-i-cule
re-tic-u-lin
re-tic-u-li-tis
re-tic-u-io-cy-to-sis
re-tic-u-lose
ret-i-form
ret-i-na
re-tin-a-lite
ret-i-nene
ret-i-ni-tis
ret-i-no-cho-roid-i-tis
ret-i-nop-a-thy
ret-i-nos-co-py
ret-i-nue
re-tir-al
re-tir-ee
ret-o-na-tion
re-tort-er
re-tract-a-ble
re-trac-tile
re-trac-tion
re-trac-tive
re-trac-tor
ret-ri-bu-tion
re-trib-u-tive
re-trib-u-tory
re-triev-a-ble
re-triev-al

re-triev-er
ret-ro-ac-tive
ret-ro-cede (v.i.)
re-tro-cede (v.t.)
ret-ro-ced-ence
ret-ro-ces-sion
ret-ro-gra-da-to-ry
ret-ro-gres-sive
ret-ro-ne-cine
re-tror-sine
ret-ro-spec-tive
ret-ro-stal-sis
ret-rous-sé
ret-ro-vert-ed
re-turn-ee
re-un-ion
re-vanche
rev-eil-le
rev-e-la-tion
re-vel-a-to-ry
rev-eled
rev-el-ry
re-veng-er
rev-e-nue
re-ver-a-ble
re-ver-ber-a-to-ry
re-vere
rev-er-ence
rev-er-ie
re-ver-sal
re-vers-er
re-vers-i-ble
re-ver-sion
re-vert-er
re-vert-i-ble
re-vet-ment
re-vil-er
rev-i-res-cent
re-vised
re-vis-er
re-vi-sion
re-vi-so-ry
re-viv-al
re-viv-i-fy
rev-i-vis-cent
re-vi-vor
rev-o-ca-ble
rev-o-ca-tion
rev-o-ca-to-ry
re-vok-a-ble
re-vok-er
re-volt-er
rev-o-lu-ble

rev-o-lu-tion
re-volv-er
re-vul-sive
Rey-kja-vik
rey-nard
Reyn-olds
rhab-do-man-cer
rham-na-zin
rham-ni-nose
rham-no-side
rha-pon-ti-gen-in
rhap-sod-i-cal
rhap-so-dy
rhe-a-dine
rhe-ni-um
rhe-ol-o-gy
rhe-om-e-ter
rhe-o-stat
rhe-sus
rhet-o-ric
rhe-tor-i-cal
rhet-o-ri-cian
rheu-mat-ic
rheu-ma-tism
rheum-ic
rhig-o-lene
rhi-ni-tis
rhi-noc-er-os
rhi-nol-o-gy
rhi-nos-co-py
rhi-zoi-dal
rhi-zom-a-tous
rhi-zome
rhi-zop-ter-in
rhi-zot-o-my
rho-da-mine
rho-da-nate
Rho-de-sian
rho-di-nol
rho-dite
rho-di-um
rho-di-zon-ic
rho-do-chro-site
rho-do-den-dron
rhom-bo-clase
rhom-bo-he-dral
rhom-boi-dal
rhum-ba-tron
rhyme-ster
rhy-o-lite
rhyth-mi-cal
rib-al-dry
ri-bi-tyl

ri-bo-fla-vin
ri-bo-nu-cle-ase
ri-bo-side
ri-bu-lose
ric-er
ri-chell-ite
ric-in-o-le-ic
rick-ett-si-al
ric-o-cheted
rid-dled
rid-er
rid-i-cule
ri-dic-u-lous
rid-ing
ri-ding (political division)
rif-fling
ri-fling
·ight-eous
right-er
ri-gid-i-ty
rig-id-ly
rig-ma-role
rig-or-ous
ri-mose
rin-der-pest
ring-er
rins-a-ble
rins-er
ri-ot-ous
ri-par-i-an
rip-en
ri-pid-o-lite
rip-pled
ris-er
ris-i-bil-i-ty
ris-ing
ris-que
rit-u-al
ri-valed
ri-val-ry
riv-et-er
Riv-i-er-a
riv-u-let
Ri-yadh
road-ster
Ro-a-noke
roam-er
roast-er
Rob-ert
rob-in (bird
ro-bin (chemistry)
ro-bi-nose
ro-bust

Ro-chelle
Roch-es-ter
rock-et-eer
rock-et-er
rock-et-ry
rock-oon
ro-co-co
ro-den-ti-ci-dal
Rod-er-ick
roe-bling-ite
roent-gen-o-graph
roent-gen-og-ra-phy
roent-gen-ol-o-gy
roent-gen-om-e-ter
roent-gen-om-e-try
roent-gen-o-scope
roent-gen-os-co-py
rog-a-to-ry
Rog-er
ro-gnon
rogu-er-y
rogu-ish
roist-er-er
Ro-land
roll-er
rol-lick-ing
ro-maine
ro-manc-er
Ro-man-esque
Ro-man-ism
ro-ma-ni-um
ro-man-ti-cism
ro-man-ti-cist
Rom-a-ny
ro-me-ite
Ro-me-o
Rom-ish
romp-er
ron-deau
ro-ne-o-graph
ron-geur
roof-er
rook-er-y
Roo-se-velt
roost-er
rop-er
Roque-fort
ro-rif-er-ous
Ror-schach
ro-sa-ceous
Ros-a-lind
Ros-a-mond
ro-sa-ry

rosch-er-ite
ro-se-ate
ro-se-o-la
ro-sette
Rosh Ha-sha-na
Ros-i-cru-cian
ros-in-ate
ros-i-ness
ro-sol-ic
ros-ter
ros-trum
ros-y
ro-tal
ro-tam-e-ter
Ro-tar-i-an
ro-ta-ry
ro-tat-a-ble
ro-ta-tive
ro-ta-tor
ro-ta-to-ry
ro-te-noid
ro-te-none
Ro-tif-er-a
ro-tis-ser-ie
ro-to-graph
ro-to-gra-vure
ro-tor
ro-tun-da
ro-tun-di-ty
rough-en
rough-er
rough-om-e-ter
rou-lade
rou-leau
rou-lette
roun-del
round-er
rout-er
rou-tine
ro-ver (robber)
rov-er
row-dy-ism
row-eled
roy-al-ist
ru-ba-to
ru-be-an-ic
ru-be-fa-cient
ru-be-o-la
rub-e-ryth-ric
ru-bes-cent
ru-bi-cun-di-ty
ru-bid-i-um
ru-big-i-nous

ru-ble
ru-brene
ru-bric
ru-bri-ca-tor
ru-di-men-ta-ry
ru-fes-cence
ruf-fi-an
ruf-fler
ruf-fling
ru-fos-i-ty
ru-fous
ru-gos-i-ty
ru-gu-lose
ru-ined
ru-in-ing
ru-in-ous
rul-a-ble
rul-er
Ru-ma-ni-an
rum-bler
ru-mi-nant
rum-mag-er
ru-mor
rump-er
rum-pled
rum-pus
run-ci-ble
ru-nic
ru-pee
ru-pic-o-lous
rup-tured
ru-ral
ru-rig-e-nous
Rus-sian
rus-ti-ca-tor
rus-tic-i-ty
rust-i-ness
rus-tler
rus-tling
ru-ta-ba-ga
ru-ta-ceous
ru-te-car-pine
Ru-the-ni-an
ru-then-ic
ru-the-ni-um
ruth-er-ford-ine
ru-tile
ru-tin-ose
ru-ty-lene
Rwan-dan
ry-an-o-dine
Ry-u-kyu-an

S

sab-a-dine
Sab-ba-tar-i-an
sab-bat-i-cal
sa-ber
Sa-bine
sab-ine (pine)
sab-i-nene
sa-bi-no
sab-o-tage
sa-bra
sab-u-lous
sa-bu-tan
sac-cha-rate
sac-char-ic
sac-cha-ride
sac-cha-rif-er-ous
sac-cha-rim-e-ter
sac-cha-rin-ate
sac-cha-rin-ic
sac-cha-rom-e-ter
sac-cha-rose
sac-er-do-tal
sa-chem
sa-chet
sac-ral
sac-ra-men-tal
sac-ra-men-ta-ry
sa-cred
sac-ri-fi-cial
sac-ri-fic-ing
sac-ri-le-gious
sac-ris-tan
sac-ris-ty
sac-ro-il-i-ac
sac-ro-sanct
sac-rum
sad-dler-y
sa-dism
sa-dis-tic
Saeng-er-fest
sa-fa-ri
safe-ty
saf-flor-ite
saf-fron
saf-ra-nine
sa-ga-cious
sa-gac-i-ty
sag-a-more

sag-a-pe-num
sag-e-nite
Sag-it-tar-i-us
Sa-ha-ra
sail-or
sa-laam
sal-a-ble
sa-la-cious
sal-ad
sal-a-man-der
sa-la-mi
sal-a-ried
sal-e-ra-tus
sal-i-cin
sal-i-cyl-am-ide
sa-lic-y-late
sal-i-cyl-ic
sa-lic-y-lide
sal-i-cyl-ize
sal-i-cyl-o-yl
sal-i-cyl-u-ric
sa-lient
sal-i-gen-in
sa-lim-e-ter
sal-i-na-tion
sa-line
sa-lin-i-ty
sa-lin-o-gen-ic
sal-i-nom-e-ter
Salis-bur-y
sa-li-va
sal-i-var-y
sal-i-va-tion
sa-li-vous
salm-on
Sal-mo-nel-la
sal-mo-nel-lo-sis
salm-ons-ite
Sal-ol
Sa-lo-me
sa-lon
sal-pin-gec-to-my
sal-pin-gi-tis
sal-si-fy
sal-ta-to-ri-al
salt-er-y
salt-pe-ter
sa-lu-bri-ous

sa-lu-bri-ty	sa-pi-ence
sal-u-tar-y	sap-o-gen-in
sal-u-ta-tion	sap-o-na-ceous
sa-lu-ta-to-ry	sa-pon-i-fi-ca-tion
sa-lute	sap-o-nin
sal-va-ble	sap-o-rif-ic
Sal-va-dor-an	sap-phir-ine
sal-vage-a-ble	sap-ro-gen-ic
sal-vag-er	sap-ro-ge-nic-i-ty
Sal-var-san	sa-prog-e-nous
sal-ver	sap-ro-pel-ic
sal-vi-a-nin	Sar-ah
sal vo-la-ti-le	Sa-ran
sal-vor	sar-casm
sam-a-ra	sar-cas-tic
Sa-mar-i-tan	sar-coid-o-sis
sa-mar-i-um	sar-col-y-sis
sam-bu-ni-grin	sar-co-ma
Sa-mo-an	sar-co-ma-to-sis
sam-o-var	sar-com-a-tous
Sam-o-yed	sar-coph-a-gus
sam-pler	sar-cop-side
sa-mu-rai	sar-co-sine
san-a-to-ri-um	sar-dine
sanc-ti-fi-ca-tion	sar-don-ic
sanc-ti-mo-ni-ous	sar-don-yx
sanc-tion-er	sar-ki-nite
sanc-ti-ty	sar-men-to-gen-in
sanc-tu-ar-y	sa-rong
sanc-tum	sar-sa-pa-ril-la
san-daled	sar-to-ri-al
sand-er	sar-to-ri-us
sand-i-ness	Sar-tri-an
san-dust	sas-sa-fras
San-for-ize	sas-so-lite
san-guin-a-rine	sa-tan-i-cal
san-gui-nar-y	satch-el
san-guin-e-ous	sa-teen
san-guin-o-lent	sat-el-lit-ed
San-he-drin	sat-el-lit-oid
san-i-dine	sat-el-lit-o-sis
san-i-tar-i-um	sat-el-loid
san-i-tar-y	sa-tia-ble
san-i-tiz-er	sa-ti-ate
san-i-ty	sa-ti-e-ty
San-skrit	sat-in-et
san-ta-lene	sat-in-ize
san-ta-lol	sat-ire
san-te-none	sa-tir-i-cal
san-to-nin	sat-i-rize
sa-phe-nous	sat-is-fac-to-ri-ly
sap-id	sat-is-fy
sa-pid-i-ty	sa-trap

sat-u-ra-ble	scar-ab
sat-u-ra-tor	scar-ci-ty
Sat-ur-day	scarf-er
Sat-urn	scar-i-fy
sat-ur-na-lian	scar-i-ous
Sa-tur-ni-an	scar-la-ti-na
sat-ur-nine	scar-let
sat-yr	scat-o-log-i-cal
sa-tyr-ic	sca-tol-o-gy
sau-cer	scat-tered
sau-ci-ness	scav-eng-er
Sau-di A-ra-bi-a	sce-nar-i-o
sau-er-bra-ten	sce-nar-ist
sau-er-kraut	sce-ner-y
saun-ter	sce-ni-cal
sau-rel	sce-no-graph
sau-ri-an	sce-nog-ra-phy
sau-sage	scent-er
saus-su-rite	scep-ter
sau-téed	sched-ule
sau-terne	schee-lite
sav-a-ble	sche-ma
sav-age-ry	sche-mat-ic
sa-van-na	sche-ma-tist
sa-vant	sche-mat-o-graph
sav-ing	Sche-ring
sav-ior	schiff-li
Sav-iour	schis-mat-ic
sa-voir faire	schist-oid
sa-vor-y	schist-ose
Sa-voy-ard	schis-to-some
sax-i-frage	schis-to-so-mi-a-sis
sax-o-phone	schiz-oid-ism
scab-bler	schiz-o-phre-ni-a
sca-bies	schiz-o-phren-ic
sca-bres-cent	schle-miel
scab-rous	schlie-ren
sca-lar	Schnei-der
scald-er	scho-la can-to-rum
sca-le-no-he-dral	schol-ar
scal-er	scho-las-tic
scal-loped	schoo-ner
scal-pel	schor-la-ceous
scalp-er	schot-tische
scam-per	schra-dan
scan-dal-ize	schrei-ner-ize
scan-dal-ous	Schro-ding-er
Scan-di-na-vi-an	schroec-king-er-ite
scan-di-um	Schweit-zer
scan-ner	schwei-zer
scant-ling	sci-at-i-ca
scap-o-lite	sci-en-tif-ic
scap-u-la	sci-en-tist

scil-i-cet
scil-li-ro-side
scim-i-tar
scin-tig-ra-phy
scin-til-la-tor
scin-til-lom-e-ter
sci-oph-i-lous
sci-re fa-ci-as
scis-sors
sclar-e-ol
scle-rec-to-my
scle-ren-chy-ma
scle-ri-tis
scle-ro-ma
scle-rom-e-ter
scle-ro-sis
scle-ro-tal
scle-rot-ic
scle-rot-o-my
scob-i-nate
scoff-er
scold-er
scol-e-cite
sco-li-o-sis
sconc-i-ble
scoop-er
scoot-er
sco-pa-rin
scoph-o-ny
sco-pine
sco-pol-a-mine
sco-po-le-tin
scop-u-lite
scor-bu-tic
sco-ri-a-ceous
sco-ri-fi-ca-tion
scorn-er
scor-o-dite
scor-per
Scor-pi-o
scor-pi-on
scor-za-lite
sco-to-ma
sco-tom-a-tous
scoun-drel
scourg-er
scrab-bler
scram-bling
scrap-er
scratch-er
scrawl-er
scream-er
screen-er

scrib-bler
scrib-er
scrip-tur-al
scriv-en-er
scrof-u-la
scrof-u-lo-sis
scro-tum
scru-ple
scru-pu-lous
scru-ti-nize
scru-ti-ny
scuf-fling
scul-ler-y
sculp-tor
sculp-tur-al
scum-bled
scur-ril-i-ty
scur-ri-lous
scur-vi-ly
scut-tle-butt
scu-tum
seal-ant
seal-er
seal-ine
seam-stress
se-ance
sea-son-a-ble
seat-er
seb-a-cate
se-ba-ceous
se-bac-ic
seb-or-rhe-a
sec-a-lose
se-cant
se-ced-er
se-clu-sive
Sec-o-nal
sec-ond-ar-i-ly
sec-ond-ar-y
sec-ond-er
se-cre-cy
se-cret
se-cre-ta-gogue
sec-re-tar-i-al
se-cre-tin
se-cre-tive
se-cre-to-ry
sec-tar-i-an
sec-til-i-ty
sec-tion-al-ize
sec-tor-al
sec- to-ri-al
sec-u-lar-ize

se-cund
se-cun-date
se-cu-ri-ty
se-dan
se-date
sed-a-tive
sed-en-tar-y
sed-i-men-ta-ry
se-di-tious
se-duc-er
se-duc-i-ble
se-duc-tive
se-du-li-ty
sed-u-lous
seed-ling
seek-er
seep-age
seg-men-tal
seg-re-ga-ble
Seid-litz
sei-gnior-age
sei-sin
seis-mic-i-ty
seis-mo-graph
seis-mog-ra-phy
seis-mo-log-i-cal
seis-mol-o-gy
seis-mom-e-ter
seis-mo-met-ric
seiz-er
sei-zin
seiz-ing
sei-zor (law)
sei-zure
sel-dom
se-lect-ance
se-lect-ee
se-lec-tiv-i-ty
se-lec-tor
sel-e-nate
se-len-ic
sel-e-nide
se-le-ni-ous
sel-e-nite
se-le-ni-um
se-le-no-bis-muth-ite
se-le-no-graph-ic
sel-e-nog-ra-phy
se-le-no-lite
se-le-no-log-i-cal
sel-e-nol-o-gy
sel-e-no-ni-um
sel-e-no-sis

self-ish
sell-er
sel-syn
Selt-zer
sel-vage
se-man-ti-cist
sem-a-phor-ist
se-ma-si-ol-o-gy
sem-blance
se-mei-ol-o-gy
se-mes-ter
sem-i-dine
sem-i-nal
sem-i-nar-y
sem-i-nif-er-ous
Sem-i-nole
Sem-ite
Se-mit-ic
Sem-i-tism
sem-o-li-na
sen-a-ry
sen-a-to-ri-al
send-er
se-ne-cic
se-ne-ci-o-nine
se-ne-ci-o-sis
Sen-e-gal-ese
se-nes-cence
sen-e-schal
se-nhor (Portuguese)
se-nile
se-nil-i-ty
sen-ior
se-nior-i-ty
se-nor
se-no-ri-ta
sen-sa-tion
sen-si-bil-i-ty
sen-sile
sen-si-tiv-i-ty
sen-si-tiz-er
sen-si-tom-e-ter
sen-so-ri-um
sen-so-ry
sen-su-al-i-ty
sen-su-ous
sen-tence
sen-ten-tious
sen-tience
sen-ti-men-tal
sen-ti-neled
sen-try
se-paled

sep-al-oid
sep-a-ra-ble
sep-a-ra-tee
sep-a-ra-tist
sep-a-ra-tor
se-phar-dic
se-pi-a
Sep-tem-ber
sep-ten-a-ry
sep-ti-ce-mi-a
sep-ti-mal
sep-tu-a-ge-nar-i-an
sep-tu-a-ges-i-ma
sep-tu-ple
sep-tu-plet
sep-tu-pli-cate
sep-ul-cher
se-pul-chral
sep-ul-ture
se-quac-i-ty
se-que-la
se-quen-tial
se-ques-tered
se-ques-tra-tor
se-ra-glio
ser-al
ser-aph
se-raph-ic
ser-a-phim
Ser-bi-an
ser-e-nad-er
ser-en-dip-i-ty
se-rene
se-ren-i-ty
ser-geant
se-ri-al
se-ri-a-tim
se-ri-ceous
ser-i-cin
ser-i-cite
se-ries
ser-i-graph
se-rig-ra-pher
se-rig-ra-phy
ser-ine
se-rin-ga
ser-in-gal
se-ri-ous
ser-mon-ize
se-ro-log-ic
se-rol-o-gy
se-ro-si-tis
se-ro-ton-in

se-rous
ser-pen-tin-ite
ser-pig-i-nous
se-rum
serv-ant
serv-er
serv-ice-a-ble
ser-vi-ent
ser-vile
ser-vil-i-ty
ser-vi-tor
ser-vi-tude
ser-vo-mo-tor
ses-a-me
ses-a-min
ses-a moid-i-tis
ses-a-mo-lin
ses-qui-pe-da-lian
ses-sile
ses-sion
se-ta-ceous
se-ti-ger
se-tig-er-ous
set-tler
sev-en-ti-eth
sev-er-al
sev-ered
se-ver-i-ty
sew-age
sew-er-age
sex-a-ge-nar-ian
sex-ag-e-nar-y
sex-tant
sex-tu-ple
sex-tu-plet
sex-tu-pli-cate
sfer-ics
sfor-zan-do
shack-led
shad-er
shad-ow
Sha-drach
sha-green
shak-er
Shake-spear-e-an
sham-bles
shank-er
shap-er
shap-om-e-ter
shar-a-ble
sharp-en-ing
sharp-er
shat-tered

shav-er
sheath-er
sheep-ish
sheet-age
shek-el
shel-lack-ing
shel-tered
shelv-ing
she-nan-i-gan
shep-herd
Sher-a-ton
sher-bet
sher-iff
shib-bo-leth
shield-er
shift-er
shi-kim-ic
shil-le-lagh
shil-ling
shin-er
shin-gled
shirk-er
shirr-ing
shiv-ered
shock-er
sho-far
shoot-er
sho-ran
short-en
short-om-e-ter
Sho-sho-ne
shoul-dered
shov-eled
shov-er
show-er-y
shriev-al-ty
Shrin-er
shrink-age
shrink-er
shriv-eled
shriv-ing
Shrop-shire
shuf-fled
shy-ster
si-a-log-ra-phy
si-al-o-li-thi-a-sis
Si-a-mese
Si-be-ri-an
sib-i-lant
sib-i-la-to-ry
sib-ling
sib-yl-line
Si-cil-ian

sick-en-ing
sick-led
si-de-re-al
sid-er-ite
sid-er-og-ra-pher
sid-er-o-graph-ic
sid-er-o-na-trite
sid-er-o-sis
sid-ing
si-dled
si-er-o-zem
Si-er-ra Le-one
siev-er
sift-er
sight-er
sig-ma-tism
sig-moid-ec-to-my
sig-moid-os-to-my
sig-naled
sig-nal-ize
sig-na-to-ry
sig-nif-i-cant
sig-ni-fi-ca-tion
si-gnor
si-gno-ra
si-lage
sil-ane
si-lenc-er
si-le-si-a
si-lex
sil-hou-ette
sil-i-cate
sil-i-ca-ti-za-tion
sil-i-ca-tor
si-li-ceous
si-lic-ic
sil-i-cide
si-lic-i-dize
sil-i-cif-er-ous
si-lic-i-fy
sil-i-co-mag-ne-sio-flu-o-rite
sil-i-con
sil-i-cone
sil-i-co-sis
sil-i-cot-ic
silk-en
sil-li-man-ite
si-lox-ane
sil-ta-tion
Si-lu-ri-an
sil-ver
sil-vi-cul-tur-al
sim-i-lar-i-ty

sim-i-le (like)
si-mi-le (music)
si-mil-i-tude
si-mon-ize
si-mo-ny
si-moom
sim-pat-i-co
sim-per
sim-pler
sim-plex
sim-plic-i-ty
sim-pli-fy
sim-u-la-crum
sim-u-la-tor
si-mul-cast
si-mul-ta-ne-ous
Si-na-it-ic
si-nap-ic
sin-a-pine
sin-ar-quism
sin-cer-i-ty
si-ne-cure
sin-ew
sing-er
sin-gly
sin-gu-lar-i-ty
Sin-ha-lese
sin-is-tral
sink-age
sink-er
si-nom-e-nine
sin-ter
sin-u-ous
si-nus-i-tis
si-nus-oi-dal
si-phon-age
si-pid-i-ty
si-ren
si-ri-a-sis
Sir-i-us
si-roc-cos
sir-up
si-sal
sis-y-phe-an
si-tol-o-gy
si-to-ste-rol
sit-u-at-ed
si-tus
siz-a-ble
siz-zled
skat-ole
skeet-er
skel-e-ton-ize

skep-ti-cal
skep-ti-cism
skew-er
ski-am-e-try
ski-as-co-py
skill-ful-ness
skimp-i-ly
skir-mish
skirt-er
skit-tish
skiv-er
skul-dug-ger-y
skulk-er
slack-ened
slak-er
slan-der-ous
slat-tern
slaugh-ter
slav-er-y
slav-ish
Sla-von-ic
sleep-er
slen-der
slic-er
slick-en-side
slick-er
slid-a-ble
slid-om-e-ter
sling-er
slith-er-y
sliv-er
slo-gan
slop-ing
Slo-vak-i-an
slov-en
Slo-ve-ni-an
sludg-er
slum-ber-ous
smart-en
smell-er
smelt-er
smi-la-gen-in
smi-lax
smith-er-eens
Smith-so-ni-an
smok-er
smol-dered
smor-gas-bord
smoth-ered
smudg-er
smug-gler
snarl-ish
snatch-er

sneak-i-ness
sneez-er
snick-er-ing
sniff-er
snif-ter
snip-er
sniv-el-er
snob-ber-y
Sno-ho-mish
snoop-er-y
snor-kel
snort-er
snuf-fled
snug-gled
soak-age
soap-er
so-ber
so-bri-e-ty
so-bri-quet
so-cia-ble
so-cial-is-tic
so-ci-a-try
so-ci-e-ty
so-ci-oc-ra-cy
so-ci-o-log-ic
so-ci-ol-o-gist
so-ci-om-e-try
so-ci-op-a-thy
sock-dol-a-ger
sock-et
Soc-ra-tes
So-crat-ic
so-da-lite
so-dal-i-ty
so-dam-ide
so-dar
so-di-um
sod-om-y
so-far
soft-en-er
soi-gne
soi-ree
so-journ-er
sol-ace
so-lan-der
so-lan-i-dine
so-la-no
so-lar
so-lar-ism
so-lar-i-um
so-lar-i-za-tion
so-las-o-nine
sol-dered

sol-dier
sol-e-cism
sol-emn
so-lem-ni-ty
sol-em-nize
so-le-noi-dal
sol-fe-ri-no
so-lic-i-ta-tion
so-lic-i-tor
so-lic-it-ous
so-lic-i-tude
sol-id
sol-i-dar-ic
sol-i-da-ris-tic
sol-i-dar-i-ty
so-lid-i-fy
so-lid-i-ty
sol-i-dus
so-lig-e-nous
so-lil-o-quy
so-li-lu-nar
sol-ip-sism
sol-i-taire
sol-i-tar-y
sol-i-tude
so-lod-ize
so-lo-ist
Sol-o-mon
sol-o-netz
so-lo-ni-an
sol-stice
sol-sti-tial
sol-u-bil-i-ty
sol-u-bi-liz-er
so-lum
sol-ute
so-lu-tion
sol-u-tiz-er
solv-a-ble
sol-ven-cy
sol-vent
sol-vol-y-sis
So-ma-li
so-mat-ic
so-ma-ti-za-tion
so-ma-to-gen-ic
som-bre-ro
som-er-sault
som-nam-bu-list
som-nil-o-quy
som-niv-o-len-cy
som-no-lent
so-na-ble

so-nar
so-na-ta
song-ster
son-ic
so-nif-er-ous
son-net-eer
son-o-buoy
so-nom-e-ter
So-no-ra
so-no-rant
son-o-res-cent
son-o-rif-er-ous
so-nor-i-ty
so-no-rous
soon-est
Soph-ist
so-phis-ti-cat-ed
soph-is-try
soph-o-mor-ic
sop-o-rif-er-ous
sop-o-rif-ic
so-pra-no
sor-be-fa-cient
sor-bent
sorb-ic
sor-bi-tan
sor-bite
sor-bi-tol
sor-bose
sor-bo-side
sor-cer-er
sor-cer-y
sor-did
sor-ghum
so-ri-tes
so-rit-i-cal
So-rop-ti-mist
so-ror-i-cide
so-ror-i-ty
so-ro-sis
sort-er
sor-tie
sor-ti-lege
so-ste-nu-to
sou-brette
souf-flé
soun-der (herd of swine)
sound-er
sou-tache
south-er-ly
south-ern-er
sou-ve-nir
sov-er-eign

so-vi-et-ism
sov-khoz
Soxh-let
so-zol-ic
spa-cious
spa-cis-tor
spa-ghet-ti
spall-er
span-drel
span-gled
Span-iard
span-iel
spank-er
sparg-er
spark-let
spar-kling
spar-si-ty
Spar-tan
spar-te-ine
spas-mod-ic
spas-mol-y-sis
spas-mo-lyt-ic
spas-tic-i-ty
spa-tial
spa-ti-og-ra-phy
spat-u-la
spav-in
spawn-er
speak-er
spe-cial-ist
spe-ci-al-i-ty
spe-cial-i-za-tion
spe-cial-ty
spe-ci-e (in sort)
spe-cie (coin)
spe-cif-i-cal-ly
spec-i-fi-ca-tion
spec-i-fic-i-ty
spec-i-fi-er
spec-i-men
spe-ci-os-i-ty
spe-cious
speck-led
spec-ta-cle
spec-tac-u-lar
spec-ta-tor
spec-ter
spec-trog-ra-phy
spec-trom-e-ter
spec-trom-e-try
spec-tro-scope
spec-tros-co-py
spec-trum

spec-u-la-tive
spec-u-la-tor
spec-u-lum
speed-er
speed-om-e-ter
speed-ster
spe-le-ol-o-gy
spel-ter
spe-lunk-er
Spen-ce-ri-an
spend-er
Spen-gle-ri-an
sper-ma-ce-ti
sper-mat-ic
sper-ma-tif-er-ous
sper-ma-tin
sper-ma-ti-za-tion
sper-ma-to-cele
sper-ma-to-ci-dal
sper-ma-to-cyte
sper-ma-tor-rhe-a
sper-ma-to-zo-id
sperm-ine
sperm-ism
sphal-er-ite
sphe-nog-ra-phy
sphe-noi-dal
spher-al
spher-i-cal
sphe-ric-i-ty
sphe-roi-dal
sphe-roid-ic-i-ty
sphe-rom-e-ter
spher-u-lite
sphinc-ter-ot-o-my
sphin-gom-e-ter
sphin-go-sine
sphyg-mo-ma-nom-e-ter
sphyg-mom-e-ter
spic-i-ness
spic-u-lar
spi-der
spie-gel-ei-sen
spiel-er
spig-ot
spike-nard
spik-i-ness
spi-lite
spill-er
spil-ler (fish)
spi-lo-ma
spi-lo-site
spi-na-ceous

spin-ach
spi-nal
spi-na-ste-rol
spi-nate
spin-dler
spi-nel
spi-nes-cence
spin-et
spin-or
spi-nose
spi-nos-i-ty
spi-nous
spin-ster
spin-thar-i-scope
spi-nu-les-cent
spir-a-cle
spi-rac-u-lar
spi-raled
spi-re-a
spi-reme
Spi-ri-fer
spi-rif-er-ous
spir-it-ed
spir-it-u-al
spir-i-tu-el
spir-it-u-ous
spi-ro-chete
spi-ro-chet-o-sis
spi-ro-graph
spi-rom-e-ter
spi-ro-met-ric
spi-ro-pen-tane
splanch-ni-cec-to-my
splen-dent
splen-did
splen-dif-er-ous
splen-dor-ous
sple-net-ic
sple-nic
sple-ni-tis
sple-ni-um
splic-er
splin-tered
spo-di-um
spod-u-mene
spoil-age
spoil-er
spo-ken
spo-li-a-tion
spon-dy-li-tis
spong-er
spon-gi-ness
spon-gi-ol-o-gy

spon-si-ble	sta-lac-tite
spon-sor	stal-ac-tit-ic
spon-ta-ne-i-ty	sta-lag-mite
spon-ta-ne-ous	stal-ag-mit-ic
spoon-er-ism	stal-ag-mom-e-ter
spo-rad-ic	Sta-lin-grad
spo-ri-ci-dal	sta-men
spo-rif-er-ous	stam-i-na
spo-ro-gen-ic	stam-pede
spo-ro-phyll	stamp-er
spo-ro-zo-an	stan-chion
spor-tive	stan-dard-i-za-tion
spor-u-la-tion	stand-ing
spor-ule	sta-nine
spout-er	stan-nite
spring-er	sta-pes
sprin-kler	Staph-y-lo-coc-cus
sprin-kling	staph-y-lot-o-my
sprint-er	sta-pler
sprock-et	starch-er
spu-mes-cence	sta-re de-ci-sis
spu-mous	star-ling
spu-ri-ous	star-lite
spur-tive	start-er
spu-tum	star-tling
squad-ron	star-va-tion
squa-lene	sta-sis
squal-id-i-ty	stat-ed
squal-or	stat-i-cal-ly
squa-mous	sta-tion-ar-y
squan-dered	sta-tion-er-y
squawk-er	sta-tis-ti-cal
squeal-er	stat-is-ti-cian
squeam-ish	stat-i-tron
squee-gee	sta-tom-e-ter
squeez-er	sta-tor
squint-er	stat-o-scope
squirt-er	stat-u-ar-y
sta-bi-la-tor	stat-u-esque
sta-bile	stat-ure
stab-i-lim-e-ter	sta-tus
sta-bil-i-ty	stat-ute
sta-bi-li-za-tion	stat-u-to-ry
sta-bi-liz-er	stau-ro-lite
sta-bled	stau-ro-scop-ic
stac-ca-to	stead-i-ness
stach-y-drine	stealth-i-ness
sta-dim-e-ter	steam-er
sta-di-um	stea-rate
staff-er	stea-ric
stag-mom-e-ter	stea-rin
stain-er	stea-rit-ic
Sta-kha-nov-ite	stea-ro-yl

stea-ryl
ste-a-tite
ste-a-tol-y-sis
ste-a-to-sis
steep-er
stee-ple
steer-age
Ste-fan
Stel-lite
sten-ciled
ste-nog-ra-pher
sten-o-graph-ic
ste-nog-ra-phy
sten-o-ha-line
ste-nom-e-ter
ste-no-sis
sten-o-typ-ist
sten-to-ri-an
Ste-phen
ste-ra-di-an
ster-co-bi-lin-o-gen
ster-co-rite
ster-cu-lic
ster-e-og-no-sis
ster-e-og-ra-pher
ster-e-o-graph-ic
ster-e-om-e-ter
ster-e-om-e-try
ster-e-o-phon-ic
ster-e-oph-o-ny
ster-e-op-ti-con
ster-e-o-scope
ster-e-os-co-py
ster-e-ot-o-my
ster-e-o-typ-er
ster-ic
ster-ile
ste-ril-i-ty
ster-i-li-za-tion
ster-i-liz-er
ster-let
ster-ling
ster-num
ster-nu-ta-to-ry
ste-roi-dal
ste-rol
ster-to-rous
ste-thom-e-ter
steth-o-scope
ste-thos-co-py
Steu-ben
ste-ve-dore
Ste-ven-son

ste-vi-o-side
stew-ard
sthen-ic
stib-a-mine
stib-ine
sti-bin-ic
stib-i-o-pal-la-di-nite
sti-bon-ic
sti-bo-ni-um
stib-o-phen
sti-chom-e-try
stick-ler
stiff-en-er
sti-fling
stig-mas-ter-ol
stig-mat-ic
stig-ma-tism
stig-ma-tize
stil-bene
stil-bes-trol
stil-let-to
stilp-no-mel-ane
stim-u-lant
stim-u-la-tive
stim-u-la-tor
stim-u-lus
sting-er
sting-y (stinging)
stin-gy (close)
stink-er
sti-pend
sti-pen-di-ar-y
sti-pes
stip-i-tat-ic
stip-pled
stip-u-la-tion
stip-ule
stitch-er
stock-ade
sto-gy
sto-i-cal
stoi-chi-o-met-ric
stoi-chi-om-e-try
stok-er
stol-id
sto-lid-i-ty
stom-ach
sto-mach-ic
sto-ma-ti-tis
sto-ma-tol-o-gy
ston-i-ness
stop-pled
stor-age

sto-ried
sto-ri-ette
storm-i-ness
sto-ver
stow-age
stra-bis-mom-e-ter
stra-bis-mus
strad-dler
strag-gler
straight-en-er
strain-er
strait-ened
stra-mo-ni-um
strand-er
stran-ger (n.)
strang-er (adj.)
stran-gler
stran-gu-late
strat-a-gem
stra-te-gi-cal
strat-e-gist
strat-e-gy
strat-i-fi-ca-tion
strat-i-graph-ic
stra-tig-ra-phy
stra-to-cu-mu-lus
strat-o-sphere
strat-o-spher-ic
stra-tum
stra-tus
streak-i-ness
stream-er
strength-en-ing
stren-u-ous
strep-o-gen-in
strep-ta-mine
strep-to-coc-cic
strep-to-coc-co-sis
strep-to-my-cin
strep-to-thri-cin
stretch-er
stri-at-ed
stric-ture
stri-dent
strid-u-lous
stri-gose
strik-er
strin-gent
string-er
strip-er
strob-i-la-ceous
strob-o-scop-ic
strob-o-tron

stro-ga-noff
strok-er
stro-mat-ic
stro-ma-tin
stron-gy-lo-sis
stron-ti-an-if-er-ous
stron-ti-an-ite
stron-ti-um
stro-phan-thi-din
stro-phe
stroph-ic
struc-tur-al
strug-gled
strum-pet
strych-nine
stub-born-ness
stu-dent
stud-ied
stu-di-ous
stul-ti-fy
stum-bling
stump-age
stu-pe-fa-cient
stu-pe-fy
stu-pen-dous
stu-pid-i-ty
stu-por
stur-di-ly
stur-geon
stut-tered
Styg-i-an
sty-let
styl-ish
sty-lis-tic
styl-ize
sty-lo-graph-ic
sty-lom-e-try
sty-lus
sty-mie
styp-tic
sty-rac-i-tol
styr-e-nate
sty-rene
sty-ryl
sua-si-ble
suav-i-ty
su-ber-ate
su-ber-ic
su-ber-in
su-ber-ose
su-ber-yl-ar-gi-nine
sub-jec-tiv-ism
sub-ju-gate

sub-junc-tive
sub-lim-a-ble
sub-li-mate
sub-lime
sub-lim-i-nal
sub-lim-i-ty
sub-li-mize
sub-merged
sub-mer-gence
sub-mer-gi-ble
sub-mer-sal
sub-mersed
sub-mers-i-ble
sub-or-di-nate
sub-or-na-tion
sub-pe-naed
sub-ro-gate
sub-scrib-er
sub-ser-vi-ent
sub-sid-ence
sub-sid-i-ar-y
sub-si-dize
sub-sist-ence
sub-son-ic
sub-stan-tial
sub-stan-tive
sub-stit-u-ent
sub-sti-tut-a-ble
sub-sti-tu-tive
sub-sump-tive
sub-ter-fuge
sub-ti-lin
sub-tle-ty
sub-tract-er
sub-trac-tive
sub-ur-ban
sub-ver-sive
sub-vert-er
sub-vert-i-ble
suc-ce-da-ne-ous
suc-ce-dent
suc-ces-sive
suc-ces-sor
suc-cin-a-mate
suc-ci-nam-ic
suc-cin-a-mide
suc-ci-nate
suc-cin-ic
suc-ci-nyl
suc-cu-lence
suck-ler
su-cre
su-crose

suc-to-ri-al
su-da-men
Su-da-nese
su-da-to-ry
su-do-rif-er-ous
suf-fic-er
suf-fi-cien-cy
suf-fo-ca-tive
suf-fra-gist
suf-fus-a-ble
suf-fu-sive
sug-ar
sug-gest-i-ble
sug-ges-tive
su-i-ci-dal
sui ge-ner-is
suit-a-ble
suit-or
su-ki-ya-ki
sul-fa-cet-a-mide
sul-fa-di-az-ine
sul-fa-gua-ni-dine
sul-fa-mer-a-zine
sul-fa-meth-yl-thi-az-ole
sul-fam-ic
sulf-am-ide
sul-fam-o-yl
sul-fa-nil-a-mide
sul-fa-nil-ic
sul-fan-i-lyl
sul-fa-pyr-i-dine
sulf-ars-phen-a-mine
sul-fat-ase
sul-fa-thi-az-ole
sul-fen-ic
sulf-hy-dryl
sul-fide
sul-fi-nyl
Sul-fo-nal
sul-fon-a-mide
sul-fo-nat-ed
sul-fo-na-tor
sul-fon-eth-yl-meth-ane
sul-fon-ic
sul-fo-ni-um
sulf-ox-ide
sul-fu-re-ous
sul-fu-ret-ed
sul-fu-ric
sul-fu-rize
sul-fu-rous
sul-fur-yl
sulk-i-ness

sul-tan-ate
sul-try
su-mac
Su-ma-tran
sum-mar-i-ly
sum-ma-rize
sum-ma-ry
sum-mit-ry
sump-tu-ar-y
sun-der
sun-dry
sunk-en
su-per-a-ble
su-perb
su-per-cil-i-ous
su-per-er-o-gate
su-per-e-rog-a-to-ry
su-per-fi-cial
su-per-flu-ous
su-per-in-tend-ent
su-pe-ri-or-i-ty
su-per-la-tive
su-per-nal
su-per-na-tant
su-per-nat-u-ral
su-per-nu-mer-ar-y
su-per-se-de-as
su-per-se-dure
su-per-sen-si-ble
su-per-son-ic
su-per-sti-tious
su-per-ve-nience
su-per-vis-ee
su-per-vi-so-ry
su-pi-na-tor
sup-ple-men-tal
sup-ple-men-ta-ry
sup-ple-tive
sup-pli-ca-to-ry
sup-port-ive
sup-pos-al
sup-po-si-tion
sup-pos-i-ti-tious
sup-pos-i-to-ry
sup-press-i-ble
sup-pres-sor
sup-pu-ra-tive
su-pra
su-prem-a-cy
sur-a-min
sur-cin-gle
sur-e-ty
sur-fac-er

sur-fac-ing
sur-fac-tant
sur-feit
sur-geon
sur-ger-y
sur-gi-cal
Su-ri-nam-ese
sur-li-ness
sur-mis-a-ble
sur-plice
sur-plus-age
sur-pris-a-ble
sur-re-al-ist
sur-ren-der
sur-rep-ti-tious
sur-ro-gate
sur-veil-lance
sur-viv-al
sur-vi-vor
sus-cep-ti-bil-i-ty
sus-pend-er
sus-pend-i-ble
sus-pen-si-ble
sus-pen-so-ry
sus-pi-cious
sus-pi-ra-tion
sus-te-nance
su-sur-rus
su-tur-al
su-ze-rain
swad-dled
swamp-er
swank-i-ness
swarth-i-ness
swas-ti-ka
sweat-er
Swe-den
Swed-ish
sweep-er
sweet-ened
swel-ter
swift-er
swin-dler
swin-dling
swin-ish
switch-er
Swit-zer-land
swiv-eled
Syb-a-rite
Syb-a-rit-ic
syc-a-more
sych-no-car-pous
syc-o-phan-cy

sy-co-sis	syn-chrop-ter
sy-e-nite	syn-chro-scope
syl-la-bar-y	syn-chro-tron
syl-lab-ic	syn-cli-nal
syl-lab-i-fi-ca-tion	syn-co-pa-tion
syl-la-bize	syn-co-pe
syl-la-ble	syn-des-mo-sis
syl-lo-gism	syn-di-cal-ism
syl-lo-gis-ti-cal	syn-di-cate
Syl-phon	syn-drome
syl-van-ite	syn-ec-do-che
Syl-ves-ter	syn-e-col-o-gy
syl-ves-trene	syn-er-e-sis
syl-vite	syn-er-gis-ti-cal
sym-bi-o-sis	syn-es-the-si-a
sym-bi-ot-ic	syn-ge-nite
sym-bol-i-cal	syn-od-al
sym-bol-ism	syn-od-i-cal
sym-bol-ize	syn-o-nym
sym-bol-o-gy	syn-on-y-mous
sym-met-ri-cal	syn-on-y-my
sym-me-trize	syn-op-sis
sym-me-try	syn-op-tic
sym-pa-thec-to-my	syn-o-vi-tis
sym-pa-thet-ic	syn-tec-tic
sym-path-i-co-trop-ic	syn-the-sis
sym-pa-thin	syn-the-siz-er
sym-pa-thiz-er	syn-the-tase
sym-pa-tho-lyt-ic	syn-thet-i-cal
sym-pa-thy	syn-thol
sym-phon-ic	syn-to-ni-za-tion
sym-pho-ni-ous	syph-i-lit-ic
sym-pho-nize	syph-i-lol-o-gy
sym-pho-ny	Syr-a-cuse
sym-phy-sis	Syr-i-an
sym-phyt-ic	sy-rin-ga
sym-po-si-um	sy-ringe
symp-to-mat-ic	sy-rin-ge-al
symp-tom-a-tize	sy-rin-gic
symp-tom-a-tol-o-gy	sy-rin-gin
syn-a-gogue	syr-in-gi-tis
syn-apse	syr-in-got-o-my
syn-ar-thro-sis	syr-inx
syn-chon-drot-o-my	sys-tem-at-i-cal
syn-chro-nism	sys-tem-a-tize
syn-chro-ni-za-tion	sys-tem-ic
sny-chro-niz-er	sys-to-le
syn-chron-o-graph	sys-tol-ic
syn-chro-nous	sy-zyg-i-al
syn-chro-ny	syz-y-gy

T

tab-ard
Ta-bas-co
tab-er-na-cle
tab-er-nan-thine
ta-bes dor-sa-lis
ta-bet-ic
tab-i-net
tab-leaux
ta-ble d'hote
tab-let
ta-bling
tab-loid
ta-boo
tab-o-ret
tab-u-lar
tab-u-la-tor
ta-chis-to-scope
tach-o-graph
ta-chom-e-ter
tach-o-met-ric
ta-chom-e-try
tach-y-car-di-a
tach-y-gen-ic
tach-y-graph-om-e-ter
ta-chyg-ra-phy
ta-chym-e-ter
tach-y-met-ric
ta-chys-ter-ol
tac-it
tac-i-tur-ni-ty
tack-ling
tac-o-nite
tac-ti-cal
tac-ti-cian
tac-tic-i-ty
tac-til-i-ty
tac-tom-e-ter
tac-to-sol
taf-fe-ta
Ta-ga-log
tag-a-tose
tag-e-tone
Ta-hi-tian
tail-er
tai-lored
Tai-wan-ese
tak-ing
talc-ose
tal-ent

ta-les (law)
tal-i-pes
tal-is-man
tal-i-tol
talk-a-tive
talk-er
tal-lage
tall-ate
tal-lith
Tal-mud-ic
tal-on
ta-lon-ic
tal-ose
ta-lus
ta-ma-le
tam-a-rack
tam-a-rind
tam-bour
tam-bou-rine
tamp-er (n.)
tam-per (v.)
Tam-pi-co
tam-pon-ade
tan-a-ce-tin
tan-a-ger
Ta-nan-a-rive
tan-dem
Tan-gan-yi-kan
tan-ge-los
tan-gen-tial
tan-ger-e-tin
tan-ger-ine
tan-gi-ble
tan-gled
tank-age
tan-kard
tank-er
tan-nom-e-ter
tan-ta-lite
tan-ta-liz-er
tan-ta-lum
tan-ta-mount
tan-trum
Tan-za-ni-a
ta-per
tap-er (device; one who tapes)
tap-es-try
ta-pe-tum
tap-i-o-ca

ta-pir
tap-ster
tar-an-tel-la
ta-ran-tu-la
ta-rax-e-in
tar-di-ness
tar-get-eer
tar-iff
tar-nish
tar-pau-lin
tar-pon
tar-sal
tars-ec-to-my
tar-sor-rha-phy
tar-sus
tar-tan
tar-tar-e-ous
tar-tar-ic
tar-tar-ous
tar-tram-ic
tar-tra-mide
tar-trat-ed
ta-sim-e-ter
Tas-ma-ni-an
tas-ma-nite
tas-seled
tast-er
tat-ter-de-ma-lion
tat-too-er
tau-rine
tau-ro-cho-late
tau-rom-a-chy
Tau-rus
tau-ryl
tau-to-log-i-cal
tau-tol-o-gy
tau-to-mer-ic
tau-tom-er-ism
tau-to-met-ric
tau-toph-o-ny
tav-ern
taw-dry
tax-i-der-mist
tax-ied
tax-i-fo-lin
tax-i-ing
tax-i-me-ter
tax-o-nom-ic
tax-on-o-my
Tche-by-cheff
team-ster
tea-seled
teas-er

tech-ne-ti-um
tech-ni-cal
tech-ni-cian
tech-nique
tech-noc-ra-cy
tech-no-log-i-cal
tech-nol-o-gy
tec-ton-ics
tec-ton-ite
te-di-ous
te-di-um
tee-ter
tee-to-tal-er
Tef-lon
teg-men-tal
Te-he-ran
Te-huan-te-pec-er
Tel-Au-to-graph
te-leg-ra-pher
tel-e-graph-ic
tel-e-ki-ne-sis
te-lem-e-ter
tel-e-met-ric
te-lem-e-try
tel-e-mo-tor
tel-e-o-log-i-cal
tel-e-ol-o-gy
tel-e-path-ic
te-lep-a-thy
tel-e-phon-ic
te-leph-o-ny
tel-e-ran
tel-e-scope
tel-e-scop-ic
te-les-co-py
tel-es-the-si-a
tel-e-vi-sion
tel-e-vi-sor
tell-er
tel-lu-ri-an
tel-lu-ride
tel-lu-ri-um
tel-lu-rom-e-ter
tel-lu-ro-ni-um
te-lome
tel-o-mer-i-za-tion
tel-pher-age
tem-blor
te-mer-i-ty
tem-per-a-men-tal
tem-per-ate
tem-per-a-ture
tem-pered

tem-pes-tu-ous
tem-plar
tem-plet
tem-po-ral
tem-po-rar-i-ly
tem-po-rar-y
tem-po-riz-er
tempt-a-ble
tempt-er
tempt-ress
ten-a-ble
te-na-cious
te-nac-i-ty
ten-an-cy
ten-ant-ry
tend-en-cy
tend-er (one who attends; ship)
ten-der (soft; offer)
ten-der-iz-er
ten-der-om-e-ter
ten-di-ni-tis
ten-don
ten-dril
ten-e-bres-cence
ten-e-brous
ten-e-ment
Ten-er-iffe
ten-et
te-nien-te
Ten-ite
Ten-nes-se-an
ten-o-de-sis
ten-on
ten-or
te-not-o-my
ten-si-ble
ten-sil-i-ty
ten-sim-e-ter
ten-si-om-e-ter
ten-so-ri-al
ten-ta-cle
ten-ta-tive
tent-age
ten-ter (drying frame)
tent-er
ten-ter-hook
te-nu-i-ty
ten-u-lin
ten-u-ous
ten-ure
te-pa-che
te-pee

teph-ro-sin
tep-id
te-pid-i-ty
te-qui-la
ter-a-con-ic
ter-a-cryl-ic
ter-a-to-log-i-cal
ter-a-tol-o-gy
ter-a-to-ma
ter-bi-um
ter-cen-te-nar-y
ter-e-ben-thene
te-reb-ic
ter-e-bin-thi-nate
ter-e-bin-thine
ter-eph-thal-ic
ter-gite
ter-gi-ver-sa-tor
ter-ma-gant
term-er
ter-mi-na-ble
ter-mi-nal
ter-mi-na-tor
ter-mi-nol-o-gy
ter-mi-nus
ter-mite
ter-mit-ic
ter-na-ry
ter-op-ter-in
ter-pene
ter-pe-nyl-ic
ter-pi-nene
ter-pin-e-ol
ter-pin-o-lene
ter-pi-nyl
terp-sich-o-re
terp-si-cho-re-an
ter-ra-pin
ter-rar-i-um
ter-raz-zo
terre-plein
ter-res-tri-al
ter-ri-bly
ter-rif-ic
ter-rig-e-nous
ter-ri-to-ri-al
ter-ror-ism
ter-tian
ter-ti-ar-y
ter-tile
tes-sel-lat-ed
test-a-ble
tes-ta-ceous

tes-ta-men-ta-ry
tes-ta-tor
test-er
tes-ter (canopy)
tes-tic-u-lar
tes-ti-fy
tes-ti-mo-ni-al
tes-ti-ness
tes-tos-ter-one
te-tan-ic
tet-a-no-gen-ic
tet-a-nus
tet-a-ny
te-tar-toi-dal
teth-ered
tet-ra-bro-mo
tet-ra-cene
tet-ra-chlo-ro
te-trac-id
tet-ra-co-sa-no-ic
tet-ra-cy-cline
tet-rad
te-trad-ic
tet-ra-eth-yl
tet-ra-gon
tet-rag-o-nal
tet-ra-he-dral
tet-ra-hy-dro-fu-ran
tet-ra-kis-a-zo
te-tral-o-gy
tet-ra-mine
tet-ra-ni-tro-meth-ane
tet-ra-ple-gi-a
tet-ra-ploi-dy
te-trar-chic
te-trar-chy
tet-ra-som-a-ty
tet-ra-thi-o-nate
tet-ra-va-lent
tet-ra-zine
tet-ra-zo-li-um
te-traz-o-lyl
tet-ra-zone
tet-ri-tol
te-tron-ic
tet-rose
te-trox-ide
tet-ryl
Teu-ton-ic
Tex-an
tex-tile
tex-tu-al
tex-tur-al

Thai-land
thal-a-mot-o-my
thal-as-som-e-ter
thal-lif-er-ous
thal-line
thal-li-um
than-a-to-sis
thau-ma-site
thau-ma-tur-gy
the-a-ter
the-at-ri-cal
the-mat-i-cal-ly
then-o-yl
the-oc-ra-cy
the-o-crat-ic
the-od-o-lite
The-o-do-si-a
the-o-lo-gian
the-ol-o-gy
the-oph-a-gy
the-o-rem
the-o-re-mat-ic
the-o-ret-i-cal
the-o-re-ti-cian
the-o-rize
the-os-o-phy
ther-a-peu-ti-cal-ly
ther-a-pist
the-ri-at-rics
ther-mal
therm-i-on-ic
therm-is-tor
Ther-mit
ther-mo-chro-mism
ther-mo-du-ric
ther-mog-ra-pher
ther-mo-graph-ic
ther-mol-y-sis
ther-mo-lyt-ic
ther-mom-e-ter
ther-mo-met-ri-cal-ly
ther-mom-e-try
ther-moph-i-ly
ther-mo-scop-ic
ther-mo-stat
ther-mo-ther-a-py
the-sau-rus
the-sis
thes-pi-an
the-tin
the-ve-tin
thi-am-ide
thi-am-i-nase

thi-a-mine
thi-a-naph-thene
thi-an-threne
thi-a-zole
thi-az-o-line
thi-a-zol-sul-fone
thick-en-ing
thiev-ish
thi-mer-o-sal
think-er
thi-o-fla-vine
thi-o-naph-thene
thi-on-ic
Thi-o-nine
thi-o-ni-um
thi-oph-e-nine
thi-o-u-ra-cil
thi-o-u-re-a
thirst-i-ness
thir-ti-eth
this-tle
thith-er
thi-u-ro-ni-um
thix-ot-ro-py
Thom-as
Tho-mism
thon-zyl-a-mine
tho-rac-ic
tho-rac-i-co-lum-bar
tho-ra-co-scope
tho-ra-cos-to-my
tho-ri-ate
tho-rif-er-ous
tho-rite
tho-ri-um
tho-ron
thor-ough
thou-sand
thrash-er
thread-er
threat-en-ing
thre-i-tol
thre-node
thren-o-dy
thre-o-nine
thresh-er
thresh-old
thrift-i-ness
thrill-er
throat-i-ness
throm-bin
throm-bo-an-gi-i-tis
throm-bo-cy-to-sis

throm-bo-plas-tin
throm-bo-sis
throm-bot-ic
throm-bus
throt-tled
thrust-er (one who thrusts)
thrus-tor (machine)
thu-co-lite
thu-ja-pli-cin
thu-jyl
thu-li-um
thump-er
thun-der-ous
thu-ri-ble
thu-rif-er-ous
thy-mi-dine
thy-mi-dyl-ic
thy-mine
thy-mol-phthal-ein
thy-mo-nu-cle-ic
thy-mus
Thy-ra-tron
thy-rite
thy-roi-dal
thy-roid-ec-to-my
thy-roid-i-tis
thy-ro-nine
thy-rot-ro-phin
ti-ar-a
Ti-bet-an
tib-i-al
tick-et-er
tick-i-ci-dal
tick-lish
tid-al
ti-di-ness
ti-ding (news)
tid-ing (tide)
Ti-flis
ti-ger-ish
tight-en-er
tig-lal-de-hyde
ti-gnon
ti-go-nin
ti-gress
ti-grine
ti-grol-y-sis
till-a-ble
till-age
till-er
tilt-er
tim-bered
tim-brel

tim-er
tim-id
ti-mid-i-ty
tim-o-rous
tim-o-thy
tim-pa-nist
tin-cal-co-nite
tinc-to-ri-al
tinc-ture
tin-der
tin-gled
tin-ker
tin-kling
tin-seled
tint-er
tin-tin-nab-u-lous
tint-om-e-ter
tip-ster
ti-queur
ti-rade
ti-rail-leur
Tish-chen-ko
ti-ta-nate
ti-tan-ic
ti-ta-nif-er-ous
ti-ta-ni-um
ti-ter
tith-er
Ti-tian
tit-il-late
ti-tled
ti-trat-a-ble
ti-tra-tion
ti-trim-e-ter
ti-tri-met-ri-cal-ly
tit-u-lar-i-ty
toast-er
to-bac-co-nist
to-bog-gan-er
to-col-o-gy
to-coph-er-ol
toc-sin
tod-dler
to-geth-er
tog-gler
To-go-lese
toil-er
toi-let-ry
to-ken
To-ky-o
tol-bu-ta-mide
tol-er-a-ble
tol-er-a-tion

tol-i-dine
tol-u-ene
to-lu-i-dine
tol-u-ol
to-lu-ric
tol-u-yl-ene
tol-yl-ene
to-mat-i-dine
tom-a-tine
to-men-tose
to-mog-ra-phy
ton-al
to-nal-i-ty
to-neme
ton-er
to-net-ics
tongu-er
tongu-ing
ton-ic
to-nic-i-ty
to-nite (explosive)
ton-neau
ton-o-log-i-cal
to-nom-e-ter
ton-o-met-ric
to-nom-e-try
ton-sil-lec-to-my
ton-sil-li-tis
ton-sil-lot-o-my
ton-so-ri-al
ton-tine
to-nus
tool-er
to-paz-ine
to-pec-to-my
to-per
to-pi-ar-y
top-i-cal
to-pog-ra-pher
top-o-graph-i-cal
to-pog-ra-phy
top-o-log-i-cal
to-pol-o-gy
to-pon-y-my
top-sy–tur-vy
tor-chon
to-re-a-dor
to-ric
to-rin-gin
tor-men-tor
tor-na-do
to-roi-dal
tor-pe-do

tor-pid-i-ty
tor-por-if-ic
torqu-er
torqu-ing
torque-me-ter
tor-ren-tial
tor-si-bil-i-ty
tor-si-om-e-ter
tor-sion-al
tor-ti-lla
tor-som-e-ter
tor-toise
tor-tu-os-i-ty
tor-tu-ous
tor-tur-ous
tos-yl-ate
tot-a-ble
to-tal-i-tar-i-an-ism
to-tal-i-ty
to-tal-iz-er
to-ta-quine
to-tem-ism
tou-ché
tough-en
tou-pee
tour-ist
tour-ma-line
tour-na-ment
tour-ni-quet
tou-sled
tout-er
tow-age
to-ward
tow-eled
tow-ered
tox-e-mi-a
tox-e-mic
tox-ic-i-ty
tox-i-co-log-i-cal
tox-i-col-o-gist
tox-i-co-sis
tox-if-er-ous
tox-i-ge-nic-i-ty
tox-in
trac-er-y
tra-che-al
tra-che-i-tis
tra-che-ot-o-my
tra-cho-ma
tra-chyt-ic
trac-ing
track-age
trac-ta-ble

trac-tile
trac-tor
trad-er
tra-dev-man
tra-di-tion-al
tra-duc-er
tra-duc-i-ble
traf-fic-a-ble
traf-fick-er
trag-a-can-thin
tra-ge-di-an
tra-ge-di-enne
trag-e-dy
trag-i-cal
trail-er
train-ee
trai-tor-ous
trai-tress
traj-ect (n.)
tra-ject (v.)
tra-jec-tile
tra-jec-to-ry
tram-meled
tramp-er
tram-po-line
tran-quil-iz-er
tran-quil-li-ty
trans-ac-tion
trans-am-i-nase
trans-at-lan-tic
trans-ceiv-er
tran-scend-ent
tran-scen-den-tal
tran-scrib-er
tran-script
trans-duc-er
trans-duc-tor
tran-sect
trans-fer-a-ble
trans-fer-ase
trans-fer-ee
trans-fer-ence
trans-ferred
trans-for-ma-tion
trans-form-er
trans-fus-a-ble
trans-gres-sor
tran-sient
tran-sil-ience
tran-sis-tor
tran-sit-er
tran-si-tion
tran-si-tive

tran-si-to-ry
tran-si-tron
trans-la-tive
trans-la-tor
trans-lit-er-a-tor
trans-lu-cen-cy
trans-mis-si-ble
trans-mis-som-e-ter
trans-mit-ta-ble
trans-mog-ri-fy
trans-mut-a-ble
tran-som
tran-son-ic
trans-par-ent
tran-spir-a-ble
tran-spi-ra-tion
tran-spire
tran-spi-rom-e-ter
trans-plan-ta-tion
trans-pon-der
trans-por-ta-tion
trans-pose
trans-ship
trans-u-da-tion
trans-ver-sal
trans-vers-er
trans-vert-er
trans-vert-i-ble
tra-pe-zi-um
trap-e-zoi-dal
trau-mat-ic
trau-ma-tism
trav-ail
trav-eled
trav-el-er
trav-el-og
tra-vers-a-ble
tra-vers-al
trav-erse (n.)
tra-verse (v.)
trav-er-tine
trav-es-ty
trawl-er
treach-er-ous
treach-er-y
trea-cle
trea-dle
trea-son-a-ble
treas-ur-a-ble
treas-ur-er
treas-ur-y
treat-er
trea-tise

tre-bled
tre-foil
tre-ha-lose
trel-lised
Trem-a-to-da
trem-bling
tre-men-dous
trem-e-tol
trem-o-lo
trem-or
trem-u-lous
trench-ant
tren-cher (board; cap)
trench-er (digger)
tre-pan
tre-phine
treph-o-cyte
treph-one
trep-i-da-tion
tre-pid-i-ty
trep-o-ne-ma-to-sis
trep-o-ne-mi-ci-dal
tres-pass-er
tres-tle
tri-an-gu-lar
tri-ar-yl-meth-ane
tri-a-zine
tri-az-i-nyl
tri-a-zole
tri-az-o-lyl
trib-al
tri-bom-e-ter
tri-bro-mo-eth-yl
trib-u-la-tion
tri-bu-nal
trib-une
trib-u-tar-y
trib-ute
tri-chi-a-sis
tri-chi-na
trich-i-no-sis
tri-chit-ic
tri-chlo-ride
tri-chlo-ro-meth-ane
trich-o-mo-ni-a-sis
tri-cho-sis
tri-chot-o-my
trick-er-y
trick-ster
tri-cli-no-he-dric
tri-cy-cle
tri-dec-yl-ene
tri-dent

tri-eth-a-nol-a-mine
tri-far-i-ous
tri-fling
trig-o-nal
tri-go-ni-tis
trig-o-nom-e-ter
trig-o-no-met-ric
trig-o-nom-e-try
tri-ha-lide
tri-he-dral
tri-hy-dric
tri-ke-tone
tri-lo-bite
tri-log-ic
tril-o-gy
tri-mer-ide
tri-mes-ic
tri-meth-yl-ene-tri-ni-tra-mine
tri-met-ro-gon
tri-na-ry
Trin-i-dad
tri-ni-tro-tol-u-ene
trin-i-ty
trin-ket
tri-no-mi-al
Tri-o-nal
tri-part-i-ble
tri-par-tite
tri-phen-yl-ene
tri-phib-i-ous
triph-thong
tri-ple-gi-a
tri-plet
trip-li-cate
trip-loi-dy
tri-pod
trip-o-dal
tri-pod-ic
trip-tych
tri-so-mic
tri-syl-lab-ic
tri-thi-o-nate
trit-i-um
trit-u-ra-tor
tri-tyl
tri-um-phant
tri-um-vi-rate
tri-va-lent
triv-et
triv-i-al
tro-car
tro-chan-ter
tro-che

troch-e-am-e-ter
troch-le-ar
tro-choi-dal
tro-chom-e-ter
trog-lo-dyte
Tro-jan
trom-bi-di-a-sis
tro-mom-e-ter
tro-nom-e-ter
troop-er
tro-pane
tro-pe-ine
troph-ic
tro-phy
trop-i-cal
tro-pism
trop-o-lone
tro-pom-e-ter
tro-po-sphere
trop-tom-e-ter
tro-pyl
trou-ba-dour
trou-bled
trou-blous
trou-sers
trous-seau
tro-ver
trow-eled
tru-an-cy
Truck-ee
truck-ling
truc-u-lent
trump-er-y
trum-pet-er
trun-cat-ed
trun-cheon
trun-dle
truss-ing
trust-ee
tru-xi-llic
tryp-a-no-ci-dal
tryp-a-no-so-ma
tryp-ar-sa-mide
tryp-o-graph
tryp-sin-o-gen
tryp-to-phan
tset-se
tsu-nam-i
tsu-tsu-ga-mu-shi
tu-bec-to-my
tu-ber-cle
tu-ber-cu-lar
tu-ber-cu-lo-sis

tu-ber-cu-lous
tu-ber-os-i-ty
tu-bi-fa-cient
tub-ing
tu-bo-cu-ra-rine
tu-bu-lar
Tuc-son
tu-fa-ceous
tuff-a-ceous
tuft-er
Tui-ler-ies
tu-la-re-mi-a
tu-lip
tum-bler
tum-bling
tum-brel
tu-me-fa-cient
tu-mes-cent
tu-mid
tu-mor
tu-mul-tu-ous
tun-a-ble
tung-sten
tung-stite
tu-nicked
Tu-ni-si-an
tun-neled
tun-nel-er
tu-pe-lo
tu-ran-ose
tur-ban
tur-bi-dim-e-ter
tur-bi-di-met-ric
tur-bid-i-ty
tur-bi-nate
tur-bine
tur-bi-nec-to-my
tur-bo-charg-er
tur-bu-la-tor
tur-bu-lence
tu-reen
tur-ges-cence
tur-gid-i-ty
tur-key
Turk-ish
tur-mer-ic

tur-nip
tur-pen-tine
tur-pi-tude
tur-quoise
tur-tle
tu-te-lage
tu-tored
tu-to-ri-al
Tu-tu-i-lan
tu-yere
tweet-er
tweez-ers
twen-ti-eth
twin-kling
twist-er
Twitch-ell
ty-ing
tym-pan-ic
tym-pa-nist
tym-pa-num
tyn-dall-om-e-ter
typ-a-ble
typh-li-tis
ty-phoi-dal
ty-phoon
ty-phus
typ-i-cal
typ-i-fy
ty-pog-ra-pher
ty-po-graph-ic
ty-pog-ra-phy
ty-po-nym
ty-poth-e-tae
ty-ra-mine
ty-ran-ni-cal
tyr-an-nize
tyr-an-ny
ty-rant
ty-ro-ci-dine
Ty-rode
Ty-ro-le-an
Tyr-o-lese
ty-ro-sin-ase
ty-ro-sine
ty-ro-sin-o-sis

U

u-biq-ui-tous
u-biq-ui-ty
u-dom-e-ter
U-gan-dan
U-krain-i-an
u-ku-le-le
ul-cer-a-tive
ul-nar
ul-na-re
u-lot-o-my
ul-ster
ul-te-ri-or
ul-ti-ma-cy
ul-ti-ma-tum
ul-tra-ma-rine
ul-tra-son-ic
ul-u-late
U-lys-ses
um-bel-lif-er-one
um-ber
um-bil-i-cal
um-bil-i-cus
um-bra-geous
um-brel-la
u-mo-ho-ite
um-pire
u-na-nim-i-ty
u-nan-i-mous
u-na-ry
un-cial
un-ci-na-ri-a-sis
un-ci-nate
un-cle
unc-tu-ous
un-dec-yl-ene
un-dec-y-len-ic
un-der-tak-er
un-du-la-to-ry
un-guen-tous
un-gui-nous
u-ni-bi-va-lent
u-nic-i-ty
u-ni-corn
u-ni-fi-ca-tion
u-ni-form-i-ty
un-ion-ism
u-nip-a-rous
u-nip-o-tent
u-nique-ly

u-ni-son
u-nit-a-ble
u-ni-tar-i-an
u-ni-tar-y
u-nit-ed
u-nit-ize
u-ni-va-lent
u-ni-ver-sal-i-ty
u-ni-ver-si-ty
u-niv-o-cal
un-prec-e-dent-ed
un-re-quit-a-ble
up-heav-al
up-hol-ster-er
Up-per Vol-tan
up-roar-i-ous
u-ra-chus
u-ra-cil
u-ra-nate
U-ra-ni-an
u-ran-ic
u-ra-nif-er-ous
u-ra-nin-ite
u-ra-nite
u-ra-ni-um
u-ra-nog-ra-phy
u-ra-nol-o-gy
u-ra-nom-e-try
u-ra-nos-co-py
u-ra-nous
U-ra-nus
u-ra-nyl
u-ra-zine
ur-ban-i-ty
ur-bi-cul-ture
ur-chin
u-re-am-e-ter
u-re-mi-a
u-re-om-e-ter
u-re-ter-i-tis
u-re-thane
u-re-thra
u-re-thri-tis
u-ret-ic
u-re-yl-ene
ur-gen-cy
u-ri-col-y-sis
u-ri-co-lyt-ic
u-ri-nal-y-sis

u-ri-nar-y
u-ri-nate
u-ri-no-cry-os-co-py
u-ri-nol-o-gy
u-ri-nom-e-ter
u-ro-bi-lin-o-gen
u-ro-fla-vin
u-ro-gen-i-tal
u-rog-ra-phy
u-ro-leu-cic
u-ro-li-thi-a-sis
u-ro-li-thol-o-gy
u-ro-log-ic
u-rol-o-gist
u-ro-poi-e-sis
u-ro-poi-et-ic
u-ro-por-phy-rin
u-ros-co-py
u-rot-ro-pine
ur-si-gram
ur-ti-car-i-a
us-a-ble
us-que-baugh
us-ti-la-gin-e-ous
u-su-al-ly

u-su-fruct
u-su-rer
u-su-ri-ous
u-sur-pa-tion
u-surp-er
u-su-ry
U-tah-an
u-ten-sil
u-ter-ine
u-ter-og-ra-phy
u-ter-us
u-til-i-tar-i-an
u-til-i-ty
u-ti-li-za-tion
u-ti-liz-er
u-to-pi-an
u-tri-cle
u-tric-u-lar
u-ve-i-tis
u-vi-ton-ic
u-vu-la
ux-or-i-cide
ux-o-ri-ous
u-zar-i-gen-in
u-za-rin

V

va-can-cy
vac-ci-na-tor
vac-il-la-tion
vac-u-ist
va-cu-i-ty
vac-u-om-e-ter
vac-u-um
va-de me-cum
vag-a-bond-age
va-gar-i-ous
va-gar-y
va-gi-na
vag-i-nal
vag-i-nec-to-my
vag-i-ni-tis
va-got-o-my
va-gran-cy
va-guish
val-ance
val-e-dic-to-ri-an
va-lence
va-len-ci-a

Va-len-ci-ennes
va-lent
val-en-tine
val-er-ate
va-le-ri-an
va-ler-ic
va-le-ryl
val-et
val-e-tu-di-nar-i-an
val-iant
val-i-da-tion
va-lid-i-ty
va-line
va-lise
val-or-i-za-tion
val-or-ous
val-u-a-ble
val-vate
val-vu-lar
val-vu-li-tis
val-vu-lot-o-my
va-nad-ic

van-a-dif-er-ous
va-na-di-um
Van-cou-ver
van-dal-ism
va-nil-la
van-ish
van-i-ty
van-quish-er
van-tage
vap-id
va-pid-i-ty
va-pog-ra-phy
va-por-im-e-ter
va-por-i-za-tion
va-por-iz-er
va-por-ous
var-i-a-bil-i-ty
Var-i-ac
var-i-ant
var-i-at-ed
var-i-a-tion
var-i-co-cele
var-i-cose
var-ied
var-i-e-gat-ed
va-ri-e-tal
va-ri-e-ty
var-i-o-lite
var-i-o-loid
var-i-om-e-ter
var-i-ous
var-is-tor
Var-i-typ-er
var-nish-er
vas-cu-lar
vas-ec-to-my
vas-e-line
vas-o-dil-a-tin
vas-o-di-la-tor
vas-o-mo-tor
vas-sal-age
vas-ti-tude
Vat-i-can
va-tic-i-nal
vaude-ville
vec-to-ri-al
veg-e-ta-ble
veg-e-tar-i-an
veg-e-ta-tive
ve-he-mence
ve-hi-cle
ve-hic-u-lar
vel-lum

vel-o-cim-e-ter
ve-loc-i-pede
ve-loc-i-ty
ve-lom-e-ter
ve-lours
ve-lum
vel-vet-een
ve-nal-i-ty
ve-na-tion
vend-ee
vend-er
ven-det-ta
vend-i-ble
ven-dor
ve-neer-er
ven-e-nif-er-ous
ven-er-a-ble
ve-ne-re-al
ve-ne-re-ol-o-gy
ven-er-y
Ve-ne-tian
venge-ance
ve-ni-al
ve-ni-re fa-ci-as
ven-i-son
ven-om-ous
ve-nous
ven-ter (abdomen)
vent-er (utters)
ven-ti-la-tor
ven-tom-e-ter
ven-tral
ven-tri-cle
ven-tric-u-lar
ven-tri-lo-qui-al
ven-tril-o-quism
ven-tril-o-quist
ven-tur-er
ven-tu-ri
ven-tur-ous
ven-ue
ven-ule
ven-u-lose
Ve-nu-si-an
ve-ra-cious
ve-rac-i-ty
ve-ran-da
ver-a-scope
ver-a-tral-de-hyde
ver-a-tram-ine
ve-rat-ric
ve-rat-ro-yl
Ve-ra-trum

ver-a-tryl-i-dene
ver-bal (adj.)
verb-al (n.) (part of speech)
ver-bal-i-ty
ver-bal-iz-er
ver-ba-tim
ver-be-na
ver-be-na-lin
ver-bi-age
ver-bile
ver-bos-i-ty
ver-bo-ten
ver-dant
ver-di-gris
ver-dur-ous
verg-er
ver-i-fi-a-ble
ver-i-fi-ca-tion
ver-i-si-mil-i-tude
ver-i-ta-ble
Ver-i-tas
ve-ri-tas
ver-i-ty
ver-mi-cel-li
ver-mi-ci-dal
ver-mic-u-lar
ver-mic-u-lite
ver-mi-form
ver-mif-u-gal
ver-mi-fuge
ver-mil-ion
ver-mi-no-sis
ver-min-ous
Ver-mont-er
ver-mouth
ver-nac-u-lar
ver-nal
ver-ni-er
ve-ron-i-ca
ver-ru-co-sis
ver-sa-til-i-ty
ver-sic-u-lar
ver-si-fi-ca-tion
ver-si-fi-er
ver-sus
ver-te-bra
ver-ti-cal
ver-tic-i-ty
ver-tig-i-nous
ver-ti-go
ves-i-cant
ves-i-ca-to-ry
ves-i-cle

ve-sic-u-lar
ves-per-al
ves-tal
vest-ed
ves-tib-u-lar
ves-ti-bule
ves-ti-bu-li-tis
ves-tig-i-al
ves-ti-ture
ves-try
ves-tur-al
Ve-su-vi-us
vet-er-an
vet-er-i-nar-i-an
vex-a-tious
vi-a-bil-i-ty
vi-a do-lo-ro-so
vi-a-duct
vi-bran-cy
vi-bra-to-ry
vib-ri-o-sis
vi-brom-e-ter
vi-bur-num
vic-ar-age
vi-car-i-ous
vice-ge-rent
vice-roy
vi-ce ver-sa
Vi-chy-ite
vi-chys-soise
vi-ci-a-nin
vi-ci-a-nose
vic-i-nage
vic-i-nal
vi-cin-i-ty
vi-cious
vi-cis-si-tude
vic-tim-ize
vic-to-ri-an
vic-to-ri-ous
vict-ualed
vict-ual-er
vi-cu-na
vi-de-li-cet
vid-e-o
Vi-et-nam-ese
vig-i-lance
vig-i-lan-te
vig-i-lan-tism
vi-gnette
vi-gnet-ter
vig-or-ous
vi-king

vi-la-yet
vil-i-fi-er
vil-lag-er
vil-lain-ous
vi-na-ceous
vin-ai-grette
vin-ci-ble
vin-cu-lum
vin-di-ca-ble
vin-di-ca-to-ry
vin-dic-tive
vin-e-gar
vin-er-y
vin-i-cul-tur-al
vi-nif-er-a
vin-ol-o-gy
vin-om-e-ter
vi-nous
vin-tag-er
vint-ner
vi-nyl-a-tion
vi-nyl-ene
vi-nyl-i-dene
Vi-nyl-ite
vi-nyl-o-gous
vi-o-la-ble
vi-o-la-ceous
vi-o-lan-throne
vi-o-la-tor
vi-o-lence
vi-o-les-cent
vi-o-lin-ist
vi-o-lon-cel-lo
vi-o-lu-ric
vi-os-ter-ol
vi-per-ous
vi-ra-go
vi-ral
vi-re-mi-a
vi-res-cence
vir-gin-al
Vir-gin-ian
vir-gin-i-ty
vir-gin-i-um
vir-i-al
vi-ri-cid-al
vi-rid-i-ty
vir-ile
vi-ril-i-ty
vi-rol-o-gy
vi-ro-sis
vir-tu-al
vir-tu-os-i-ty

vir-tu-o-so
vir-tu-ous
vir-u-lent
vi-rus
vis-aged
vis-cer-al
vis-cid-i-ty
Vis-co-liz-er
vis-com-e-ter
vis-co-scope
vis-cose
vis-co-sim-e-ter
vis-cos-i-ty
vis-cous
vis-i-bil-i-ty
vi-sion-ar-y
vi-sioned
vis-it-ant
vis-it-a-tion
vis-i-tor
vi-sor
vis-ta
vis-u-al
vis-u-al-i-ty
vis-u-al-iz-er
vi-tal-i-ty
vi-tal-ize
vi-ta-min-ol-o-gy
vi-ta-scope
vi-tel-lin
vi-ti-at-ed
vit-i-cul-ture
vit-i-li-go
vit-rain
vit-re-ous
vi-tres-cence
vi-tres-ci-ble
vit-ri-fi-a-ble
vit-ri-fi-ca-tion
vit-ri-ol
vit-ri-o-lat-ed
vit-ri-ol-ic
vi-tu-per-a-tive
vi-va-cious
vi-vac-i-ty
vi-van-dier
vi-vant
vi-var-i-um
vi-va vo-ce
viv-id
vi-vid-i-ty
viv-i-fi-ca-tion
viv-i-par-i-ty

vi-vip-a-rous
viv-i-sec-tion
vix-en-ish
vi-zier
Vlad-i-vos-tok
vo-ca-ble
vo-cab-u-lar-y
vo-cal-ist
vo-cal-iz-er
vo-ca-tion
voc-a-tive
vo-cif-er-ous
voic-ing
void-ance
vol-a-til-i-ty
vol-a-til-i-za-tion
vol-can-ic
vol-ca-no
vo-cod-er
vo-lem-i-tol
vo-li-tion
volt-age
vol-ta-ic
vol-tam-e-ter
volt-am-me-ter
vol-u-bil-i-ty
vol-ume
vol-u-me-nom-e-ter
vo-lu-me-ter
vol-u-met-ric
vo-lu-mi-nous
vol-un-tar-i-ly
vol-un-teered
vo-lup-tu-ar-y

vo-lup-tu-ous
vo-lute
vol-u-tin
vol-vu-lus
vo-mer-ine
vom-it-er
vom-i-tus
voo-doo
vo-ra-cious
vo-rac-i-ty
vor-tex
vor-ti-ces
vor-tic-i-ty
vot-a-ble
vo-ta-ry
vot-er
vo-tive
vouch-er
vow-el
vox po-pu-li
voy-ag-er
voy-a-geur
vul-can-ite
vul-can-i-za-tion
vul-can-iz-er
vul-gar-i-an
vul-gar-ism
vul-gar-i-ty
vul-ner-a-ble
vul-pine
vul-pin-ic
vul-tur-ous
vul-vi-tis

W

wad-dled
wad-er
wa-fer
waf-fle
waft-age
wa-ger (bet)
wag-er (competitor)
wag-es
Wag-ne-ri-an
wag-on-er
wag-on-ette
wain-scot-ing

wait-er
wait-ress
waiv-er
wak-en-er
walk-er
wal-lop-er
Wal-tham
waltz-er
wam-pum
wan-der
wan-gled
wan-ton

wap-i-ti
war-bler
war-den
ward-er
war-fa-rin
war-i-ness
warm-er
warp-age
war-rant-ee
war-rant-er
war-ran-tor (law)
war-ran-ty
war-ri-or
wash-a-ble
Wash-ing-to-ni-an
wasp-ish
was-sail
Was-ser-mann
wast-age
wast-er
was-trel
wa-ter me-ter
watt-age
wave-me-ter
wa-ver (sway)
wav-er (waving)
Wa-ver-ley
wax-en
weak-ened
weak-ling
weap-on-eer
wear-a-ble
wea-ri-ness
wea-ri-some
wea-seled
weath-ered
weath-er-om-e-ter
weav-er
Web-er
Web-ste-ri-an
Wechs-ler
wed-ding
Wedg-wood
Wednes-day
weed-er
weep-er
wee-viled
weight-i-ness
Weight-om-e-ter
Wei-mar-an-er
weld-er
wel-kin
welsh-er

wel-ter
welt-er (worker on shoes, etc.)
west-er-ly
west-ern-er
West-min-ster
West-pha-li-an
weth-er
whal-er-y
wharf-age
wheat-en
whee-dled
wheel-er
wheez-i-ness
wher-ev-er
wheth-er
whi-lom
whim-pered
whim-si-cal
whim-sy
whirl-er
whirl-i-gig
whisk-ered
whis-kies
whis-ky
whis-pered
whis-tler
whis-tling
whit-en-ing
whith-er
whit-ish
whit-tled
whor-tle-ber-ry
wick-ed-ly
wick-ered
wick-et
wick-i-up
wid-en
widg-eon
widg-et
wid-ow-er
wie-ner schnit-zel
Wies-ba-den
wie-sen-bo-den
wild-er
wil-der-ness
Wil-helms-ha-ven
Wil-helm-stras-se
Wil-lam-ette
will-ful-ness
Wil-liam
Wil-ton
wind-age
wind-er

wind-i-ness
win-dow
wind-row
Wins-low
win-some
win-ter-ize
win-try
wip-er
wir-i-ness
Wis-con-sin-ite
wise-a-cre
wis-tar-i-a
Wis-te-ri-a
witch-er-y
with-al
with-ered
wit-ti-cism
wiz-ard-ry
wiz-ened
wob-bu-la-tor
woe-ful-ness
wolf-ra-min-i-um
wolf-ram-ite
wol-las-ton-ite
wol-ver-ine
wom-an
wom-bat
wom-en

won-dered
won-drous
wood-en
woof-er
wool-en
wool-ly
Worces-ter
word-ster
work-er
wor-ri-some
wor-shiped
wor-ship-er
wor-sted
wor-thi-ly
wor-thy
wo-ven
wran-gler
wreck-age
wres-tler
wres-tling
wretch-ed
wring-er
wrin-kled
wrist-let
writ-er
Wy-an-dotte
Wyc-liffe
Wy-o-ming-ite

X

xan-tha-mide
xan-thate
xan-the-nyl
xan-thine
xan-tho-gen-ate
xan-tho-ma
xan-tho-ma-to-sis
xan-thom-a-tous
xan-thom-e-ter
xan-tho-phyll
xan-thop-ter-in
xan-thous
xan-thox-y-le-tin
xan-thy-drol
Xa-ve-ri-an
xe-ni-al
xen-o-lith
xe-non

xen-o-pho-bi-a
xen-yl
Xe-res
xe-ric
xe-ro-gel
xe-ro-graph-ic
xe-rog-ra-phy
xe-ro-phyte
xe-ro-phyt-ic
xe-ro-sis
xiph-oid
xi-phop-a-gus
xy-lem
xy-lene
xy-le-nol
xy-le-nyl
xy-lic
xy-li-dine

xy-lin-de-in
xy-lo-graph-ic
xy-log-ra-phy
xy-loid
xy-lol-o-gy
xy-lom-e-ter
xy-loph-a-gous

xy-lo-phone
xy-lo-side
xy-lot-o-my
xy-lo-yl
xy-lu-lose
xy-lyl-ene
Xy-ris

Y

Yak-i-ma
Yak-u-tat
ya-men
Yan-kee
Ya-qui
yard-age
yaw-me-ter
Ya-zoo
year-ling
yeast-i-ness
yelp-er
Yem-en-ite
yeo-man
yes-ter-day
yield-a-ble

yo-del-er
yo-gurt
yo-him-bine
yo-kel
yon-der
Yo-sem-i-te
young-ster
y-per-ite
yp-sil-i-form
yt-ter-bi-um
yt-ter-bous
yt-trif-er-ous
yt-tri-um
yt-tro-tan-ta-lite
Yu-go-slav

Z

Zach-a-ri-ah
Zam-bi-an
za-ni-ness
za-pa-te-a-do
zeal-ot
zea-lot-i-cal
zeal-ous
ze-a-xan-thin
ze-bra
ze-nith
ze-nog-ra-phy
ze-o-lite
ze-ol-i-tize
zeph-yr
Zep-pe-lin
ze-ro-ize
ze-ros
zib-el-ine

zinc-ate
zinc-if-er-ous
zin-cog-ra-phy
zinc-oid
zin-ger-one
zin-gi-ber-ene
Zi-on-ism
zirc-ite
zir-con-ate
zir-co-ni-um
zir-co-nyl
zith-er
Ziz-i-phus
zlo-ty
zo-an-thro-py
zo-di-ac
zo-di-a-cal
Zo-is-i-a

zois-it-i-za-tion
Zoll-ver-ein
zon-al
zon-ar-y
zon-ate
zo-nif-er-ous
zo-og-a-my
zo-o-gen-ic
zo-ol-a-ter
zo-o-log-i-cal
zo-ol-o-gy
zo-om-e-ter
zo-on-o-sis
zo-o-phyte
zo-os-co-py
zo-os-ter-ol
zo-ot-o-my
Zo-ro-as-tri-an
Zou-ave
Zo-ys-i-a

zu-mat-ic
zun-yite
zwie-back
zwit-ter-i-on
zyg-a-de-nine
zy-gal
zy-go-mat-ic
zy-gote
zo-got-ic
zy-mase
zy-min
zy-mo-gen-ic
zy-mog-e-nous
zy-mo-hy-drol-y-sis
zy-mol-o-gy
zy-mom-e-ter
zy-mo-sis
zy-mos-ter-ol
zy-mos-then-ic
zy-mur-gy

Punctuation Guide

Punctuation Guide

Punctuation is used in writing and printing for the purpose of clarification of meaning. The standardized marks and signs normally used help to separate sentences, clauses and phrases into understandable parts of the whole.

While correct punctuation clarifies the meaning of the written word or printed language, well-planned word order requires a minimum of punctuation. A good rule of thumb is — when in doubt about the need for punctuation, eliminate it. But there are times when punctuation is necessary for a sentence or thought to be clearly understandable. These are the times when it is essential to understand the correct usage.

Generally, if the use of punctuation does not clarify the text it should be omitted. The sole aim in the choice and placing of punctuation marks should be to bring out more clearly the author's thought. Punctuation should aid in reading and prevent misreading.

A rigid design or pattern of punctuation cannot be laid down except in broad terms. However, whatever style is adopted for use must be consistent and be based on sentence structure.

Punctuation marks with conventional applications are listed below in alphabetical order.

Apostrophes and Possessives

To make a singular or plural noun possessive when it does not end in s add an apostrophe and s.

man's, men's
child's, children's

The possessive case of a singular or plural noun ending in s or with an s sound is formed by adding an apostrophe only.

students'
Cos.'
Jones'

Joint possession is indicated by placing an apostrophe on the last element of a series.

soldiers and sailors' home
Brown and Nelson's store

Individual or alternative possession requires the use of an apostrophe on each element of a series.

editor's or proofreader's opinion
Roosevelt's or Truman's administration

Generally the apostrophe should not be used after names of countries and other organized bodies ending in s.

United States control
editors handbook

Possessive pronouns do not take an apostrophe.

>its
>theirs

Possessive indefinite or impersonal pronouns require an apostrophe.

>one's home
>each other's books

The singular possessive case is used in such general terms as the following:

>arm's length
>cow's milk
>printer's ink

An apostrophe is used to indicate contractions.

>don't
>I've

An apostrophe is used to indicate the omission of figures and letters.

>class of '92
>spirit of '76

An apostrophe is used to indicate the coined plurals of letters, figures and symbols.

>49'ers
>OK's
>2 by 4's (lumber)

The plural of spelled out numbers is formed by adding s or es. However, 's is added to indicate the plural of words used as words if the omission of the apostrophe would cause difficulty in reading.

>twos
>threes
>ins and outs
>   BUT
>do's and don'ts
>which's and that's

The possessive case is often used instead of an objective phrase even though ownership is not involved.

>day's labor (labor for 1 day)
>for charity's sake

Do not use the possessive where one noun modifies another.

>day labor (labor by the day)
>State rights

Nouns ending in s or ce and followed by a word beginning with s form the possessive by adding an apostrophe only.

Mr. Hughes' service
for conscience' sake

Brackets

Brackets, not parentheses, are used to enclose things that are not specifically a part of the original quotation, omissions and editorial comments. They can also be used as a caution that an error has been reproduced literally.

The general [Washington] ordered him to leave.
Do you know these men [handing witness a list] ?
He came on the 3d [2d] of July.

When material in brackets makes more than one paragraph, start each paragraph with a bracket and place the closing bracket at the end of the last paragraph.

Colon

The colon is used before a final clause which extends or amplifies the preceding matter.

Railroading is not a variety of outdoor sport: it is service.
We have one action left: we must work.

Use a colon to introduce a complete sentence, question or quotation.

In his speech, the President said: "We have nothing to fear..."

The colon is used after a formal salutation.

My Dear Sir:
Ladies and Gentlemen:
To Whom It May Concern:

The colon is used to express clock time.

10:20 p.m.

The colon is used to separate book titles from their sub titles.

Financial Aid for College Students: Graduate
Germany Revisited: Education in the Federal Republic

Comma

The comma is probably used the most frequently of all the punctuation marks and its overuse can produce confusion.

If there is any doubt as to whether the comma is needed for clarification, the best suggestion is to eliminate it. But where it is properly used, the comma greatly enhances understanding of the written word.

Use the comma to separate two words, figures or clauses which might otherwise be misunderstood.

> Instead of hundreds, thousands came.
> February 10, 1927
> In 1930, 400 men were dismissed.
> What the difficulty is, is not known.

Following an introductory phrase or before a direct quotation, use a comma.

> He said, "Now or never."
> After dinner, the speaker was called upon.

Use a comma to indicate the omission of a word or words.

> Then we had much; now, nothing.

A comma is used after each of a series of coordinate qualifying words.

> Supplies included paper, pens, paper clips and manila folders.

Use a comma both before and after personal titles.

> Henry Smith, Jr., chairman
> Motorola, Inc., factory
> Brown, A.H., Jr.

Parenthetic words, phrases or clauses are set off by commas.

> It is obvious, therefore, that this office cannot function.
> Mr. Jefferson, who was then Secretary of State, favored the location of the National Capital at Washington.

Commas set off words or phrases in apposition or in contrast.

> Mr. Green, the lawyer, spoke for the defense.
> James Roosevelt, Democrat, of California.

Use a comma after a noun or phrase in direct address.

> Senator, will the measure be defeated?
> Mr. Chairman, I will reply to the gentleman later.
> Yes, sir, he did see it.

Use a comma after an interrogative clause, followed by a direct question.

> You are sure, are you not?
> You will go, will you not?

Use a comma between the title of person and name of organization in the absence of the words of or of the.

> Chief, Division of Finance
> colonel, 7th Cavalry
> president, Yale University

Use a comma inside closing quotation marks.

> "Freedom is an inherent right," he insisted.

In writing numbers, use a comma to separate thousands, millions, etc., in numbers of four or more digits.

> 4,230
> 50,123
> 1,270,123

The comma is used after the year in complete dates within sentences when used parenthetically.

> The reported dates of September 11, 1943, to June 12, 1944, were proved erroneous.

Omit the comma before:

> ZIP postal delivery number
> between month and year in dates (June 1938)
> between the name and number of an organization
> (General U.S. Grant Post No. 25)
> before a dash
> whenever possible without danger of ambiguity

Dash

Mark a sudden break or abrupt change in thought with a dash.

> He said – and no one argued – "The battle is lost."

A dash is used to indicate an interruption or an unfinished word or sentence.

> "Such an idea can scarcely be –"
> Observe this closely –

At times, the dash may be used instead of commas or parentheses, if the meaning may thus be clarified.

> These are shore deposits – gravel, sand and clay – but marine sediments underlie them.

Use a dash before a final summary clause.

> Freedom of speech, freedom of worship, freedom from want, freedom from fear – these are a fundamental of moral world order.

The dash is used after an introductory phrase to indicate repetition of that phrase.

>I recommend –
>That we accept the rules;
>that we also publish them; and
>that we submit them for review.

Ellipses

Ellipses may be three asterisks or three periods. They are used as an indication of omission of part of material quoted or as omission of words needed to complete a sentence.

>He called * * * and left.
>He called . . . and left.

When an ellipsis appears at the end of a sentence, a period is used.

>He called * * * .
>He called . . . .

Exclamation Point

Emphasis is achieved through the correct use of the exclamation point to mark surprise, incredulity, appeal or other strong emotion.

>He acknowledged the error!
>How beautiful!
>"Great!" he shouted. [Note omission of comma.]

Hyphen

The hyphen as a punctuation mark is used to connect the elements of certain compound words.

>right-of-way
>ill-advisedly

The hyphen indicates the continuation of a word divided at the end of a line. Do not hyphenate for one single letter.

>continua-
>tion

Use a hyphen between the letters of a spelled word.

>c-e-n-t-s

Use the hyphen to eliminate confusion as to meaning.

>re-form (in contrast to reform)

Parentheses

Use parentheses to set off matter not intended to be part of the main statement or not a grammatical element of the sentence but important enough to be included.

The result (see Fig. 2) is most surprising.

Use parentheses to enclose an explanatory word.

the Erie (Pa.) News
Portland (Oreg.) Chamber of Commerce

Enclose letters or numbers designating items in a series with parentheses.

The order of delivery will be: (a) food, (b) clothing and (c) tents.

Enclose a figure inserted to confirm a statement given in words if double form is specifically requested.

The contract shall be completed in sixty (60) days.

Period

Use a period at the end of a declarative sentence or after an imperative sentence.

Stars are suns.
Do not be late.
On with the dance.

A period should be used after an indirect question or after a question intended as a suggestion and not requiring an answer.

Tell me how he did it.
May we hear from you.
May we ask prompt payment.

Use a period in place of parentheses after a letter or number denoting a series.

a. Bread well baked.
1. Index thoroughly.

Omit the period after the following:

Lines in title pages.
Center, side and running heads.
Continued lines.
Boxheads of tables.
Scientific, chemical or other symbols.

This rules does not apply to abbreviation periods.

Also omit the period after a short name which is not an abbreviation of a longer form such as Alex; after Roman numerals used as ordinals such as King George V; after words and incomplete statements listed in columns.

Question Mark

Use a question mark to indicate a direct query, even if not in the form of a question.

> Did he do it?
> He did what?
> Can the money be raised? is the question.
> Who asked, "Why?"

Use a question mark to express more than one query in the same sentence.

> Can he do it? or you? or anyone?

Use a question mark to express doubt.

> He said the boy was 8(?) feet tall. (No space before question mark)

Quotation Marks

Quotation marks enclose direct quotations of spoken dialogue or reproduced material. They are used at both the beginning and end of the quotation.

> The answer is "No."
> "Did you send the letter?" he asked.

Quotation marks are also used following such words as entitled, the word, the term, marked, designated, named, endorsed or signed.

> Congress passed the act entitled "An Act . . ."
> After the word "treaty", insert a comma.
> The check was endorsed "Jonathan Derek".

Use quotation marks to enclose titles of addresses, articles, books, captions, editorials, essays, plays, poems, subjects, etc. All principal words should be capitalized in such titles.

> "The Conquest of Mexico," a published work
> The subject was discussed in "Courtwork" (chapter heading)
> The editorial "Haphazard Budgeting"

When quoting poetry, each stanza should begin with quotation marks. However, only the last stanza should end with them.

Note: The comma and the final period will be placed inside the quotation marks. Other punctuation marks should be placed inside the quotation marks only if they are a part of the matter quoted.

> Ruth said, "I think so."
> "The President," he said, "will veto the bill."
> Who asked, "Why?"

Semicolon

The semicolon is used to separate independent clauses not joined in a sentence by a coordinating conjunction.

> He angered me; I was sorry he was there.

Use the semicolon to separate clauses containing commas.

> Mr. Peters, president of the First National Bank, was a director of New York Central; Harvey D. Jones was a director of Oregon Steel and New York Central; Thomas Harrison was also on the board of Oregon Steel Co.

> The office manager, an excellent executive, was pleased with the survey; she regretted losing good workers.

Use the semicolon to separate statements that are too closely related in meaning to be written as separate sentences, and also statements of contrast.

> Yes; that is right.
> It is true in peace; it is true in war.

Set off explanatory abbreviations or words which summarize or explain preceding matter with a semicolon.

> Three metal producers were involved; Jones, Armco and Kennecott.

Avoid using a semicolon where a comma will suffice.

Single Punctuation

Single punctuation is used wherever possible without ambiguity.

> 124 U.S. 321 (no comma)
> Sir: (no dash)
> Joseph replied, "It is a worthwhile effort." (no outside period)